Jews in Transition

PUBLISHED WITH SUPPORT FROM THE

EDWARD F. WAITE PUBLICATION FUND

of the University of Minnesota Press

The purpose of the Waite Fund is to further the publication of books on the subject of race and race relations broadly conceived. The fund was established in 1944 by George B. Leonard of Minneapolis to honor the career of Edward F. Waite, retired judge of the district court in Hennepin County, Minnesota. Throughout a long life of service to the community, Judge Waite has always shown, in word and deed, an admirable social consciousness and a keen appreciation of the importance of friendship and understanding among peoples of all races everywhere.

JEWS IN TRANSITION

by Albert I. Gordon

UNIVERSITY OF MINNESOTA PRESS, Minneapolis

LONDON · GEOFFREY CUMBERLEGE · OXFORD UNIVERSITY PRESS

To
DOROTHY

Preface

SINCE the year 586 B.C.E., when the kingdom of Judah was conquered by the Babylonians, Jews have lived in all lands other than their own. As a people they have held steadfastly to certain ways of thinking concerning God and man. These ways have set them apart from other peoples and religions. As a minority, however, they have been obliged to adapt some phases of their life and thought to the culture of the people in whose lands they have lived. They would otherwise have long ago ceased to exist as a people.

This book is a study of the changes that have occurred in the beliefs, practices, and institutions of the European Jews who took up residence in Minneapolis, Minnesota. It is concerned with adaptations in the original cultural patterns of the Jews as a result of contact with the cultures of other peoples; and with why and how these adaptations occurred.

The Jews of Minneapolis have been chosen as the subjects of this study primarily because the author, as a resident of the community, had the opportunity to study every phase of its life. For a number of reasons the city seemed highly suitable for an investigation of cultural change. Minneapolis, with a total population of approximately 500,000 and a Jewish population of 20,000, contains about the same proportion of Jews (4 percent) as the country as a whole. Minneapolis has a comparatively stable population. There is little transiency in the city. This holds true for the Jewish community also. The number of Jewish families that move in from the eastern and larger centers of Jewish population is comparatively insignificant.

Sixteen years were spent in gathering the material. From 1930 to 1946 the author served as the rabbi of Adath Jeshurun Synagogue. As a settled member of the community, he was in an excellent position to participate in the Jewish community as well as to observe and study it in the framework of the larger community. Such a long period of residence within the community; association with the Jewish groups in many different roles; and an intimate knowledge of many, if not most, of the Jewish families within the community have made it possible, it seems accurate to say, to know the community well.

This study is based on the technique commonly referred to by social anthropologists and sociologists as the "participant-observer technique." The advantages of this technique have been well described by Florence Kluckhohn:

First, it affords access to the data which come from observation in the current situations in which the community members are involved . . . The range of available data is likely to be increased in a second respect. There are in all groups certain kinds of data which are guarded more closely than others. Direct questions regarding such information may be met with evasions if not outright misrepresentations. Indirect questions may also fail. Simulation of behavior made possible by participation may, however, open the door to this guarded realm . . . The ready access to gossip is the third respect in which participant observation serves to increase the range of information. Gossip is an important source of information both for what is said and for what is not said . . . Moreover it is especially important to listen to gossip if one wants to discover the patterns of "socially approved" behavior . . . The fourth respect in which range is increased . . . lies in the advantage derived from being in the position of the person who is being taught. It has long been an argument of field research workers that the prestige of being an outsider is of great importance, that people talk because they are flattered by attention from an outsider. This does apply to a certain type of person, but it may be added that all people, even the simplest, have "egos." While some individuals are flattered by attention and are happy for the opportunity to talk at length, the egos of research workers themselves have led to over-emphasis of this factor and to too little regard for the detrimental effects of a suspected attitude of superiority and condescension . . . [1]

Throughout the study, however, the author has sought to avoid the pitfalls that may result from such close participation in

community life. He believes that, in the main, he has avoided the
kind of subjectivity with which such a study may be plagued.
When it has been necessary to express value judgments, the
author has done so, believing that nonstatistical studies must,
inevitably, allow for a degree of subjectivity on the part of an
author.

The comments of individuals within the Jewish group, quoted
in this study, have been gathered over a period of ten years.
They were seldom if ever written down as they were made. The
author simply "listened in" to the conversation going on about
him — at meetings, in the privacy of small gatherings, in the
homes of innumerable people, in study and discussion groups, on
the golf course, on fishing trips, or even while driving along the
highways of Minnesota.

These ideas, comments, and reactions were later written down,
sometimes verbatim, at other times paraphrased. At all times,
however, an effort was made to capture the spirit in which the
words were uttered.

Another important source of information consisted of formal
statements made by persons who were well aware of the use to
which their statements would be put. Wherever such statements
can be ascribed to their authors, this has been done. Excerpts
from speeches and reports have also been used in this study, the
sources for which are acknowledged in the Notes at the back of
the book.

Interviews and personal meetings with many of the leaders of
the Jewish community were responsible for much information
that could not be obtained from printed reports, minute books,
and other formal sources. This helped to fill in the bare spots in
the story and to cast light on the thinking of the leaders themselves.

The directories of Minneapolis, beginning with the first community directory published in 1858, were carefully examined,
first, for a detailed picture of the total community and then for a
record of the earliest Jewish residents. Local histories and bio-

graphical sketches of the early settlers were also examined and when useful were recorded.

The life of the total community in all its phases was examined, as were the records of other ethnic groups in Minneapolis. This information made it possible to understand the status and position of the Jewish residents in Minneapolis.

Annual reports of the departments of the city government were examined, as were the earliest records of juvenile delinquency, with particular reference to Jewish children.

Marriage records, filed with the clerk of the district court of Hennepin County, in which Minneapolis is located, were also studied. In order to discover the exact number of marriages among Jews for a particular year, a copy of each marriage license recorded in that year was examined. Each marriage at which a rabbi officiated was then recorded. When there was some uncertainty as to whether the persons were Jewish, the names of the witnesses were recorded and checked on as a further means of identification. In other cases the names were discussed with certain of the older members of the Jewish community, men and women who "knew everybody." The number of cases of this type was, however, extremely small.

In order to ascertain the number of divorces for specified years in the Jewish community, the author undertook a truly formidable task. Because official marriage and divorce records do not indicate religious or national backgrounds, local official statistics could not provide anything more than grand totals for both marriage and divorce. It was necessary, therefore, to make a careful search for Jewish names on each judgment issued and recorded with the clerk of the district court. When doubts arose concerning the Jewishness of any of the parties, the names were discussed, as in the case of marriages, with certain of the oldtimers until the doubts had been resolved.

As a further check on the accuracy of this procedure, newspaper files were consulted for all divorces granted during specified years. A record was kept of all names known to be Jewish. A period of one year elapsed between these two independent examinations. The totals secured by the first method were found to agree with the totals obtained from the second method.

Wherever possible, records and documents pertaining to the institutional life of the Jewish community were gathered and examined. The anniversary programs, the minute books, the membership lists of synagogal and other groups were studied. The records of the Minneapolis Federation for Jewish Service, the Jewish Family Welfare Society, and other organizations dealing with the needs and activities of the Jewish community were read. Surveys and Jewish population studies made at various times in the history of the community were consulted.

One of the best ways of presenting the changes that have occurred in all phases of the life of the Jews of Minneapolis is the medium of personal life histories. Four old-timers who settled in Minneapolis in the 1880's were chosen as the persons most likely to provide the desired information. Each of them represented a distinctive type of national origin and cultural and economic background. In addition, all were well acquainted with the author, and it seemed likely they would not require too much prompting to tell their stories.

In the first interview the author explained that he was seeking to record the stories of a select few of the earliest Jewish settlers in Minneapolis, that it would be helpful if the interviewee would tell something of his family background, the kind of town or village from which he came, his early experiences, his religious and secular training, what caused him to come to the United States and then to settle in Minneapolis, his early experiences both general and religious in his new community, and any and all information that seemed to him to be pertinent.

The interviews, in all but one case, took place in the home of the interviewee. Except for questions put to the interviewee by the author in order to secure the specific information, the stories practically told themselves. In no case did the interviewee write his own story. The author, listening to the story as it was being narrated, would jot down dates, names, words, and phrases that would help to individualize the life histories. No essential facts have been changed except as it was necessary to maintain the anonymity of the interviewee.

After each interview the author prepared a transcript of the life history. Questions and uncertainties regarding certain statements were cleared up in subsequent interviews. It required three separate meetings with each interviewee in order to secure the full story.

For three of the interviewees the author was able to follow the same procedure with his son or daughter and grandchild. In one case the story does not get beyond the second generation. Because the story of the second generation was in this instance so different from the others, it was included in the series.

Though every effort was made to secure letters, written by or to the interviewee when he was still in the old country, the author met with no success along these lines. Nor was he able to secure any other written documents such as diaries which might add details to the life stories.

The records of the district court from 1901 to 1945 were consulted for the various name changes that have officially been recorded for Minneapolis. These records, plus a long acquaintance with the Jewish community and a knowledge of "typically" Jewish names, offered, if not the exact number, at least the type and form of name changes which have officially been recorded.

It is of interest that the author was incorrectly told by several members of the clerk of court's office that most of the changes in surnames were made by Jewish persons. A careful examination of the files indicates that, in the vast majority of cases, the original surnames were of Polish origin. When this fact was pointed out to the clerk of court, he told the author that some years ago a Polish-American attorney had carried on an intensive campaign among the newly arrived Polish immigrants in an effort to induce them to change their surnames to ones more characteristically American.

PREFACE

The daily newspapers of Minneapolis were frequently used in order to check on the accuracy of the statements made by interviewees. The names of persons alluded to as having played some role in the community affairs, as well as dates and places concerning which there remained some uncertainties, were checked in this manner.

The Anglo-Jewish weekly publication, the *American Jewish World*, published and edited in Minneapolis since 1912 and containing a detailed account of the week-to-week goings and comings of the Jewish community — as well as the activities of every religious, cultural, and social group in the Jewish community — proved especially helpful. The smaller clubs, about which little might otherwise be known, frequently recorded their programs and other activities within its columns.

Births, marriages, and deaths were also listed here, as were the names of children who participated in such religious rites as Bar Mitzvah and confirmation. News concerning divorces was never recorded in this or any other official Jewish publication.

This magazine proved helpful also in other ways. The editorials were carefully scanned in order to ascertain the major interests or issues that seemed important to the editor. Repetition of certain themes, such as overseas-relief needs, Palestine and Zionism, Hebrew education, the Minneapolis Talmud Torah (Hebrew school), and anti-Semitism, helped to highlight the special interests and concerns of the community. The frequency with which pictures and stories about various local persons were printed called attention to these persons who were regarded as the leaders of the Jewish community. Social positions in the community were thus defined.

The early files of other Anglo-Jewish weekly newspapers, such as the *American Israelite*, published in Cincinnati, Ohio, and the *American Hebrew*, published in New York City, were used frequently. These publications, among the earliest published by Jews in the United States, representing Reform and Conservative religious tendencies respectively, were national Jewish publications. Each of these papers carried news of various local Jewish communities in the United States almost weekly. Local correspondents were thus frequently responsible for providing sidelights on news that could not be obtained otherwise.

On occasion, bits of information concerning the local Jewish community were gleaned from magazines and newspapers published in the German language in Vienna, Austria. This is particularly true of items involving Zionist activity and interest. For example, the presence of Rabbi Stephen S. Wise in Minneapolis to deliver a discourse on Zionism, though not mentioned in the local press, was recorded in great detail in a Vienna Jewish newspaper.

The author does not assume that the Jewish community of Minneapolis is typical of all American-Jewish communities. He believes that certain trends in thought and action that characterize this community will be found in other American-Jewish communities as well, in varying degree.

Jews in Transition calls attention to the cultural changes that are occurring in a Jewish group in a midwestern community. It represents a serious attempt to describe life as it was and is now being lived by American Jews who are Americans even as they are Jews.

ALBERT I. GORDON

March 1949

Acknowledgments

THIS book could not have been written without the active co-operation of many of Minneapolis' citizens. Information gathered from persons who represented the interests and activities of the Jewish community during a period of many years constitutes the basic source of the materials used in the preparation of this study. Any attempt to name each of these sources of information would be doomed to failure because the total number was so large.

I do, however, wish to express my sincere appreciation for the interest and assistance that was given me by many of the rabbis and lay leaders of the Jewish community. They permitted me to examine the records of their organizations, which provided helpful information and sidelights on the community as a whole. I am especially grateful to the late Dr. George J. Gordon, who, shortly before his passing, spent many full days in my company, describing in great detail the life of the Jewish community of Minneapolis from its earliest days. I am deeply indebted, too, to my friends Joseph H. Schanfeld, David C. Jeffery, Amos Deinard, and Meyer D. Mirviss, who contributed of their vast and intimate knowledge of the total community to this study.

Charles I. Cooper, executive secretary of the Minneapolis Federation for Jewish Service, was a gracious consultant on many phases of the organizational life of the community. The assistance of Mrs. Florence Kunian, Mrs. Sadye Kantrowitz, Michael Finkelstein, and the late Reuben Latz, who provided detailed information concerning certain phases of the organizational life of the community, is gratefully acknowledged.

The files of the *American Jewish World*, the Anglo-Jewish weekly newspaper published in Minneapolis, were made available to me by Leo Frisch, the editor. I am deeply indebted to the staff of librarians in the Reference Room of the Minneapolis

Public Library for their ever-gracious assistance. I am grateful, too, to my secretary, Mrs. Muriel A. Baumwoll, for her work in the preparation of the maps.

This study could not have been completed without the assistance of such men as the late Judge Fred Wright, judge of the Hennepin County juvenile court, B. K. Wasmuth, clerk of the district court of Hennepin County, W. W. Thomas, a member of Mr. Wasmuth's staff, Wilfred Leland, and other public officials whose assistance I sought. Senator Hubert Humphrey, Jr., former mayor of Minneapolis, was particularly helpful to me in making available the reports of the Mayor's Council on Human Relations before their publication.

For obvious reasons I cannot here list the names of the persons who provided me with their personal biographies. Their contributions are, I believe, invaluable and help materially to round out this study on the Minneapolis Jewish community.

I am deeply indebted to my friend, Dr. David Mandelbaum, professor of anthropology at the University of California, for the role he played in arousing my interest in the field of anthropology, as well as for his advice and assistance.

To Dr. Louis Finkelstein, president of the Jewish Theological Seminary of America, and Dr. Mordecai M. Kaplan, professor of homiletics at the Jewish Theological Seminary of America and leader of the Society for the Advancement of Judaism, who read the manuscript critically; to Ruth Sawtell Wallis, whose criticisms and valued suggestions are incorporated in this study; and especially to my dear friend and counsellor, Professor Wilson D. Wallis, head of the department of anthropology at the University of Minnesota, whose advice and encouragement have made this study possible, I owe my heartfelt appreciation.

Finally, let me say that this study owes more than words can tell to the inspiration and encouragement of my dear wife, Dorothy Davis Gordon.

A. I. G.

Table of Contents

JEWS IN TRANSITION

REFERENCE MATTER

Part I THESE ARE
THE PEOPLE

Chapter 1   The Setting

◄§ A YANKEE *with a round Puritan head, an open prairie heart,
and a big Scandinavian body.* [1]

I T is understandable why citizens of Minneapolis, the largest
city in the state of Minnesota, speak of it with affection and
pride. It is as typical of midwestern America as the Mississippi
River, whose waters course through the city, or the yellow fields
of grain covering the rich farming areas which border on the
city.

Minneapolis is a pleasant city in which to live. Its close to
500,000 citizens, of whom 41 percent live in their own homes,
appreciate the quiet and beauty of its tree-lined streets. They enjoy and use the five lakes within the city limits, where they
may take full advantage of both summer and winter sports.
They enjoy the hundreds of lakes around the city and speak
of the entire area as a hunting and fishing paradise. They may
live on the outskirts of the city and yet be no more than half
an hour's drive from the Loop, the business center of Minneapolis.

Though Minneapolis is the twin of neighboring St. Paul, there
is little political or social contact between these two largest cities
in the state of Minnesota. One may drive from Minneapolis into
St. Paul without being aware that the city of St. Paul has been
entered, but roads do not in themselves tie cities' interests together. Each of the twin cities has a distinctive personality.

Minneapolitans take pride in the fact that the city is the
home of the state-controlled University of Minnesota, with its
thirty thousand students [2] and feel a sense of cultural well-being
because it supports several art museums, excellent school and

library facilities, the Minneapolis symphony orchestra, and an "Artists Course" that brings the world's greatest musicians and lecturers to the city.

It is true, of course, that the city may become unbearably hot in the summer and that during the winter the temperature will drop to twenty and even thirty degrees below zero. However, Minneapolitans, those who can afford it, escape to the northernmost lake-dotted ends of the state in the summer, and they insist that sub-zero winter temperatures are really less penetrating and uncomfortable than above-zero temperatures in New York City.

Since its incorporation in 1856, Minneapolis has been known as an important industrial center. In its early days mining, milling, quarrying, logging, shipping, and fishing were its chief activities. From the iron range in northern Minnesota came the iron ore which was destined to play a major role in reshaping the industrial future of the country. From the farming areas to the west and south came the rich harvests of grain which were converted into fine flour and gave the city the name "Flour City." The great mills of Minneapolis utilized the inexpensive water power generated by the waters of St. Anthony Falls, above which the city was built. From the great forests to the north came the logs which were floated down the Mississippi to the city's mills and converted into lumber or used for the manufacture of paper. From its solid stone hills came the granite which was hewed into building stone.

To this midwestern country came the sons of old New England families to establish vast industrial empires. There came also the lumberjacks, the traders, the merchants, as well as the thousands of men and women who were looking for land and the chance to live a better, freer life.

The first permanent dwelling within the boundaries of the original corporate city is known to have been erected in 1849. The village of St. Anthony, located on the east bank of the Mississippi above St. Anthony Falls, appeared for a brief while

4

to be the likely center of the greatest population in the area. However, the rapid growth of Minneapolis on the west bank of the river made it inevitable that the two towns be combined, and consolidation took place in 1872.

Waves of immigration began to sweep the Upper Midwest as early as 1850. The greatest growth of the population in Minneapolis occurred in the decade from 1880 to 1890. During that period the city acquired almost 130,000 new residents.

Just as Minneapolis is typical of midwestern cities in the manner of its living, its economic and cultural interests, so it is typical also in the mixture of the people who are its citizens. From all the countries of the Old World, men and women have come to Minneapolis. Swedes, Norwegians, Germans, Irish, Russians, Poles, Czechs, Rumanians, Greeks, English, Negroes, Roman and Greek Catholics, Protestants and Jews — all have lived together for many decades in this metropolis of the Midwest. While each ethnic group has contributed to the growth and development of the community, each has preserved certain ethnic characteristics that are distinctly its own.

It is the 20,000 Jews of Minneapolis, who constitute 4 percent of the city's total population, with which this study is directly concerned.

TODAY'S JEWISH COMMUNITY

A study of the Jewish population made in 1936 showed that 49 percent of the total Jewish population of the city had resided in Minneapolis for twenty-five years or more.[3] Since well over a decade has passed since this fact was ascertained, it is evident that, except for the several hundred "refugee" families who arrived in the city just before or during World War II, the length of continued Jewish residence in Minneapolis has risen considerably.

The sons and daughters of the same families whose names are recorded in the early history of the community reside in Minneapolis today and take their places in the life of the Jewish community. Young people may attend out-of-town schools or universities but they usually return and establish themselves as residents of the city.

As one walks the streets of the city or visits the campus of the University of Minnesota, it is often difficult to distinguish the children and grandchildren of the early Jewish immigrants from the rest of the local population on the basis of physical appearance alone. Boas would have found in Minneapolis added support for his view that the children of European immigrants tend to assume the physical characteristics of the people in whose midst they live.[4] The sons and daughters of the early Jewish settlers are usually taller than their parents. Many are blonde and blue-eyed, almost Scandinavian in appearance. Their love of sport, hunting, swimming, fishing, and the outdoor life so characteristic of the region surprises even their parents.

On the North Side of Minneapolis live 59 percent of the city's Jewish citizens.[5] Thirty-six percent reside on the near North Side, the area into which the first Jewish settlers migrated, located only a short distance from the downtown business district. Though many own the homes which they built many years ago, the area has lost its original attractiveness and now stands but one step removed from what may be termed a slum area. The families are larger, the crowding is greater. A foreign atmosphere is noticeable on the eastern fringe of the district, which borders the largest center of Negro population in the city. A large part of this "area of heavy concentration of structures unfit for human habitancy — many without central heat, adequate toilet facilities, baths or gas or electric services"[6] was torn down as a part of the federal slum clearance project. In 1936 the new Sumner Field Housing Project with 613 living units was officially dedicated to take its place. Of a total of 400 families that had lived in this area, 126 were Jewish.[7]

The North Side also has a better residential section, the Homewood district, an upper middle-class area that is almost entirely Jewish. Here 23 percent of the city's Jewish population live more or less closely and comfortably. About 80 percent of them own the homes in which they reside. To the west of this area are a city park and a golf course, which constitute the western boundary of the city.

Forty-one percent of the total Jewish population reside on either the West or South sides of the city. The South Side area was the earliest home of the Rumanian immigrants. At present only about 4 percent of the total Jewish population live on the South Side, approximately 65 percent of them in homes which they own. The Jewish population on the South Side is rapidly decreasing in size. The children of the original settlers of this neighborhood move, along with many from the North Side, to the newer centers of Jewish population on the West Side, in the vicinity of the four lakes: Calhoun, Harriet, Lake of the Isles, and Cedar.

An even newer development is forming just west of the city limits in what is known as St. Louis Park. Here Jews have moved into their own homes, in the main from the West Side. Even though the number of apartment buildings and apartment hotels is greater on the West Side, it is estimated that 60 percent of its Jewish residents own their homes. In all about 70 percent of the Jewish population are believed to own the homes in which they reside. As we shall see, the reason for the purchase of homes has less to do with the wealth of the population than with the inability to secure homes other than through outright purchase.

The size of the average Jewish family in Minneapolis is 3.82 persons,[8] slightly larger than for the community as a whole (3.45). The average size of the family on the old North Side is only a little greater than that of other neighborhoods.

The average person in the Jewish community has reached the senior grade in high school. Eighteen percent have received only an elementary school education; 32 percent have attended college and 13 percent have graduated. The number of college graduates is increasing rapidly. The average Jewish person has also received more than five years of Jewish education; 17 percent have attended a Jewish school for more than eight years.[9]

7

JEWS IN TRANSITION

Though an exact statistical record of the vocations of the heads of Minneapolis' sixty-one hundred families has never been made, the records of the Minneapolis Federation for Jewish Service throw some light on the matter. From it we learn that Jews are, in high proportion, members of the white-collar class: proprietors of retail businesses, salesmen, office workers, manufacturers of women's clothing and other lines of apparel, including furs. Jews are to be found as proprietors of wholesale meat distributing establishments, cleaning and laundering establishments, jewelry and furniture stores, as managers of retail chain stores, as operators or managers of motion picture theaters. They are distributors and bookers of motion pictures; they are in the liquor business (wholesale and retail), the scrap iron industry, the grocery, produce, and drug industries. Jews predominate in the jobbing of merchandise of all kinds. In the professions there were in 1946 ninety-two Jewish lawyers, fifty-nine physicians and surgeons, thirty-nine dentists, one hundred and seventy-three pharmacists, thirty-two accountants, thirteen teachers in the Minneapolis public school system, and five newspapermen. There was only one firm of architects, consisting of two Jews, although there may have been several others employed in this field.

A survey prepared in 1947 under the sponsorship of the Minneapolis Mayor's Council on Human Relations substantiates the earlier study and gives additional information about the main occupational groups of Minneapolis Jews compared with white Gentiles and Negroes. (See Table I.) Table II gives the age distribution of the Jewish population in 1936, as compared with the population as a whole in 1930.

During World War II Minneapolis Jewry contributed of its resources, not only by war work and the purchase of war bonds, but in human terms as well. As of April 11, 1946, the record indicates that 2327 Jewish men from Minneapolis served in the armed forces. Of these 490 were commissioned officers and 1837 were enlisted personnel, including noncommissioned officers. Forty-six Jewish young women also served in the armed forces,

TABLE I. PERCENTAGE DISTRIBUTION OF EMPLOYED WORKERS IN PRESENT JOBS, BY MAIN OCCUPATIONAL GROUPS, FOR WHITE GENTILES AND THE MINORITIES, MINNEAPOLIS, 1947 [10]

Main Occupational Groups	Present or Last Job		
	White Gentile	Jewish	Negro
Total Employed	*100.00*	*100.00*	*100.00*
Professional and semi-professional workers....	2.75	1.53	5.62
Proprietors, managers *	1.83	6.06	1.12
Clerical, sales, and kindred workers...........	26.61	43.95	10.11
Subtotal	*31.19*	*51.54*	*16.85*
Craftsmen, foremen, and kindred workers.....	21.10	9.01	5.62
Operatives and kindred workers..............	26.60	31.83	16.85
Subtotal	*47.70*	*40.84*	*22.47*
Domestic service workers *	0.92	.00	2.25
Protective service workers...................	3.67	1.53	1.12
Service (excluding domestic and protective) ...	7.39	4.56	46.07
Subtotal	*11.93*	*6.09*	*49.4*
Laborers, excluding farm and mine...........	8.26	1.53	11.24
Other occupations	0.92	.00	.00

* Our study of individual employees excluded the self-employed and the domestic service workers *in homes*.

TABLE II. TOTAL POPULATION, 1930, AND JEWISH POPULATION, MINNEAPOLIS, 1936, BY AGE-GROUP [11]

Age-group	Total Population (1930)		Jewish Population (1936)	
	Number	Percent	Number	Percent
All ages	*464,356*	*100.0*	*16,260*	*100.0*
Under 5	34,177	7.4	873	5.4
5–9	38,685	8.3	1,147	7.1
10–14	36,986	8.0	1,147	8.9
15–19	37,008	8.0	1,747	10.7
20–24	43,308	9.3	1,832	11.3
25–34	81,852	17.6	2,641	16.2
35–44	78,272	16.0	2,465	15.2
45–54	53,310	11.5	2,048	12.6
55–64	33,212	7.2	1,178	7.2
65–74	20,158	4.3	584	3.6
75 and over.............	7,185	1.5	154	0.9
		less than		
Unknown	203	0.1	144	0.9

9

of whom forty were enlisted personnel and six were commissioned officers.

One hundred and sixty Jewish youth were casualties of the war. Sixty-eight were killed in action or died in service, eight were prisoners of war, and eighty-four were wounded. Two hundred and forty-one of the men and women in the armed forces received medals or awards for distinguished service.[12]

There were in 1936 ninety-four Jewish organizations and agencies in Minneapolis.[13] These included all religious institutions, Hebrew schools, fraternal, philanthropic, social, Zionist, and other organizations and clubs, both public and private, and their auxiliary bodies. The total membership of these organizations and institutions was approximately 20,000.[14] This means that each adult Jew in Minneapolis was a member on the average of two Jewish organizations.

The Jews of Minneapolis are philanthropically minded. In 1945 $504,010 was contributed through the Minneapolis Federation for Jewish Service by 4993 persons for the support of local causes such as the Minneapolis Talmud Torah, Jewish organizations, and hospitals, and for world causes such as support of war victims and displaced persons, and rehabilitation work in Palestine. The per capita contribution in that year for the entire Jewish population was $24.35. In 1946 almost a million dollars was contributed to the same causes, and a million and a half dollars was also given for the building of the Jewish-operated Mount Sinai Hospital. In 1948 the federation reported contributions of $1,250,000 from 6200 contributors. In addition various campaigns were conducted for special causes, notably those associated with the rebuilding of Palestine as a Jewish homeland.

Seventeen buildings in which the varied Jewish communal interests are housed cost $1,157,492. Seventy-five percent of this capital outlay is invested in synagogue buildings. Two of the synagogues are presently conducting building campaigns for a total of $500,000, and the Minneapolis Talmud Torah is seeking to raise an additional $250,000 in order to secure new quarters.

10

THE SETTING

Economic conditions of Minneapolis Jewry were not always as good as they are today. Indeed, in 1933, as a result of the general depression, only $18,832 could be raised by the federation in its annual fund-raising campaign. On March 1, 1936, there were 639 unduplicated active cases of relief of economic need recorded for the Jews of Minneapolis. There was and still is a vital need for such Jewish agencies as the Jewish Family Welfare Association, the major Jewish social agency, whose services comprise relief and case work to needy families and unattached individuals (the aged, homeless, transients), economic adjustment by means of vocational guidance, placement and loans, and care of dependent and neglected children in their own and foster homes. The association also supports in part the Hebrew Sheltering Home, which gives shelter and food to Jewish transients; the Jewish Home for the Aged of the Northwest, which provides institutional care for approximately fifty aged men and women; and the relief and free loan societies in the community.

The Jews of Minneapolis have no central, over-all community organization. The closest approach to such an organization is the Minneapolis Federation for Jewish Service, on whose board sit representatives of the major Jewish organizations and religious institutions of the city. As the name implies, it is a federation of many organizations over whom there is no control other than the expressed approval or disapproval of the Jewish community as a whole. Since 1930, the year of its organization, the federation has grown in prestige and importance so that each local organization, while maintaining complete autonomy, seeks its counsel and approval of acts which it believes may affect the Jewish community as a whole.

All groupings in the Jewish community, despite numerous differences in opinion and constituency, cooperate to a high degree in what is generally regarded as a satisfactory manner. Differences in religious belief and practice or economic and social status are seldom permitted to obstruct cooperative action in matters pertaining to the welfare of the entire community.

Chapter 2   Community in the Making

◄§ A COMMUNITY *might be defined as that form of social organization in which the welfare of each is the concern of all, and the life of the whole is the concern of each.*[1]

THE Jews of Minneapolis regard themselves as members of a united Jewish community. They point with pride to their many cooperative activities and enterprises. While respecting differences in opinion or point of view, they do nevertheless make every effort to plan and think as a community. But it was not always so!

In its early days there were, in fact, several separate Jewish communities in the city. There were the German Jews, who lived as members of a self-contained community. Then there were the East European Jews: the Russians, Lithuanians, and Poles, who lived in another section of the city in a tightly knit community of their own, and the Rumanians who lived in a third section almost entirely by themselves. Each group developed its own institutions and went its own way. Not until strong and understanding leadership developed within these groups and certain critical situations requiring mutual cooperation pressed hard upon them, did they begin to unite as a single Jewish community.

In this chapter we shall discuss the origin and history of the Jewish community, the early settlers, where they came from and why they came, where and how they lived, the conditions that obliged them to unite, and those persons whose efforts made a united community possible.

The names of the first two persons known to be Jews who took up residence in Minneapolis are recorded in the *Directory of Minneapolis and St. Anthony* published in January 1867:

'E. Altman & S. Lauchheim — Clothing. Wholesale and Retail. Bridge Square between 1st and 2nd." It is apparent that these men were residents of the town during 1866, just ten years after the official incorporation of Minneapolis. There were about seven thousand residents in Minneapolis when Emanuel Altman and Samuel Lauchheim established their clothing store in the little downtown business section.

Other Jews, both individuals and families, began to settle in Minneapolis beginning in 1869. The earliest known Jewish settlers came from Germany, Austria, Hungary, and Bohemia.[2] Some of them, though born in the United States, were children of immigrants from Western Europe who had settled in the eastern part of the country.

THE GERMAN JEWS

The German Jews began their migration to the United States before 1840. Between that date and 1880 the German-Jewish wave of immigration was highest. The reasons are not hard to find. Anti-Jewish prejudice in Germany, coupled with autocratic government, left its mark on the Jewish population. Poverty was rife. Then too a new philosophy of freedom for the individual swept through the world in the second half of the eighteenth century. Everywhere men had begun to take seriously American democracy and the French motto of liberty, equality, and fraternity. Western Europe, however, was not ready to grant its Jews the same rights and privileges that had, at least in theory, been granted to all other citizens. The failure of the German Revolution of 1848 made it abundantly clear to the Jews of Western Europe that political and economic freedom could be obtained only by emigration to the New World and especially to the United States.

The Middle West, which was then undergoing rapid expansion, was quite naturally looked upon with favor by these immigrants. Jewish communities developed in Cincinnati, Cleveland, Indianapolis, Chicago, and Memphis, and continued their westward advance — first to St. Paul and then to Minneapolis. By 1880, 103 names that are known to be Jewish were recorded in the Minneapolis directory.[3]

Contrary to the experience of other communities, these Jews did not begin their business careers in Minneapolis as peddlers. Most of them had lived for a while in eastern or southern communities before they came to Minneapolis, and they were able to establish themselves in business with the capital which they had acquired. They opened clothing, dry goods, and general furnishings stores. They helped in some measure to supply the needs of the thousands of men who came to the city from lumber camps in the north. They exchanged merchandise for furs and beadwork brought in by trappers and Indians and supplied the goods needed by the ever-increasing number of workmen in the flour mills and other industries.

Early records indicate that most of the German-Jewish families lived in the better residential section of the growing city. Theirs was in no sense a ghetto. They lived in close proximity to their business establishments along Hennepin Avenue between First and Third streets, along Nicollet Avenue to Third Street, and along Washington Avenue, south to Fourth Street and north to Fifth Street. First and Second avenues north and Third to Sixth streets were the most popular residential quarters.

Because the German Jews were the merchant class, they were in a position to enjoy comforts equal in most respects to those enjoyed by all other merchants of the community, except the very wealthy. They lived in good homes. Their children went to the public schools — grade school, high school, and some to the University of Minnesota. They were on friendly terms with their non-Jewish neighbors.

An earnest desire to conform to the American standard, to be integrated into the American cultural pattern, and to avoid as many external differences as possible characterized these early immigrants. With few exceptions they had received little more than an elementary Hebrew training. To be sure, the homes in

14

which they had been reared in the old country were pious and God-fearing. Jewish ceremonialism, including the observance of the dietary laws and the Sabbath as a day of rest, had been respected. These, however, were matters that could be and were easily compromised when the occasion demanded.

In America most families had little to do with Jewish ceremonialism. Although in a few cases the dietary laws were observed in the home, little attention was paid to such things outside the home. Instead of the aristocracy of Hebraic learning which characterized East European Jewish communities, there was an aristocracy based upon business or professional success — a characteristic of the larger community as well. That is not to say that learning per se was not highly regarded. Yet surely Hebraic learning did not play a major role in the life or in the thinking of this group.

The language of conversation with minor exceptions was English, though it was often spoken with a German accent. Of course, German was frequently used in conversations between husband and wife, and German expressions were to be heard.

Except, then, for occasional attendance at services in their house of worship and for participation in various Jewish organizations, there were no marked differences between these early settlers and their Christian neighbors. They were on the whole well adjusted and quite ready and able to take their places in their new community. These people were, however, Jews and wished so to be regarded.

The members of the German-Jewish community tended to live self-contained lives, associating for the most part with their own kind. There were visits, home parties, and socials to occupy their time. The men were busy in their various business pursuits. The women cared for their homes, taking great pains in the preparations for the numerous home socials. One of the early settlers reports: "I remember that for several days before company would come over my mother was very busy in the kitchen preparing all kinds of delicacies and special foods for the occasion."

In addition to attending public school with their non-Jewish friends, children attended dancing-school classes arranged for them by their parents once a week. They studied their Jewish history in their Sunday school classes at the temple. In the early days there were no special clubs or social organizations for the young people. Outings were arranged for by hiring a horse and buggy.

There were in the 1880's several social clubs for the men. One of the most active was the Apollo Club, which existed for several years, to be followed by the Phoenix Club, which had attractive quarters in the old Lyceum Theater building. Social affairs took place in most instances in the homes of the various members of the community. However, from time to time halls were rented for the purpose of giving larger social affairs or dances in the interest of raising money for various charitable causes.

The women of the German-Jewish community played an important role in its development. They began their philanthropic activities through the medium of the Baszion Benevolent Society, later renamed the Hebrew Ladies' Benevolent Society. In addition in 1903 they organized the ladies' auxiliary of Temple Shaarei Tov, the first Reform temple in Minneapolis. They joined forces with their husbands for the purpose of meeting the debts incurred as a result of building the new temple.

Another of the early organizations which played a major role, not only in the life of Temple Shaarei Tov and its membership but in the community as a whole, was the Council of Jewish Women, organized in 1893.[4] "Through the work of the Council, the Minneapolis women have been stimulated to the study of the Bible, their race and its history. Religion, literature and philanthropy have been included in the Council's work."[5]

Members of the council attended study classes each Saturday afternoon. Once a month during the winter season the council held a public entertainment "of a high character." Later, when it felt that the North Side community required aid, the council established a sewing school for young girls in that district and provided a corps of teachers from among its members who taught from 100 to 125 pupils in its several classes. The council also started a day nursery on the North Side, and later a Sunday School which met in the Kenesseth Israel Synagogue. The Jewish community began to develop those institutions, religious, philanthropic, cultural, and social, that served to provide the people with outlets for their particular interests.

THE EASTERN EUROPEAN JEWS

The Jews of Russia, Poland, Lithuania, and Rumania are among those who may be classed as East European Jews. Many of them came to the United States during the veritable tidal wave of immigration between 1880 and 1920. The reasons for their coming are well known.

Tzarist Russia was a land of reaction, of bitter opposition to the growing liberalism and democratic tendencies of the West. During the reign of Nicholas I Jews for the first time in Russia were conscripted into military service. The "statute of conscription and military service" promulgated in August 1827 provided that Jews were to supply recruits for the army to serve a term of twenty-five years and to produce juvenile conscripts—"cantonists"—from the ages of 12 to 25. Jewish communities were required to fill these quotas under penalty of severe punishment in the event of failure. The Pale of Settlement, a region containing certain locales and provinces in which Jews were compelled to live, was clearly and definitely fixed by a regulatory code in April 1835.

Jews of Russia and Russian-controlled Poland distrusted the Russian government. They knew of the missionizing tactics employed to convert young Jewish soldiers to Christianity. They knew they could not maintain the customs and ceremonies of their religion, including observance of the dietary laws and the Sabbath, as members of the Russian army. They knew of the desire of the Russian government to rout out all vestiges of Jewish Talmudical learning.

To make things worse, the Church regarded the Jews as its enemy and on many occasions, particularly on the Easter festival, its clergy aroused the general populace to such a frenzy that pogroms were not infrequent. Jews remained in mortal fear of their lives and during religious festivals actually barred the doors of their homes against intruders.

The Russian pogroms of 1881 finally caused great numbers of Jews to make their way to America. In most instances they were young men seeking to escape from conscription and thus they came to this country singly, rather than in families.

The Jews of Rumania were no better off than those of Russia and Poland. In 1860 there were more than two hundred thousand Jews in Rumania, most of them descended from Polish-Jewish emigrants who had begun their migrations in the first half of the seventeenth century. The great mass of Jews lived in Rumanian cities and villages under conditions not dissimilar to those in Russia. Anti-Semitic agitation was rife; mob attacks on Jews were common and frequent expulsions of Jews took place.

East European Jews as a group made their first appearance in Minneapolis in the 1880's. With minor exceptions they turned to peddling as a means of earning their livelihood. As has been indicated, most of the original settlers came without their families. For a few weeks after their arrival, they would pick up any odd job that was available. Artisans as well as those who had spent their entire youth in study in the various academies of higher Jewish learning turned to manual labor as the surest and quickest way to earn a few dollars. They took up residence in the homes of their fellow East Europeans and after earning small sums of money sought the aid of one of several Jewish dry goods jobbers in the city. The jobber provided the immigrant with various small articles and notions. With his merchandise in a basket tied over his shoulders the immigrant was then escorted to the city limits along some country road and told to "peddle."

COMMUNITY IN THE MAKING

The newcomer seldom had any command of the English language. He might pick up a word here and there, but for the most part he trusted entirely to his own ingenuity and determination. He walked down dusty country roads and peddled his wares at the farmhouses along the way.

As his earnings increased the immigrant first purchased a few new articles of clothing for himself on credit. He then arranged with the *Schiffskarten* (steamship ticket) agency for the transportation of wife, children, and parents whom he had left behind in the old country. The third step in the process of acquiring a foothold in a new land was usually that of purchasing a horse and wagon, which would make the peddling tasks a bit easier and help the peddler to carry more merchandise.

The newly arrived immigrants settled in different sections of the city according to nationality groups, separate from the German Jews and from each other. The Rumanian Jews established themselves on the South Side around Franklin Avenue and Fifteenth Street. A colony of Russian, Polish, and Lithuanian Jews developed on the near North Side of the city. The Russians developed their own synagogues, as did the Lithuanians and Poles.

Thus Minneapolis, like most other communities, gradually saw the development of a form of self-segregation among the East European Jews. Variations in religious practices, though minor, were often regarded as of the utmost importance by the Jews of the community. Memories associated with the "old home" required that persons who knew of the places of which the immigrant spoke should be at hand or easily available. The reasons for this self-segregation appear to be (1) the similarity of language and custom, (2) the greater opportunity to observe religious practices and duties in the company of like-minded individuals, (3) the characteristic inability to pay high rentals for homes, (4) the refusal of native residents to rent other than the poorest homes to immigrants, and (5) the convenient location of the new residences from the point of view of distance to work. (It should be noted that even though the homes into which the immigrants moved were not of the very best, they were in practically all instances better by far than the homes in which these people had lived in Europe.) The German-Jewish community had been able to avoid establishment of a voluntary ghetto because it possessed superior financial means and the ability to speak English.

The center of Jewish settlement on the North Side was first located in the vicinity of Washington Avenue and Fifth Street. Most of the Jews lived in two- or three-room frame houses, which in many instances held more than one family. Few if any of these homes had inside plumbing. None of them was lighted by gas.

One of the early settlers has related the following account of life in this district:

"All our homes were lighted by kerosene lamps which we used all the time. Of course this was no different from what we had been accustomed to in the old country. Still, many of us got burned because of these lamps. I still have a scar on my face as the result of a lamp tipping over when I was trying to light it.

"I remember that we lived in three rooms and we paid $8.00 a month rent. We got along very well. We raised our children in this, our first home in Minneapolis. When we moved around 1900, other Jews were also moving into the Oak Lake district, which was around Eighth Avenue North and Lyndale. Many of our friends did not live quite as far up in the new neighborhood. My husband had developed a nice grocery business and so we were able to afford a better home, which we rented. This home had six rooms and we felt much happier about it because our family was increasing.

"I still remember the way in which the shul (synagogue) was the center of our lives. My husband, after he got through working in the store and having his supper, would be among those who would go to the shul and study the Blatt (Talmud). My mother, who lived just a short distance from the shul, would bring in refreshments for the men — there were about forty of them who studied every day in the synagogue. Each morning my mother would actually prepare coffee and make fresh rolls which she would bring over for these men.

"I remember how a few of the women would gather food from individuals like myself and from Jewish storekeepers, so that they could take it to the very poor Jews who lived in our neighborhood. Particularly on the Sabbath they wanted every Jew to have a good Sabbath meal. I always baked extra loaves of bread on Friday so that I could give some to the poor. Our families were much larger in those days. It seems that all my friends had at least four children. In many cases there were many, many more.

"I remember that we used to call a doctor to take care of our sick children around the year 1900, and even after, and we paid him fifty cents for each visit. Life was certainly much different in those days, yet we enjoyed it. We were all busy and we were all happy with what we had. America for us was the land of hope and we wanted to give our children every chance to do and become those things which we had never been able to have for ourselves in the old country."

The immigrant Jews of the North Side did not readily adjust themselves to the practices and manners of their non-Jewish neighbors. They strictly maintained their religious customs in their homes and synagogues. Some even clung tenaciously to the garb that had characterized them in their East European communities, long black coats and the broad black hat which was characteristic of the Talmudical student. Many of the men wore long beards. The married women frequently wore sheitels (wigs traditionally worn by married Jewish women). In other ways, including their inability to speak English and the use of Yiddish as the language of conversation, they were looked upon as strange creatures by other members of the community, including their fellow Jews from Western Europe. As a consequence, their relationship with their non-Jewish neighbors, who were themselves of lower middle-class origin, was frequently strained, and often open warfare broke out among them:

"The Jews of the North Side used to be afraid to walk anywhere above Fifth Street North. It was actually dangerous to go there, because the Germans and the Irish lived there. There was a lot of beard pulling and name calling. The children of these Germans and Irish people would very often tip over the apple carts or wagons of the Jewish peddlers and in general they made life miserable for them."

21

JEWS IN TRANSITION

The customs as well as the dress of these people began to show a marked change when their children started to go to public school. Through the children parents became aware of the differences and changes resulted. Beards began to disappear. Old-fashioned garb was discarded in favor of American made and styled clothes. The younger girls, upon their marriage, never put on the traditional sheitel, and parents did not object. Only within the confines of the home were the traditional practices and religious rites retained.

In Eastern Europe the scholar and learned Jew was regarded as an aristocrat among his people. Parents so prized Talmudical learning that they sought, when at all possible, to marry their daughters to yeshivoh bochurim (Talmudical students). Boys and men who possessed such learning were not expected to earn a living for themselves or their families. Sometimes they were supported by the parents or parents-in-law. It was also common practice for the wives of scholars to conduct various small businesses so that the husband could devote himself to Jewish learning.

This emphasis was soon changed when these Jews came to America. Earning a livelihood necessarily became of primary importance and Jewish study could be engaged in only after working hours or on the Sabbath. Status in the community was acquired less frequently on the basis of scholarship. One of the early settlers describes the situation as follows:

"Once upon a time it was the hope of every Jewish mother that her son would be a rav (rabbi). Today when you speak to some of these Jewish mothers about why their children do not attend Hebrew school, they ask: '*Nu, vos veht ehr sein — a rav?*' (Well, what do you expect him to become — a rabbi?)"

Among the peddler class men still spoke of differences among them with respect to the kind of Jewish learning to which each could lay claim. This, however, eventually gave way to an outright acceptance of the monetary standard as the deciding factor in the society of these people. The peddler class usually associated with its own kind. The small-merchant class, owners of groceries and candy stores and dry goods establishments, constituted a separate group. Owners of the larger stores which catered to the peddler and the small merchant became a third class. Distinctions between these groups were, of course, not hard and fast. Often the traditional attitude and respect for Jewish learning or concern for the welfare of a landsman tended to obviate certain of these distinctions.

The synagogues of the North and South sides were centers of the cultural life of the more learned East European Jews. The synagogue was used not only for prayer, but for study and social purposes as well.

Many peddlers were forced by circumstances to give up religious practices such as observance of the dietary laws, cessation of work on the Sabbath, and the recital of daily prayers with the wearing of phylacteries. Yet they yearned to be associated with their fellow Jews and many of them made every effort to return to the city for the Sabbath. It was their delight to worship with other Jews and in the synagogue to be called up to the reading of the Torah and to exchange a word of "torah" (biblical or rabbinic learning) with their friends.

The first institution to be established was in every instance the synagogue. The early congregations usually met in a spare room over somebody's store. The benches were hard, the accommodations poor, yet they were at least as good as those in their European village communities.

The problem of training the children in the ways of their fathers, teaching them the language of the Bible, and providing an intimate knowledge of its books, was of immediate concern to these parents. Resorting at first to the age-old method of securing a rebbi (teacher) for their children, many parents soon discovered that it required more than a learned Jew to provide adequate education for children growing up in an American environment. Such teachers, who would come to the homes of their pupils, were often unprepared to teach American youth. They were, indeed, frequently men who had failed in business ventures and turned to teaching as a means of subsistence. As a consequence several of the synagogues on the North Side established the cheder (Hebrew school) which met after school hours, usually in makeshift classrooms and taught by teachers who were inadequate as pedagogues.

Impressed by the resultant educational chaos, George J. Gordon, who later became a practicing physician in Minneapolis, rallied the more progressive Jewish members of the North Side and by the sheer force of his zeal and personality finally succeeded in establishing a modern Hebrew school, which met after regular school hours in a synagogue building. This school, known as the Minneapolis Talmud Torah, was organized in 1894. It has grown in importance and influence so that today it is recognized as one of the finest Hebrew educational institutions in the country.

Philanthrophy occupied the attention of several organizations on the North Side. Such societies as the Sisters of Peace, the Russian Hebrew Charity Association, and the Bikur Cholim of the North Side, a society dispensing a sick-benefit fund, were of direct assistance to the East European immigrants who were arriving daily. For the most part, however, charity was dispensed by several highly respected Jewish matrons in the community. They would collect money from friends and neighbors and give it to various needy persons, known only to the matron. Often they prepared chicken soup and other delicacies and brought supplies in their baskets to the homes of the poor. Fraternal organizations were important to the East Europeans, not only in developing the social life of the people but also indirectly in the important work of Americanizing its members.

The Jewish youth of the North Side community began to organize social and cultural activities. The Gymal Doled Club was begun for purely social reasons in 1908 on the North Side by a group of boys who were then attending the University of Minnesota. It established club rooms in the downtown area. This group consisted entirely of American youth from 18 to 30 years of age.

COMMUNITY IN THE MAKING

Different activities centered around their own social interests, but from time to time they became concerned about such problems as juvenile delinquency in the Jewish community.

Another group of Jewish youth organized several months after the Gymal Doled Club and assumed the name of the Atlas Club. This separate society was formed by young men who were "working boys," rather than students at the university, and who were thus not invited to join the Gymal Doled Club. It too carried on a program of social and athletic activities. In 1921 these two organizations joined forces and were known as the Gymal Doled Club until 1945, when the name was changed to the Standard Club.

In addition to these organizations the synagogues of the community had their special youth groups. There was the Hatikvah Society of Kenesseth Israel Synagogue, organized in 1912, which gave various affairs for "charity"; during World War I it raised funds for war relief, as well as for the maintenance of the synagogue.

The Clara de Hirsch Club, an outgrowth of the Sabbath school conducted on the North Side by members of the Shaarei Tov Congregation, its sisterhood, and the Council of Jewish Women, was a club for girls. It met at the homes of its members and regarded itself as a literary club. In addition to its literary efforts, it attempted to "do social work."

The Talmud Torah had numerous clubs, the most important of which seems to have been the Ner Tamid Club, whose purpose was "to establish and maintain a social center for the Jewish community of the North Side." It conducted social affairs, dances, and teas, and sponsored minstrel shows, all for the purpose of raising funds for the Talmud Torah.

One other society, the Jewish Literary Society, consisted of young men who were students at the University of Minnesota and met regularly on the campus. Beginning in 1905, it discussed Jewish life and affairs. In 1911 it became affiliated with the newly established National Menorah Society and carried on a program intended to enrich the lives of Jewish youth on various college campuses throughout the country.

Interest in the rebuilding of Palestine and the re-establishment of a Jewish state was a characteristic of the East European community from its very early days. As early as 1897 the following notice appeared in a Cincinnati paper:

An association to be known as "The Sons of Zion" has been organized at Minneapolis, Minnesota. The aim is to work in connection with the Zionist Movement inaugurated by Mr. Theodore Herzl of Vienna.[6]

This item associated the beginning of Zionist interest in Minneapolis with the rebirth of the Zionist movement through the efforts of the Viennese journalist, Theodore Herzl.

It is not hard to find reasons for the interest in Zionism in Minneapolis. The East European immigrants were Orthodox Jews who understood their history and tradition well enough to know that the hope for Zion restored was Bible-centered. They remembered the promise made by the Lord to the patriarchs, even as they felt at one with the psalmist who wrote, "If I forget thee, O Jerusalem, Let my right hand forget her cunning." Three times daily in their prayers they recited, "O may our eyes witness Thy return to Zion."

But it was not solely their religious tradition which made them think in terms of Zion. These East Europeans had been the victims of pogroms and massacres, had themselves experienced the feeling of being strangers in their native lands. They knew what it was like to live in exile. Little wonder that they found in the modern Zionist movement a source of both strength and unity. Zionism became for them a common denominator, a uniting factor which was stronger than distinctions based on national origin.

We have reason to believe that Zionist interest continued during the early days and that several other clubs and societies were organized after the Sons of Zion. By far the most important was the Poale Zion (Labor Zionists), which established a chapter of the National Workers Zionist Society in Minneapolis in 1907.

COMMUNITY IN THE MAKING

The Poale Zion believed that only through manual labor could the soil of Palestine be redeemed. Many of its members were socialistically inclined. All were vitally interested in helping to reestablish a vital Jewish life in Palestine. Some twenty-five men, all of them artisans or small shopkeepers in the community and all of East European origin, were the original organizers. At first they held regular meetings on Friday nights. Though some were entirely divorced from Jewish religious life and openly violated certain traditional practices, the majority were hardly of that type.

"At first there were a good many of us who would have nothing to do with religion. We held our meetings on Friday nights, but we didn't do it because we were irreligious. For example, we never smoked cigarettes at our meetings on the Shabbas. Later on we came to be more religious. We used Yiddish at all our meetings and we carried on all our conversations in that language. We tried to the very best of our ability to prepare people to emigrate to Palestine, not because we didn't like America, but because we felt that the only way in which we could rebuild Palestine would be to get as many people, Jews, from whatever land they lived in, to help in the important work of building up the land of Israel."

Interest in Zionism has continued and grown through the years. Men, women, and even young people have organized societies whose primary purpose is to foster the idea of rebuilding the land of Palestine. Other phases of the story of Zionist interest and activity in the community are recorded elsewhere.

THE COMMUNITY EXPANDS

Around 1900 the first major shift of the Jewish population of the North Side took place. The Oak Lake district, to which Jews began to move in ever-increasing numbers, bordered the older Jewish neighborhood, just a bit to the west. This district, which had been plotted in 1880, was still sufficiently removed from the city to make it an "exclusive" district.

Oak Lake Addition was a beautiful area, hilly on its west side

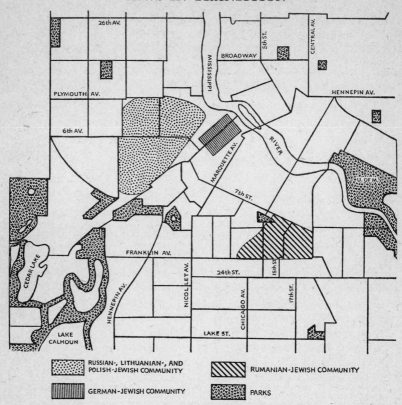

DISTRIBUTION OF THE JEWISH POPULATION OF MINNEAPOLIS
IN 1900

and heavily wooded. . . . In its early days, it was considered the
finest section of town and comprised only the "best people."
However, the people settling the district could not be considered
as the most "elite" of Minneapolis, but they were a substantial
upper middle-class type of people engaged in such occupations
as those of bank cashiers, newspaper editors, attorneys, doctors,
and real estate men. . . . Most of the homes constructed in Oak
Lake were large, spacious dwellings. . . .

By 1900 Minneapolis had increased in population to 202,718,
representing a growth of about 50,000 people during the preceding ten years, and an increase of approximately 150,000 people
from 1880. This growth, of course, was not due to a natural increase, but was due mainly to immigration. . . .

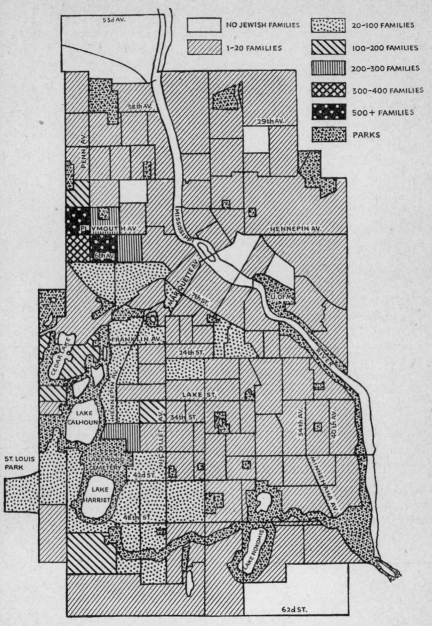

LEGEND:

NO JEWISH FAMILIES
1-20 FAMILIES
20-100 FAMILIES
100-200 FAMILIES
200-300 FAMILIES
300-400 FAMILIES
500+ FAMILIES
PARKS

DISTRIBUTION OF THE JEWISH POPULATION OF MINNEAPOLIS
IN 1945 (BY CENSUS TRACTS)

29

The pressure of numbers caused the Jews to expand and the movement was westward. They worked south from Eighth Avenue North to Sixth Avenue North and then to Lyndale Avenue. By 1900 the presence and pressure of the Jews began to be felt in Oak Lake. At first there was bitter opposition to the Jewish invasion. . . .

After the peripheral invasion of the Oak Lake district the mere presence of the Jews seemed to melt the bitter opposition. People became alarmed and frightened at the number of Jews. Many of the Jews were small dealers, some rag peddlers, some fruit men, and still others dealers in junk. . . . Even the pride and dignity of Highland Avenue finally humbled and succumbed to this affront. In 1912 the first Jewish family moved into the Highland district. To close an estate, one of the large residences was sold to a chicken dealer. From this time on, the whole Oak Lake district was rapidly taken over by the Jews. . . .

Meanwhile another segregation on the North Side had commenced. By 1910 the number of Negroes in Minneapolis had increased to 2,592. The original segregation of Negroes occurred around "Seven Corners," but due to lack of houses and high rents the Negroes began a migration to the North Side. The Jews, having vacated the district immediately north and east of Sixth Avenue North, offered to the Negroes a great number of homes at very cheap rents. . . .

Simultaneous with the influx of the Negro into the territory adjacent to Oak Lake, a new residential area, Homewood, was opened. This addition was intended to be exclusive . . . and was not intended for Jews. In spite of all the residents of Homewood could do, the wealthier Jews were able to buy into the new plot. Other Jews in Oak Lake in 1912 to 1914 took a cue from their wealthier neighbors, or perhaps due to the presence of the Negro, and moved north of Sixth Avenue towards Plymouth Avenue. . . . Today Oak Lake is pointed out as one of the bad housing spots in Minneapolis.[7]

The Homewood district, as was pointed out earlier, is today the residential area of the middle- and upper-class Jews on the North Side. It is the center of an area of beautiful, well-maintained homes, owned by their occupants.

Another population shift began around 1915, when the German Jews first began to move to the West Side. This area now is the largest growing Jewish neighborhood in the city. It owes its growth to the ever-increasing number of Jewish families who have moved from the South and North sides. The South Side Jewish community, though decreasing in size, still remains in the vicinity of its original settlement, Franklin Avenue and Fifteenth Avenue South.

THE COMMUNITY UNITES

Thus far in the story of the development of the Jewish community, we have called attention to the schisms and divisions that characterized the group until the turn of the century.

German Jews looked down upon the later immigrants, the "refugees" as they called them. Russian and Rumanian immigrants and their children were not often invited to join the organizations or participate in the activities of the older group, and when such participation occurred it was generally frowned upon. It is true that the Council of Jewish Women and the Hebrew Relief Association undertook certain very helpful and necessary tasks in the interests of the children of the North and South sides. Yet the temper of the times seems to have been one of toleration, rather than of complete and wholehearted acceptance.

The German Jews frequently misunderstood the needs of the "refugees":

We have here eight Russian refugees to take care of and some of them are pretty unmanageable, especially when advised to begin working and getting their $10.00 a week, which is an easy thing in this growing city. They want land and nothing but land, as if they knew anything about husbandry or as if tillage were easier than any other work. Who can provide all these people with farms, houses, oxen, horses, provisions for a year, implements for a guide, etc.? We have gathered $360.00 and have formed a Relief Society, having spent more than half this amount and are at a loss how to deal with the problem without some advice and material help from the East.[8]

The new immigrants, while accepting whatever aid the German community could give, felt that it spelled for them a position of dependence, if not of inferiority. Hence there was an undercurrent of resentment and an uneasiness about the situation.

The first step in the process of unification came when the North Side community began to feel the need of maintaining its independence. Up to that point, these people had depended upon the active assistance and cooperation of certain members of the German Jewish community. Except for their synagogues, there was little in an organizational sense which they could call their own. The belief that they were quite capable of conducting their own affairs started to develop in 1893, when Dr. George J. Gordon arrived in the city.

Dr. Gordon, a Lithuanian Jew who had studied at the renowned Talmudic academy of the town of Telz, soon became the recognized leader of the North Side Jewry. As a physician who went into the homes of the newer immigrants and as the prime mover and later director of the Minneapolis Talmud Torah (the modern Hebrew school), he wielded great influence upon his neighbors. For many he became the symbol of the spirit of independence that began to manifest itself on the North Side. He resisted the tendency to accept a lower status in the eyes of the German Jewish community. He insisted that Orthodox Jewry must build or create those institutions that it required without falling back upon others for advice and help. With the aid of some of the more progressive members of the Orthodox community, he developed a program of social service and Hebrew education that commanded the attention and respect of the German Jews.

The new attitude of independence whenever possible on the part of the North Side Jews began to have its effect upon the German Jews. They found in Dr. Gordon a man worthy of their respect. He had acquired status, not solely as the leader of the East European Jews but also as a physician and generally a man of culture. He was turned to for advice and counsel by the leaders of the older Jewish community. His role in helping to bring about a certain rapprochement between the two segments of the community cannot be overestimated.

Fortunately for the community, another outstanding person, Dr. Samuel N. Deinard, came to Minneapolis. In 1901 Dr. Deinard received a call to serve as the rabbi of Temple Shaarei Tov, a post he was to hold for twenty years. As the rabbi of a Reform temple, whose members were German Jews, it was hardly expected that he would assume the role of liaison between the German and Russian Jewish communities. Yet he did perform this function in an admirable manner.

Though a Reform Jew, unorthodox in his practices and beliefs, he was himself of East European origin, which may explain his understanding of and sympathetic approach to his Orthodox brethren. Dr. Deinard was a Zionist when the members of his congregation were non-Zionists. He was a scholar of note, thoroughly familiar with Hebraic literature and tradition and able to speak many languages including Yiddish. Though his own temple observed but one day of a holy day that was celebrated by the Orthodox Jews for two, he made it a practice to attend some Orthodox synagogue on the second day of the festival and usually accepted invitations to address the congregation. It was but natural that he should have won the respect and admiration of the East European Jews.

Dr. Deinard acted also in the capacity of interpreter to his own people of the spirit and the needs of the more recent Jewish arrivals. Through his efforts, his people came to understand these strange "foreigners" from East Europe who also spoke of themselves as Jews.

Believing that a newspaper would serve to bring about a union of the various groups by expressing the interests of the total Jewish community, Dr. Deinard in 1904 undertook the publication of an Anglo-Jewish news magazine for Minneapolis and St. Paul. Accordingly he established a weekly, the *Jewish Progress*. This first venture did not prove successful. In 1905 he introduced another weekly newspaper called the *Judaean,* which apparently was also a failure, for in 1907 a third weekly, the *Scribe,* first saw the light of day. In order to overcome the problem which arose from the fact that the number of English-speaking Jews in Minneapolis was still not very large, the *Scribe* published a weekly four-page supplement in Yiddish. In spite of its special feature this paper too ceased publication after several years.

Finally in 1912 the first financially successful Anglo-Jewish news weekly appeared in the Twin Cities. This news magazine, the *American Jewish World,* was also edited by Dr. Deinard. It had the support and backing of various Jewish lay leaders from the community as a whole.

The present number of subscribers to the *American Jewish World* has not been disclosed. Yet its news columns are read by all elements of the community, and the fact that all Jewish organizations, religious and secular, seek to publicize their activities through its columns seems to indicate that it plays an important role in the Jewish community.

The Zionist movement in Minneapolis received vigorous support from Dr. Deinard. Believing firmly in the need for establishing a Jewish state in Palestine, he soon found many enthusiastic supporters of the modern Zionist movement in the community — co-workers who came mainly from the North Side group. It is related that shortly after Dr. Deinard began his ministry in Temple Shaarei Tov, his enthusiastic support of Zionism began to trouble some members of his congregation. The president of the temple, a man of German origin, spoke to Dr. Deinard about his Zionist activities and "threatened that if he talked about Zionism any more, he would lose his post." Dr. Deinard refused to be intimidated and continued his work on behalf of the Jewish state.

In 1918 he was instrumental in establishing a local branch of Hadassah, the national women's Zionist organization which sought "to foster Zionist ideals through Jewish education." Hadassah has expressed its interest in Zionism through the years by assuming responsibility for the physical well-being of Jews

COMMUNITY IN THE MAKING

living in the Holy Land. After the issuance of the Balfour Declaration in 1917, it began to provide medical units to minister
to the needs of Palestinian Jewry and of the Arab population as
well. Later it built a great medical center on Mount Scopus, just
outside Jerusalem, and established a network of medical stations
throughout the country.

The local chapter of Hadassah had grown by 1948 to a membership of 1900 women. In addition a chapter of Junior Hadassah, for unmarried women, has been established. Their interest
in Zionism expresses itself not only through the excellent medical
program which the local chapters support, but also through
active participation in the work of supporting and rehabilitating
Jewish refugee children in Palestine. This phase of the program
is known as Youth Aliyah (Youth Immigration). Locally Hadassah, with the cooperation of other Zionist organizations in Minneapolis and St. Paul, has established Herzl Camp, a summer
camp which provides a program of Jewish activities for the
young people of the Twin Cities and environs.

Another of the early leaders who helped to create a united
Jewish community was the leader of the Kenesseth Israel Synagogue, Rabbi S. M. Silber. For twenty-three years (1902 to 1925)
Rabbi Silber served as the religious leader and arbiter of the
Orthodox Jews. Had he been content to confine himself to
the problems and interests of his own congregants alone, it is
doubtful if the process of unification of the Jewish community
could have come about as quickly as it did. A learned Jew of
the old school, Rabbi Silber's interests were city-wide. Though
in complete disagreement with the religious views and practices of the Reform Jews, he soon won their respect and approval
by his active participation in every phase of Jewish communal
life.

A fourth leader in the unification of the community was
Joseph H. Schanfeld, who concerned himself with the very seri-
ous problems created by the mass immigration of Jews from
Eastern Europe in the early 1900's. Though valiant efforts had

been made in Minneapolis, particularly by a small group of German Jews, to assist the newly arrived immigrants, general dissatisfaction still existed. Schanfeld, a member of the South Side community and the son of Rumanian immigrants, undertook to help the new arrivals by providing them with shelter and then with jobs. He gathered about him a group of young men, all sons of immigrants, who recognized the importance of the work, and soon they had created an active, though loosely organized, body.

In 1903 Schanfeld's work attracted the attention of the Jewish Immigration Society of New York and he was invited to act as their representative in Minneapolis. This official recognition coupled with an awareness of the work he and his co-workers had already done, had an unexpected but important result. Schanfeld was invited to become a member of the local B'nai B'rith Lodge.

B'nai B'rith, founded in New York in 1843 as a national Jewish fraternal order, had as its purpose "the instilling of the principles of morality among the followers of the Mosaic faith, and of inculcating charity, benevolence and brotherly love as the highest virtues." The local lodge of the order had been established in 1877 and was composed entirely of German Jews. Schanfeld was the first East European to "make the grade."

Sometime before, B'nai B'rith had established its Free Employment Bureau to help recently arrived immigrants find means of earning a livelihood. Schanfeld's interest in this work undoubtedly made him a valuable asset, and under his direction B'nai B'rith developed an expanded program of aid and assistance to immigrants.

Max Seham, a young medical student who became director of the employment bureau in 1908, has described how he and Schanfeld located jobs for the immigrants:

"I used to get up at 5 o'clock in the morning to meet the immigrants when they arrived. Most of them were single persons. We placed these immigrants in a house on Sixteenth Avenue

South around Fifth or Sixth Street, which we had rented for this purpose. Mr. Schanfeld and I would make the rounds of the various factories and if some worker did not show up for work, we would place these immigrants. I placed about twenty-five immigrants a month this way.

"We provided food and other necessities for these people until they were settled and were able to go on their own. There was a continual turnover in the home. New immigrants kept arriving daily. I would take care of all those who needed jobs and many of them would line up in Mr. Schanfeld's insurance office each morning and he would interview them. Between the two of us and with the help of the B'nai B'rith and the Immigration Society we managed to do a quite important piece of work."

Another young man, Arthur Brin, born of Lithuanian parents in Chicago, was attracting attention. He too had become a leader of some prominence because of his interest in Jewish communal affairs. Like Joseph Schanfeld, a selfless individual, devoted to the ideal of assisting his fellow man, Arthur Brin too attracted the attention of B'nai B'rith and in 1905 he was invited to join the local lodge.

Neither Joseph Schanfeld nor Arthur Brin cared much about the national origins that seemed so important to their elders. They paid little attention to the economic successes of certain members of the community and little more to the divisiveness resulting from different religious philosophies. They focused their attention and energy on the numerous problems that required solutions. There were the immigrants, arriving daily, who had to be cared for and given a proper start in their new land. There were problems of adjustment of the residents to their new environment, as well as other vexing educational, religious, and social problems. Both men later distinguished themselves for their efforts not only on behalf of the Jewish community, but in the larger community as well.

The story of the growth of the Minneapolis Jewish community would hardly be complete if it did not take cognizance of the role played by Dr. Moses Barron, a physician and Jewish lay leader of note. While still a student at the University of Minnesota, Moses Barron was a guiding spirit in Jewish student affairs. Throughout the years, however, his interest in Zionism was most marked. At the university he was primarily responsible for the interest displayed in the modern Zionist movement by his fellow students. After his graduation from medical school Dr. Barron helped to fire the imagination of numerous other persons in the Jewish community with respect to Zionism.

It was he, together with his devoted wife, who bridged the gap that existed between the Poale Zion (Workers for Zion) and the general Jewish public. The Poale Zion, a small but devoted group who were manual workers and laborers, was often regarded with suspicion by other Jews because many of its members spoke of themselves as socialists. Realizing that if Palestine was to be rebuilt physically and culturally, it would certainly require the active cooperation of all classes of Jews, Dr. Barron lent his support to this group, even though he was himself a member of the general Zionist organization.

Respected because of his high scholastic and medical attainments, as well as for his devotion to Zionist ideal, Dr. Barron became the symbol of modern Zionism in the community. Through him there developed closer ties on the Zionist level between the members of the faculty of the university and all elements in the Jewish community. For many years Dr. Barron served as the president of the Friends of the Hebrew University, an organization of Minneapolitans and St. Paulites, in the main, professional men and their wives, which assisted in providing financial support for the Hebrew University in Jerusalem.

These men have been singled out because the Jewish community, as it looks back upon its history, has often expressed the belief that they were the real leaders of the younger generation of Jews in Minneapolis. This chapter is intended, not to record the name of every man or woman who made a contribution to the Jewish community, but rather to call attention to the typical leaders, the men whose point of view and effort helped to overcome the divisiveness and create a single community of interest.

The next important step in the development of unity within the Jewish community came in 1910. In that year the Associated Jewish Charities of Minneapolis was organized. This is how it happened.

In September 1909 the Minneapolis Lodge B'nai B'rith, apparently as a result of its experience with the Jewish Free Employment Bureau and its work on behalf of the Russian immigrants, appointed a committee to "canvass the situation in regard to the advisability of federating all Jewish charities under one head." Then B'nai B'rith invited the following then-existing Jewish organizations to become part of the association: the Hebrew Ladies' Benevolent Society, the Sisters of Peace, the Jewish Loan Society, B'nai B'rith Free Employment Bureau, the Sheltering Home for Transients, and the Jewish Free Dispensary, which had been established to furnish medical service by private physicians for indigent Jewish families. In addition to these local organizations the Minneapolis committees for the National Jewish Hospital for Consumptives and the Jewish Consumptives' Relief Society, both of Denver, were invited to send their representatives. Representatives of all these groups created the Associated Jewish Charities.

Though the first president, vice-president, and treasurer of the organization were members of the German-Jewish community, the secretary was a Russian Jew. Of the five-man executive committee, four were Russian Jews and one was a German Jew. The first committees that were appointed indicate the nature of the work which was to be undertaken. There was a relief committee, a committee on the Sheltering Home, a juvenile committee (apparently to concern itself with programs of juvenile delinquency), a committee on subscriptions, and an auditing committee. In 1914 a trained social worker, Anna L. Fox, was invited to come to Minneapolis to become superintendent of the new organization. In 1915 Miss Julia Felsenthal became the superintendent. She played an important role in the development and integration of all philanthropic activities within the Jewish community. Minutes of the organization indicate that twelve thousand dollars was spent by the Associated Jewish Charities in 1915 for the relief of Jewish families.

In 1918 the Community Fund of Minneapolis invited the association to participate and from that time on the financial obligations of the Jewish charities were assumed by the Community Fund. Something of the nature of the changes which have occurred within the organization itself may be gathered from the fact that in 1924 the Associated Jewish Charities changed its name to the Jewish Family Welfare Association and that in 1946 the name was changed once again to the Jewish Family Service Society.

The history of this organization represents the first clear-cut organizational activity carried on by all the elements within the Jewish community under one banner. It demonstrated to the Jewish community that there were many areas of activity which could be undertaken jointly by all elements despite their religious differences.

The story of the Emanuel Cohen Center, a neighborhood house located in the Oak Lake district, represents another step in the unification of the Jewish community. In 1910 the members of the Gymal Doled Club noted that there were a great number of young people in the Jewish community who were likely to become delinquents. They took account of the petty gambling and other vices among the Jewish youth of the North Side and accordingly invited a social worker from Chicago to consult with them as to the best means to overcome this situation. One of the prime movers in this effort relates:

"This social worker, whose name I do not happen to remember, told us that he believed that the only way in which we could break up some of the gangs of North Side Jewish boys that were then in existence would be to start a program of activities that would keep them busy and out of mischief. We talked the matter over and decided to appeal to a well-known Jewish lawyer, Mr.

Emanuel Cohen. We told him our story and he gave us the assurance that money would be forthcoming for such a project."

It was, however, through the Minneapolis Talmud Torah that the center finally came into being. In 1914 the Talmud Torah began to lay plans for the provision of recreational facilities for its own students and alumni, as well as for other young people in the community. There was an urgent and increasing plea on the part of the Gymal Doled Club, the Associated Jewish Charities, and the members of the then-existing YMHA and YWHA, for the completion of the Talmud Torah gymnasium. As the result of this pressure representatives of fifteen organizations were called together to formulate a program of activities for the Jewish youth of the North Side. This meeting resulted in the organization of the Talmud Torah Social Service Department and the release by the Associated Jewish Charities of their supervisor, Miss Julia Felsenthal, to establish the department as an educational and recreational agency.

The program at first consisted mainly of English classes, Friday evening services, and a few clubs. By 1921 activities and attendance had expanded to such an extent as to require the services of a trained worker. Three years later the Talmud Torah quarters had become entirely inadequate for the social service department and a new building was purchased and remodeled — the Talmud Torah gymnasium, swimming pool, and auditorium being still available for larger group activities. The purchase was made possible by the transfer of funds left to the Jewish Family Welfare Association by the late Emanuel Cohen to establish a recreational and social agency. In recognition of this assistance the name of the institution was changed from the Talmud Torah Social Service Department to the Emanuel Cohen Center.

The development of a Jewish community spirit was finally assured with the organization of the Minneapolis Federation for Jewish Service in 1930. This over-all body has on its board representatives of all major Jewish organizations, groups, and philosophies in Minneapolis.

JEWS IN TRANSITION

A word too should be said about the religious leadership of the community. Minneapolis is fortunate in having had .the benefit of rabbinic leaders who, despite their loyalties to specific institutions and philosophies, have always cooperated with each other in the interest of building a better Jewish community.

Finally, it should be noted that, as the economic differences between the members of the community have leveled off — the German Jews being no better or no worse off financially than Russian, Lithuanian, Polish, or Rumanian Jews — distinctions that divided the community in an earlier day have largely disappeared. The Oak Ridge Country Club and the temple, formerly the possession of German Jews, now have numerous members who are the sons and daughters of East European parents.

The Jewish community is little concerned today with questions concerning the country of origin or religious grouping of particular persons. It asks only that there be a readiness to serve the needs of the community as a whole.

Chapter 3   The Jew and His Neighbor

☞§ THE *problem of anti-Semitism which confronts the Jews of the western world has two aspects, that of mitigating such prejudices as already exist and of forestalling their unfortunate consequences in the Jewish personality.*[1]

Consider the case of the Jews in Minneapolis! The average Jew knows court records will support his belief that he and his children are law-abiding citizens. He believes that he maintains his home and family life in a manner that reflects credit upon his community. He contributes liberally to the Community Fund.[2] He is among the active supporters of and contributors to the Minneapolis symphony orchestra and other cultural activities. He provides his sons and daughters with opportunities for higher education. He believes that he conducts his business affairs on a high ethical plane. He is aware of the fact that there are a few notorious "characters" in the community who happen to be Jews by birth and he deplores their presence, yet he knows that the number of such Jewish persons in the community is limited.[3] He has built and contributed to the maintenance of the numerous temples and synagogues in the community and has not failed to accept any call to serve on civic and other committees within the community.

He is the proprietor of many of the smaller shops and businesses of the city, but the larger department stores and industrial establishments have been and are in the hands of non-Jews. He does not control or share in the control of the milling, mining, lumber, or banking industries. He does not own or control the local newspapers. He may be liked personally. His business is actively solicited.

43

He is told that he is a "good fellow," that he is generally regarded as a good citizen — but he knows that Minneapolis has, despite this, not completely accepted him. He feels that he is still an outsider. He believes that Carey McWilliams may have been more right than he knew when he termed Minneapolis the "capitol of anti-Semitism in the United States." [4]

In his article McWilliams says:

One might even say, with a measure of justification, that Minneapolis is the capitol of anti-Semitism in the United States. In almost every walk of life, "an iron curtain" separates Jews from non-Jews in Minneapolis. Nor is this "iron curtain" a matter of recent origin; on the contrary, it seems to have always existed. So far as I know, Minneapolis is the only city in America in which Jews are, as a matter of practice and custom, ineligible for membership in the service clubs. In fact, Jews have never been accepted into membership in the local Kiwanis, Rotary, Lions, or Toastmasters organizations. . . . Even the Automobile Club in Minneapolis refuses to accept Jews as members. Mr. Hugh Craig, secretary of the club, recently declined to accept the application of a well-known and highly respected rabbi. So far as I know, there is not another automobile club in America which pursues a similar policy.

McWilliams calls attention to the fact that "at a recent meeting of the national realty boards, the Minneapolis delegation made much of the fact that Jews are not eligible for membership on the local realty board"; that, although "years ago, a few Jews were accepted, as life members, in the Minneapolis Athletic Club. . . . the board of the club, contrary to a long established practice, has of recent years refused to recognize the transfer of these memberships to the sons of deceased members and has stated that it will not accept further Jewish applications." He calls attention, too, to the established policy of certain business concerns, notably some of the chain stores, of not interviewing Jewish applicants and understates the case when he says that "Jews have experienced considerable difficulty in buying residential property in Minneapolis." McWilliams quotes Douglas Hall, attor-

THE JEW AND HIS NEIGHBOR

ney for the CIO in Minneapolis, to the effect that "anti-Semitism
has been a rather serious problem in the local trade unions."

He points out further:

The most striking aspect of anti-Semitism in Minneapolis,
however, consists in the lack of significant Jewish participation
in the dominant economic activities of the city. In milling, lum-
bering, transportation, private utilities, banking, insurance, and,
even to a degree in the field of department-store merchandising,
Jews do not figure as an important element. Despite the fact
that a sizable Jewish community has existed in Minneapolis for
many years, Jews have not acquired an economic position com-
parable to that which they occupy in other cities of approximately the same size. . . . While Jews participate in local civic
affairs, they are seldom represented on the boards of civic organizations. That local residents, seeking to minimize this statement, should emphasize the fact that a Jew was recently selected
as head of the Council of Social Agencies, merely underscores the
existence of a general exclusionist policy. With the exception of
an alderman elected from a predominantly Jewish district, there
are no Jewish office-holders in Minneapolis.

Selden C. Menefee, reporting for the *Nation* in 1943 on the
trend of public opinion in the United States, said about Minneapolis: "I found almost no evidence of anti-Semitism in the
Northwestern and West Central States. *Except in Minneapolis*
no one considered it a serious problem." [5]

In his book, *Assignment: U.S.A.*, Menefee writes further about
Minneapolis:

Minneapolis, unlike most Western and Midwestern cities, is
highly stratified along class lines, with little social intercourse
between the major social groups. . . . The most prominent Minneapolis citizens, financially and socially, have little in common
with the great Scandinavian- and German-stock middle classes.
. . . Signs of militant anti-Semitism I found to be almost entirely lacking in the Middle West, as in the South and West —
except for Minneapolis. . . . In Minneapolis, however, a professional man of liberal viewpoint told me, "Anti-Semitism is stronger
here than anywhere I have ever lived. It's so strong that people
of all groups I have met make the most blatant statements

45

against Jews with the calm assumption that they are merely stating facts with which anyone could agree. After more weeks of mere listening than I am proud of, I finally began taking a stand every time an anti-Semitic statement was made in my presence. The bombshells have been something to see and hear." [6]

As early as 1922 the subject of anti-Semitism in Minneapolis was a source of disturbance if not of frustration to the Jewish population of Minneapolis. In that year Dr. Maurice Lefkovits, writing in the *American Jewish World,* said:

Minneapolis Jewry enjoys the painful distinction of being the lowest esteemed community in the land so far as the non-Jewish population of the city is concerned. And that is what I mean by "objective evaluation," — the evaluation of the Jewish community by the non-Jewish population of the city. In this respect, Minneapolis Jewry is way below par of the other communities in the land. [7]

Anti-Jewish feeling seems to have existed in Minneapolis since the arrival of the first Jewish settler. As early as 1890, when the Jews of East Europe began moving into the North Side, they were obliged to create minor ghettos for themselves, not alone because of their limited financial means, but because other neighborhoods were already occupied by Irish and German residents, themselves comparative newcomers to the community.

"It was dangerous for any Jew to move above Fifth Street, North, because the Irish and the Germans lived there. If we went into their neighborhood, they might start a fight and beat up any Jew, young or old, who was passing by."

Such things do not happen in Minneapolis today. Yet it must be recorded that the Jewish owner of a new home in a fashionable section of the city was recently obliged to call for police protection when, shortly after he moved into his home, the windows were shot through with buckshot. Jews have been approached by neighborhood committees who have urged them not to purchase homes in their particular neighborhoods, because "this is a Christian neighborhood." There are whole sections in the city that to this day are "wisely restricted," that is, restricted to Jews. These areas happen to be owned not by the ignorant or by the manual workers of the city or even by the Fundamentalist-Christian groups, but rather by members of the upper middle-class "fashionable set" of Minneapolis.

Unless the residence be in the poorer sections of the city, or in a neighborhood already predominately Jewish, Jews find it difficult, if not impossible, to rent an apartment or a home in many sections. In his early days in Minneapolis the author spent many hours trudging the streets of Minneapolis attempting to rent an apartment, only to be told time and again, "We don't rent to Jews," in a definitely Scandinavian accent.

This fact, perhaps more than any other, explains why Jews, in even larger proportion than is true of the general public, are obliged to purchase their own homes. One or two Jewish families (they may be among the most cultured and even native born) move into a given neighborhood and the non-Jewish neighbors begin a general hurried departure, not unlike the Exodus from Egypt. That is not to say that each neighborhood in Minneapolis is either Jewish or Christian. There are, of course, many understanding souls within the community who frown upon such tendencies. There are even many close friendships between Jewish and Christian neighbors, but the picture with respect to housing must be recorded as dark.

To take another, more encouraging aspect of the intergroup relationship, it can be reported that the Jews of Minneapolis are active participants in the general community program.

While there are few exact statistics regarding Jewish participation in the activities conducted under public auspices, it is the impression of the leaders of the public school, library and park board systems that their respective facilities are utilized by the Jewish population in the same degree as by the general population.[8]

There is in addition a substantial amount of Jewish participation in the activities of private agencies: the YWCA and YMCA, the settlement houses, and the Girl Scouts and Boy Scouts. There is a rather larger proportion of Jewish youth participating in the Scout movement than in other activities. It is of interest to note that Jewish participation in general community activities is largely in the physical activities — swimming, camping, and other forms of athletics.

Jewish women are members of such organizations as the College Women's Club, the League of Women Voters, and the Women's International League for Peace and Freedom, though their number is not large. Both men and women are members of the Foreign Policy Association, sponsors of the Minneapolis symphony orchestra, and members of the Council of Social Agencies.

In the main there appears to be a friendly spirit, at least outwardly, among Jews and Christians in business and the professions, but there is little intermingling of the groups socially. "Most of my business associates are Jews," reports a Christian businessman. "Whenever I see them, they invite me to play golf with them at their golf club. I have accepted their invitations on many occasions. But it has never occurred to me to invite them to join me in a game of golf at my golf club." He might have gone further and pointed out that he would have been the object of unfavorable comment among his friends had he invited his Jewish associates to his club.

Although there is no positive evidence that Jews are not wanted in the Minneapolis public school system, there are only nine Jewish elementary school teachers, four high school teachers, one music supervisor, and one high school principal who was at one time an assistant superintendent of schools. All that can be stated is that there are, strangely, fewer Jewish teachers than one would expect in a city where Jews comprise 4 percent of the total population.

There are, however, a goodly number of Jews on the faculty of the University of Minnesota. They range from instructor to full professor and are to be found in practically all faculties, with the largest number in the school of medicine.

48

THE JEW AND HIS NEIGHBOR

The university is comparatively free from anti-Semitism. An interesting and revealing analysis of this situation was made by Dr. Leo Rigler, professor of roentgenology at the University Hospitals, in a letter published in one of the local newspapers. He pointed out the

striking difference between the attitude of the University of Minnesota and the city in which it is located. There is no Jewish quota in any college of the University. Beyond the exclusion of Jewish students from most of the sororities and fraternities, over which the administration and faculty have no control, there is virtually no discrimination, or even any recognition of differences in race or religion. The lack of prejudice, the fairmindedness, the really democratic spirit of the university are so outstanding as to merit special recognition.

This admirable state of affairs has not always existed on the campus. Anti-Semitism became something of a problem in the early 1930's. At that time pacifism was an important if not a major issue. Among the pacifists were certain Jewish youths who actively opposed the use of force and vowed never to bear arms. (They did, however! During World War II many of the pacifists of an earlier day distinguished themselves in the armed forces of the United States.) Their oratorical efforts aroused the anger of a number of people, both on the campus and in the community as a whole. Jews then were accused not of being warmongers, as they were in the days before World War II, but of being pacifists, which, it seems, was just as bad.

The decade of the thirties brought several bad outbreaks of anti-Semitism to Minneapolis. The city-wide strike of 1934, engineered and dominated by the AFL Truck Drivers Local 574, is a case in point. When this union, led by the three Dunne brothers, literally took control of the city and for several days actually directed traffic in the downtown streets, it was whispered that the Jews had taken over Minneapolis. At the invitation of warring employer and employee groups, the author was invited to arbitrate the issues. Peaceful relations in certain of the strike-bound industries were restored in some degree, and as a result twenty-three industries invited the author to be impartial arbitrator. Later handbills were mysteriously distributed around the city asking, "Why, Rabbi Gordon, do you control the unions of Minneapolis?" with the intent of making it appear that the author, with diabolical cleverness, was actually responsible for the numerous strikes.

About 1935 the ugly head of organized anti-Semitism was raised in the community. To the city there came, among others, Elizabeth Dilling with her addresses on the "Red Network" in which Jews figured prominently. Her first addresses were delivered in the First Baptist Church, of which the late Dr. W. B. Riley was the minister. From his pulpit and from others like that of the evangelist Luke Rader there came a series of attacks against the Jews.

The Silver Shirts, led by William Dudley Pelley, and a variety of other organizations known for their anti-Semitic tendencies, began to put in their appearance in 1937. They met first in private homes and later in public halls to which "select" individuals from the community were invited.

It is noteworthy that at a Silver Shirt meeting so prominent a citizen as George K. Belden, president of the Associated Industries of Minneapolis, an employers' group, and president of the Automobile Club, was present. News of his presence, when called to the attention of the people of Minneapolis on the front pages of local newspapers, met with mixed response. The unions and their leaders saw for the first time that anti-Semitism was the bait by which anti-unionism was being sold to the people. They wrote official letters of thanks and offers of continued support to the author, who had called attention to the issue.

Others, led principally by Dr. Riley, who undertook to act as public defender, made it appear that there was an attempt to deprive Mr. Belden, in some mysterious way, of his constitutional right to attend any meeting he so desired. The Associated Industries, meanwhile, hastily convened its board and wrote an official letter pointing out that if its president did attend such a meeting he did so as a private individual. Belden telephoned the author at the time and explained that he appeared at the Silver Shirt meeting only out of curiosity, though the story of the Silver Shirts and their Jew-baiting tactics had been front page news for many months.

The Minneapolis *Journal* sent one of its reporters, Eric Sevareid, later to become an outstanding radio reporter of World War II, to several of the Silver Shirt meetings. Sevareid's series of articles, ridiculing the organization, produced a startling effect, less upon the general community than upon many of the Jews themselves. Some regarded the publicity as dangerous. Others, a majority of the Jewish community, though frightened in some degree by the disclosures, were grateful for the publicity that had been given the issue.

The statewide campaign in 1938 in which Harold Stassen undertook to wrest the governorship from Elmer Benson was in large measure built around the issue of a "Jew-controlled state capitol." At first in a whispering campaign, then in the form of a never-to-be-forgotten pamphlet entitled "Are They Communists or Are They Catspaws?" each Jew who had worked in the state capitol under Governors Floyd Olson and Elmer Benson was singled out for attack and by indirection made to appear as a Communist. Just before the election the Minneapolis *Journal* (the predecessor of the Minneapolis *Star,* then owned by other interests) devoted a page of its rotogravure section to photographs of the men who surrounded Governor Olson. Most of those whose pictures were used were Jews, though they represented only a small fraction of the governor's intimates.

"It isn't because we thought that these Jewish politicians were all such wonderful people that we objected and were so hurt by the attack. If there are Jews who violate the law they ought to be punished. But if the things they did were so very dreadful why did the newspapers and all these righteous citizens wait all those years and only decide to blast these persons in particular just before the campaign? No. The fact is, we believed then and

51

we believe now that anti-Semitism was being used to get rid of the Farmer-Labor administration."

So vicious did the attack become that several Jewish Republicans visited Harold Stassen and urged him to make a public repudiation of those people who used the anti-Semitic argument during the campaign. In his concluding radio address, delivered the night before election day, Stassen declared that he did not wish to identify himself with those responsible for the attack.

There are people in the community who insist that the gubernatorial campaign served as the testing ground for a technique which was to be used with great effectiveness on the national scene during the days when "Clear it with Sidney" (Hillman) was a battlecry to be reckoned with.

The problem of anti-Semitism is felt among Jewish members of the various labor unions, both AFL and CIO. There are three Jewish business agents in the city, two for AFL unions and one for the CIO. Of the seventy-five members of the Cap Makers Union, sixty are Jews. Though Jewish women are members of the Amalgamated Clothing Workers and the International Ladies Garment Workers, they do not constitute a majority in either case. There are Jewish members in practically all other unions in Minneapolis. It has been estimated that there are about a thousand Jewish union members in Minneapolis.

In spite of the supposed bond among workers, reliable information makes it clear that anti-Semitic feeling expresses itself in many of the unions. Though two of the Jewish business agents are active in labor affairs, and even though the unions they serve are not predominantly Jewish (indicating that these men are highly regarded by the membership), derogatory remarks about them as Jews are often heard.

Minneapolis employers are believed to have anti-Semitic tendencies, and it is regarded as bad policy for Jews to take their places in the picket line. One non-Jewish business agent has said:

"Employers like to see Jews in the picket lines. Then they can argue that all their troubles are brought about by Jews. I once had to take some Jewish members off the picket line in the case of a strike against a Gentile employer, because he was calling everyone's attention to the fact that Jews had caused the strike, when as a matter of fact there are really very few Jews in that union."

Another source indicates that anti-Semitism among both employers and union members has increased since 1935.

"The propaganda-spreading anti-Semitism is conducted in a more subtle and palatable manner, and the recipients of the poison are getting it in a very generous and systematic manner. Because of that the movement is more deeply imbedded and harder to counteract than in former years."

In the city of Minneapolis there are understanding and liberal clergymen and laymen who are profoundly disturbed by these manifestations of anti-Semitism and who are sometimes aroused sufficiently to fight back. There are, however, few clergymen whose indignation causes them to lead a militant fight within their own churches. One important clerical leader sadly confessed that anti-Semitism was rife in his own church but that there seemed to be little he could do about it. This clergyman was once advised by his congregation to devote less time to "good will" activities if he wished to retain the favor of his congregants.

A part of the Fundamentalist-Baptist group has been and remains the local leader in the attacks upon the Jews. The Lutheran clergy, owing to its theological position, is passive on the issue. It does not generally cooperate in communal activities where Jews are represented. One result of the attitude of the Lutheran and Fundamentalist-Baptists is the difficulty Jewish women often experience in hiring domestic workers, since a large number of maids and houseworkers come from these two groups. It is not uncommon for someone who wishes to employ "help" to be told, "We don't work for Jews." One Jewish woman reported the following incident:

"I happened to meet a young Lutheran girl who had just come from a small town in Minnesota and I offered her employment as a maid in my home. She accepted the position and seemed quite happy. I not only told her the location of the Lutheran church in our neighborhood, but saw to it that she was introduced to the group by a girl who had once worked for me. Imagine my surprise when after several weeks, this girl showed me a letter she had received from the pastor of her home-town church, to whom she had apparently written, denouncing her, in no uncertain terms, first for joining a church, even though Lutheran, that belonged to a synod different from hers, and second, for working for 'God-forsaken Jews.' I never realized that such things were possible in this day and age."

There is little contact between the Jews and Negroes of Minneapolis, except for the Lyndale and Sixth Avenue district on the near North Side, where Negroes and Jews live in close proximity to each other. Despite their proximity in this area there have been few occasions where ill feeling developed on matters related to difference of color. The Sumner Field housing project on the near North Side is occupied by both Negroes and Jews. At no time has there been ill will between these groups.

On occasion Negroes have complained of the tactics and practices of individual Jewish landlords whose houses they may rent, yet they have often turned to various Jewish leaders, rabbinic and lay, to resolve these differences. Rabbi Albert G. Minda of Temple Israel has for many years served as an active member of the local board of the Urban League, the national association working for the betterment of the Negro. The leaders of the Negro community feel that even though Jewish individuals or families may at times show a spirit of intolerance, this does not represent the attitude of most Jews.

Who is responsible for the anti-Jewish feeling that appears to be so marked in Minneapolis? Why is it that its next-door neighbor, the twin city of St. Paul, knows no such problem?

Various answers suggest themselves. For one thing, the world Fundamentalist movement has its headquarters in Minneapolis and the Northwest Bible School, one of the major Fundamentalist schools, is located in the city. There is a large Lutheran population in Minneapolis, almost twice as large as the Lutheran population of St. Paul. On the other hand, St. Paul has a considerably larger Roman Catholic population and Roman Catholics play a greater role in the civic affairs of St. Paul than they do in Minneapolis.

The spirit of isolationism is far greater in Minneapolis, despite the fact that it is peopled by the sons and daughters of the old world. Religious and social ideas that had taken root in Europe were part and parcel of the luggage, both material and cultural, which all immigrants brought with them. The large Scandinavian population of Minneapolis knew few Jews in the countries of their origin and many of them still think of the Jew as the very incarnation of the devil.

The dominant economic activities of Minneapolis were developed and controlled by New Englanders and their descendants are still in control of the major industries. In St. Paul Jim Hill, the "empire builder" and dominant industrial giant, befriended Irish-Catholic immigrants, and as a result they played a major role in the economic and political development of the city.

It is the author's belief that much of the responsibility for social anti-Semitism in Minneapolis must rest with the descendants of the New Englanders, who still set the patterns for the community. These people are, surely, not to be regarded as anti-Semites in any sense. They are rather a self-contained and, one may even say, a self-sufficient class, unaware that the problem exists or, if aware, choosing rather to ignore it and go about their own affairs. Thus those groups and persons who are anti-Semitic for reasons theological, political, economic, or national are provided with the opportunity to carry on their anti-Semitic campaign, for the real leaders of the community appear not to be too concerned about the issue.

There is, however, cause for hope that conditions will improve. Under the leadership of Hubert H. Humphrey, former mayor,[*] a

* Humphrey, who was elected to the United States Senate from Minnesota in 1948, has continued to be identified with civil rights on the national scene. At the

Mayor's Council on Human Relations was organized to fight discrimination in all forms. The council, consisting of representative citizens of different faiths and interests and guided by social scientists, has thus far prepared an excellent study of majority-minority relations in such areas as housing, employment, labor unions, schools, and hospitals and medical care. The reports on each phase, along with recommendations for the improvement of existing conditions, have been published in mimeographed form.

Humphrey, in cooperation with the city council, was also responsible for a local fair employment practices ordinance. This ordinance, passed by the city council by a vote of twenty-one to three, was put into effect on February 5, 1947. It is administered by a permanent Commission of Job Discrimination, consisting of a chairman and four other members, all appointed by the mayor and confirmed by the council. Violation of the provisions of the ordinance constitutes a misdemeanor and subjects the guilty person to a fine of one hundred dollars or imprisonment in the workhouse for ninety days. Between May 1947 and June 1948 the commission handled thirty-three cases of alleged job discrimination against Negroes, Jews, and other minorities. Nine of the cases involved alleged discrimination against Jews. In no case was it necessary to recommend any complaints to the city attorney for prosecution.

According to one of the members of the commission, the ordinance has had a marked effect upon the general attitude of business leaders of the community. Not only have the number of instances of discrimination been reduced, but there is apparent a marked desire to cooperate in improving human relations. For example, the Dayton Company, the largest department store in Minneapolis, owned and operated by Christians, just before the passage of the ordinance announced a change in its employment policy and is now hiring Negroes as salespeople. About a

1948 convention of the Democratic party, he was instrumental in convincing the delegates to accept a minority committee report and thus write a strong civil rights plank into the platform.

dozen business firms are making an annual contribution to the commission.

At the University of Minnesota Professor Theodore Brameld, then a member of the College of Education, developed intercultural workshops for teachers and other interested persons which studied the sociology of racial and religious conflict. The public school system under the leadership of Willard Goslin, former superintendent, and the school board, headed by the Reverend Morris Robinson, has also undertaken a program of intercultural education which augurs well for the future.

The Minneapolis Round Table, the local branch of the National Conference of Christians and Jews, directed by the zealous and devoted Reverend Carl Zietlow, a Christian clergyman, is also contributing its share toward understanding between the groups. The Central Labor Union, composed of all AFL unions, has recently officially recorded its determination to boycott all construction jobs on buildings which are covered by racial or religious restrictions.

The local newspapers too have both editorially and in their news columns made evident their desire to rid Minneapolis of anti-Semitism. The McWilliams article, with minor deletions, was reprinted in the Minneapolis *Journal*. This act indicates the spirit of its publishers and editors.

Among hopeful signs for the future the following should also be mentioned:

1. Strong efforts by Republican Governor Luther Youngdahl to enact a state fair employment practices law. FEPC legislation has the endorsement of both major political parties in Minnesota. An FEPC bill was defeated in the 1949 legislature by a small majority, but the chances seem good that it will be passed in the next session.

2. The existence of a statewide interracial commission, established by former Governor Edward J. Thye. The commission's program has consisted for the most part of publishing pamphlets on the status of some of the minority groups in Minnesota.

3. The July 1948 change in policy of the Minneapolis Automobile Club, admitting Jews to membership.

4. The educational efforts of the Minneapolis Round Table, the Minnesota Jewish Council, the Minneapolis Town Meetings, and other religious, civic, and labor groups.

5. The numerous invitations extended to Jewish spokesmen to address non-Jewish meetings on the subject of the Jew in Minneapolis.

6. A greater awareness on the part of industrial and economic leaders of the city that the future growth and development of Minneapolis depends in a measure upon the elimination of the conditions that gave rise to the appellation, the "capitol of anti-Semitism."

7. The rise of a younger generation, all sons of the Midwest, who themselves believe fervently in democracy for all and who appear to mean what they say. Notable in this group is the Junior Association of Commerce, which has never restricted its membership.

Though these positive factors alone may not root out the evils of anti-Semitism, they will serve to discourage a continuation of the evil on as high a level as in the past.

But they are all portents for the future. In the meantime anti-Semitism continues to take its toll of a large part of the Jewish community. Because the problem affects them so directly, the subject of anti-Semitism occupies a large share of the thinking and attention of many Jews. There are indeed many persons who see an anti-Semite under every bed. They have the jitters. Some, anxious to demonstrate that they are just as good as their non-Jewish neighbors, emulate not only the virtues of their neighbors but their vices as well. Their number, however, appears to be small. Others would escape into a world of their own making. They avoid whenever and wherever possible any direct contact with persons who are likely to add to their insecurity. Here too the number is extremely small.

The young people are as much concerned with the problem

and often quite as insecure as their elders. In a sampling study of the Jewish student body at the university, made in May 1942, 159 students were studied in an effort to discover the extent of a feeling that they had been "let down," relegated to an inferior position in society and deprived of those social and economic opportunities to which they believe themselves entitled.[9] Of these students 153 were born in the United States, 3 in Canada, and 3 in Europe. They ranged in age from 16 to 30, with 74.2 percent falling into the 18 to 21 group. Of the total number 50.9 percent were graduates of a Hebrew or religious school; 64 percent were members of Hillel Foundation, the Jewish youth organization on the campus. Three fourths came from families of moderate income. Their fathers were principally engaged in business. Table III gives the twenty statements which were prepared for the purpose of testing the degree of frustration that characterized these students.

In reply to a further statement — "Whenever I read a list of names in the newspaper, I always look for the Jewish names. If the news is good, I am proud of the Jews. If the news is bad, I am personally upset and disturbed about it" — 64.1 percent of the students replied in the affirmative, indicating their sense of responsibility for the acts of their fellow Jews.

It is noteworthy that, despite a deep awareness of the problem of anti-Semitism and its personal implications for them, these young people clearly do not wish to withdraw either from the Jewish people or from the life of the larger community. They intend rather to seek their places in the various phases of American organizational life, economic, political, or social, which interest them.

What are the Jews of Minneapolis doing about the problem of anti-Semitism? How are they meeting the challenge that results from their present sense of insecurity?

Membership in organizations, local and national, that are openly fighting the menace is one such method. Membership is sought in the Minneapolis Round Table and the Minnesota

TABLE III. PERCENTAGE OF AGREEMENT AND DISAGREEMENT OF JEWISH STUDENTS
WITH FRUSTRATION-IMPLYING STATEMENTS

	Agree	Disagree
1. I sometimes wonder whether most of the accusations made against the Jews might not be true...................	31.4	68.6
2. I wish that I could break the tie that binds me to the Jewish people	8.1	91.9
3. I sometimes resent the fact that my parents brought me up in the world as a Jew............................	6.2	93.8
4. I almost hate the Jewish group because I am forced to share its fate	3.1	96.9
5. As a Jew, I often feel like an unwanted child............	13.8	86.2
6. I often feel that even the best of Gentiles are not to be trusted when it comes to their attitudes toward Jews....	28.9	71.1
7. I feel that the whole world is hostile toward me because I am a Jew	9.4	90.6
8. I believe that it would be better if Jewish students did not gather in the Coffman Memorial Union because that makes for anti-Semitism	43.4	56.6
9. I believe that being born a Jew means that you have two strikes against you	30.1	69.9
10. I am convinced that anti-Semitism is likely to interfere with my search for personal success and happiness.......	40.2	59.8
11. I often feel a great personal insecurity because of existing discriminations	45.9	54.1
12. I find life as a Jew unsatisfactory because of existing discriminations	11.3	88.7
13. I feel that my opportunity for getting the job I would really like is seriously restricted because I am a Jew....	33.9	66.1
14. I feel that at any moment my feelings may be hurt because I am a Jew	22.6	77.4
15. I feel that I should refrain from participation in any and all organizations, economic, political, or social because of possible manifestations of anti-Jewish prejudice.........	1.8	98.2
16. I feel that I am barred from many worthwhile friendships because I am Jewish	16.9	83.1
17. According to Jews, I am an American. According to Americans, I am Jewish, though I haven't much of an idea about what being Jewish really means. Frankly, I'm neither here nor there	22.6	77.4
18. If I could somehow conceal my Jewish background, I would certainly do so	8.1	91.9
19. I often worry lest anti-Semitism take on more violent forms in the United States..........................	59.7	40.3
20. I feel that if I associated exclusively with Jews, I would be better off	3.7	96.3

THE JEW AND HIS NEIGHBOR

Jewish Council, an organization consisting of representative Jews from various cities throughout the state of Minnesota in which Jews reside. The local B'nai B'rith lodges have grown by leaps and bounds in recent years, from a membership of two hundred and fifty in 1932 to fifteen hundred in 1946. Jews, by and large, believe that all forms of prejudice and intolerance must be fought. Hence, they actively support these and all other organizations that will, in their opinion, make for better human relations.

Other Jews seek, wherever consistent with their dignity as Jews — for they do not wish to lose their self-respect — to reduce to a minimum all points of difference between themselves and their neighbors. Consider, for example, the changes in surnames among members of the Jewish community.

The earliest Jewish names were biblical in origin. Not until the Middle Ages did Jews begin the practice of adopting names identical in character with those of the people in whose midst they lived. In 1787 an order was issued by the Austrian empire compelling Jews to adopt surnames. Since then Jews have adopted names or had names unceremoniously thrust upon them. Wherever he has lived the Jew has taken on the protective coloration of the surnames most common to the country of his residence. Thus many of the names that are said to be distinctly Jewish are actually Russian or Polish or German, anything but Jewish.

An examination of the name changes officially recorded in the district court of Hennepin County indicates that in the majority of cases the Slavonic name suffix was dropped in order to shorten the name. In other cases exact translations of the Hebrew plus Slavonic suffix are made: Yonkelovich, which literally means "Son of Jacob," became Jacobson. In still others names were given American translations such as Weisman to Whiteman or Whitman. In a good number of cases a major operation was performed which changed the name completely. (For a list of name changes see the Appendix.)

Difficulties with pronunciation also produced unofficial name changes.

"We came here from London, England. I had a very pronounced English accent. On the first day of school, I took my little sister to school and we both enrolled. The principal of the school heard me speak and she made quite a fuss over my accent. Now my last name was Jaffe. But the principal apparently misunderstood me or perhaps she decided that the name wasn't appropriate for me, so she enrolled me as Jeffrey, because that name to her was really English. For some time after that my father still went by the name of Jaffe and it wasn't until I complained because the two of us were known by different names that he changed his name to Jeffrey. It would have been too much trouble to get the school to change its records, so I figured."

It is the author's belief that in many cases these name changes have little, if any, relationship to Jewish frustrations. They are rather a normal part of the Americanization process. The name changes recorded in Hennepin County for Jews are less in number than those for non-Jewish immigrant families from Poland, Lithuania, and Russia.

There are persons in the community who look askance upon name changes, whether of individuals or of organizations. Consider the case of the recent name change by the Gymal Doled Club. For approximately ten years a campaign was undertaken by members of this business and professional men's club to change the name to "something more appropriate." Though the name Gymal Doled has no special meaning other than that these two words are the names of the third and fourth letters respectively of the Hebrew alphabet, the change of name aroused considerable debate among the members of the club. A letter that appeared in the *American Jewish World* focuses attention upon certain psychological factors which may have had something to do with inducing the desire for a change in name:

. . . For 37 years the Gymal Doled Club has rendered the civic service to the people of Minneapolis equaled by no other similar organization. In this time the name Gymal Doled has become

a by-word for civic good, social comraderie, and general good
will to all. Together with thousands of others I feel the
name has *that* definite significance and meaning to both Jew
and non-Jew. The community as a whole is conscious and proud
of the name Gymal Doled and its civic connotations. War
Bond Drives — Jewish Federation — Community Chests — and
its many other good deeds for civic betterment, done by
and through its name.

Hard to pronounce — Gymal Doled? Have we so soon forgotten the names in World War II? Buchenwald, Lidice, Dachau,
Iwo Jima, Okinawa, Bataan. Are they easy to pronounce? What
was their significance before making new history? Now they have
a definite meaning. Will the war horrors of these places or the
hallowed ground where lie our dead need easier or different
names to help us remember the sacrifices made, that democracy
might live? And what about the names of Levinski, Papanaoala-
pous, Kyszinski, or Bobricini, and thousands of similar unpro-
nounceable names — names of our American heroes many of
whom made the supreme sacrifice on foreign battle fields? Shall
we forget these names, or be ashamed of them and the things
they stand for, because we can't pronounce them easily? . . .

Behind all the campaigns for changing the name there was
always the unspoken FEAR: a fear of the innate Jewishness of
the name. That is at the root of all the agitation. FEAR. This
bogey-man, FEAR, was exposed by and will forever be heard in
the stilled voice of our late beloved Franklin Delano Roosevelt
in his immortal "we have nothing to fear but fear itself." It isn't
necessary to be "scared to death" to fear. Fear is a conscious
or subconscious emotion caused by an imaginary danger which
we try to disguise by fortifying ourselves with an outward display of bravery, like "whistling in the dark" or perhaps by
changing one's name because it sounds like "an Hebraic Chinese
tong joint." Deeds, not words, is the real import and significance. . . .

Despite this eloquent plea, the name was officially changed
in 1945 to the Standard Club. An editorial published in the
Standard News, the official publication of the club, in May 1946
presents another point of view:

Slowly we accustom our ears to the sharp sounding "Standard" as over against the liquid-vowel-rich "Gymal Doled" which

was our name but yester-year. It was indeed a long drawn dispute which finally achieved our present appellation — a campaign embracing more than a decade punctuated by many a pitched forensic battle and continued by gusty private arguments galore. These things are now become part of our almost two-score years of history.

Those who experienced the years bear living witness to an inevitable transition. Otherwise America will not have become the melting pot for which our fathers longed — and which concept some of their sons now reject, or seek to modify under the concept called multiple or pluralistic cultures.

The editor has expressed the belief that within the Jewish community there exists a difference of concept concerning the basic definition of Americanism. Shall each of the cultures acquired and brought to these shores by immigrant groups be poured into the great melting pot, from which there will come a new amalgam, wholly American? Or shall each maintain, to as great extent as possible without infringement upon the rights and privileges of the others, its own way of life, and is this cultural pluralism in keeping with the American spirit and tradition? The conflict, to date, remains unresolved.

Another approach to the problem of human relations is represented by the recently completed local campaign for the building of a Jewish hospital which will be nonsectarian in character. More than two and a half million dollars has already been raised for this project. The hospital, which will be known as "Mount Sinai," is intimately associated with the problem of anti-Semitism in Minneapolis, though other factors play an important role.

For a period of years many Jewish doctors in Minneapolis have been unable to become members of various hospital staffs. As a result, it is often difficult for them to get their patients admitted to hospitals. Excellent surgeons and physicians have found themselves frozen out, with no assurance that they can carry on their practice successfully. Jewish interns have found it difficult to secure the opportunities for internship which they desire. It should be observed that this practice applies only to the private hospitals in Minneapolis, not to the University of Minnesota Hospitals or the city General Hospital. These factors have tended to make both the doctors and the Jewish public aware of the fact that some way must be found to keep the better trained professionals, who would otherwise leave, within the community.

There are almost as many opinions on what Jews ought to do about the problem of anti-Semitism as there are Jews in the community. Debate on this subject is often heated. Varied suggestions and counter arguments are advanced.

"I think that it was wrong for us to bring any refugees into the city of Minneapolis. There's enough anti-Semitism as it is. When you bring these people in you simply give the anti-Semite more reason for argument."

The humanitarian aspects of the refugee problem are thus lost sight of by some Jews in the community.

Should Jews avoid their responsibilities as citizens by refraining from holding public office?

"I think the whole problem of anti-Semitism would be solved if Jews stayed out of public life. They should know their place. Now mind you, I'm as good as anyone else and I think I have a right to hold any job or office I'm capable of holding, but if the anti-Semite will use that fact to point out that we Jews are holding office or getting into the affairs of government, then we ought to be the first to stay out of it all."

How one determines which positions and offices Jews may accept without endangering the welfare of an entire people remains an open question.

Still others suggest:

"I think we Jews ought to clean house of all the dead beats among our own people. There are Jews who are getting their names in the paper for one thing or another. We ought to either turn them over to the police when we hear about some Jew doing something shady or we ought to run them out of town. Anyhow, we ought to do *something*."

Exactly what the Jews of Minneapolis ought to do and what they have the power and right to do is of course quite another problem. Inasmuch as the religious power of excommunication is now practically never utilized, and even when used has no effect, it is questionable whether Jews can do more than what they are already doing — refusing to associate with known law violators and further keeping them from joining their social organizations. As a matter of fact, when one person of questionable reputation applied for membership in the Oak Ridge Country Club, his application was rejected. This, in a case where no violation of the law had actually been proved against the person in question. Public opinion has its effective usage and is actually being utilized by the Jews of Minneapolis.

"Jews of shady character ought not to be permitted to join synagogues and temples. They have no right to be a part of a religious body."

But who is there to say that any man, no matter what he has done or contemplates doing, should be deprived of the benefits of his religion? If religion is to become the property of the "good" people, what is there left for any religious teacher to do?

"Jews ought to watch their manners in public. They ought not to speak loudly or do some of the vulgar things they do on occasion."

To which Jews answer:

"Correct! Not only should Jews not be ostentatious and otherwise vulgar, but all people should be less vulgar. All we can do, when we see such displays is to remind the offender that he is bringing disgrace upon an entire people. And *that* we already do."

Differences in religious practice are also discussed:

"Jews should stop being different in their religious practices. If we stopped following our rituals, such as observing the dietary laws and other practices which make us different, we would not be disliked."

To this argument one hears the reply:

"But as a matter of fact, we have discovered that despite their statements, the anti-Semite really makes no such fine distinctions between observant and nonobservant Jews as you infer. As a matter of fact, Hitler was just as harsh with so-called 'assimilated' Jews as he was with the most Orthodox. Just how then will further nonobservance help the Jewish people to survive?"

Finally, there is the argument:

"Get rid of those Jews who are shady in their business dealings. Such people have brought disgrace upon us."

To which we hear the reply:

"Shady practices bring disgrace and dishonor upon all peoples. Yet one does not hear of Christians feeling a personal sense of responsibility for every petty thief who happens to be born of Christian parentage. There are police and courts to arrest and bring the guilty to the bar of justice. It is no one's right, whether he be a member of a minority people or not, to take the law into his own hands and become both prosecutor and judge of any other man."

There are some Jews in Minneapolis who believe that total assimilation is the only solution. The number of persons who leave the Jewish fold or are converted to another faith is extremely limited, yet there are many whose assimilation takes one or all of the following forms: (1) intermarriage, (2) refusal to belong to a synagogue or temple or even a social club where Jews predominate, (3) avoidance of Jews socially and instead developing friendships exclusively among non-Jews, and (4) refusal to participate in or contribute to specifically Jewish organizations or causes.

By far the majority of Jews, however, take another view of the matter. They say:

"All we Jews can do is to lead as normal a life as possible. Go about our business in a decent, upright fashion. Conduct ourselves as self-respecting individuals, attend our synagogues and temples, maintain our religious schools and other cultural activities and organizations, and hope that sooner or later men will learn that prejudice and bigotry are inimical to the best interests of America. The problem of anti-Semitism is not a Jewish problem at all. It is a problem for all America to solve. Jew-hatred is but one form of the tendency to dislike the unlike."

By and large the Jewish community accepts this standard. It believes in the need to accommodate its Jewish self to the life and standards of the larger community, not just because accommodation is necessary, but rather because it finds the American standards to be right for this age. On the other hand, it refuses to assimilate, if by that we mean giving up identity with Jewish life and culture.

The largest proportion of the present Jewish community believes that those who speak for complete assimilation are misinterpreting the spirit of Americanism. They believe that neither the Constitution nor the American people expect any minority group to discard all aspects of its tradition in order to become more American. They believe rather that living in two cultures is not only necessary but even desirable, if America is to continue to grow spiritually and culturally.

Whatever the feeling among Minneapolis Jews with regard to assimilation, it cannot be denied that certain changes are occurring in the pattern of Jewish life and thought. These changes are most marked in the traditional practices associated with religion. Over a period of many years the author has had the opportunity to listen to statements made by many Jews of Minneapolis who represent a cross section of the total Jewish community. He has also had the opportunity to watch the practices of other Jews as they pertain to religious and general cultural values.

There can be no doubt that the process of acculturation has been at work. The Jews of Minneapolis today are markedly different in many ways from the immigrant generation. In the succeeding chapters we shall examine all phases of the life of the Jews in the eight and more decades of their history in Minneapolis, in an effort to see how the contact of cultures has affected them.

Part II **A PEOPLE
IN TRANSITION**

Chapter 4   Beliefs and Practices

⁋ RELIGIOUS *faith, in the sense of a theistic world outlook, is in many regards the neglected aspect of the Jewish heritage . . . For Jews, like Christians, have been exposed to all the influences which account for the general advance of secularism in modern times.*[1]

THE Jewish religion, like all other religions, has two important elements. Jews have a faith, that is, a particular kind of belief concerning God, man, and the universe. They have also certain forms of observance and practice by which their beliefs are expressed. Both belief and practice are based upon the Torah or Bible.

The Orthodox Jew believes that there is in reality a dual law: the written law, or Bible, and the oral law, consisting of the Talmud. "He believes that in addition to the Written Law given on Mount Sinai an interpretation of its difficulties was simultaneously revealed to Moses, and that this interpretation, handed down through an unbroken chain of authority," was recorded in that great Hebraic work called the Mishnah.[2] This compendium of law, relating to all aspects of life and all branches of religious observance, was completed about the year 200 c.e.

The Mishnah was subjected to even further discussion and examination in the academies of Babylon and Palestine for a period of three centuries. The compilation of these discussions and decisions was known as the Gemarah or "completion." Together the Mishnah and the Gemarah are known as the Talmud.

The Talmud provides the exposition of traditional Jewish law, the decisions with respect to Jewish law and the discussions and debates that preceded these decisions. Its monumental character made it almost impossible for most persons to really know what

71

ritual practices were required of the Jew who wished to be observant. Hence it was reduced, first by Moses Maimonides in the twelfth century to a code known as the Mishnah Torah. Still regarded as unwieldy, it was further reduced and codified by Rabbi Jacob ben Asher in the middle of the fourteenth century. Finally it was still further reduced in the sixteenth century by Rabbi Joseph Caro. This code, known as the Shulchan Aruch ("Prepared Table," for the law was carefully digested and arranged) became the standard of Jewish law.

"The Shuchan Aruch" thus forms the final repository of law and only they who scrupulously conform to its regulations are regarded as orthodox Jews in the strictest sense. It expounds the duties of the Jew to man and his Maker; it governs his acts in all the relations of life, private and public, domestic and social, from the cradle to the grave; it enacts in minute detail how he shall dress and how he shall walk; what he should eat and what he should drink; how he should kill the animals fit for his consumption, and prepare their flesh for food; how he should pray and how he should study; how he should keep the Sabbath and celebrate the feasts and fasts, how he should bake the unleavened bread for Passover and build the booths for Tabernacles; what his duties are to his wife and his children, his parents and his teachers, to his neighbors and the community, to the orphans, the sick, the poor, to the living and to the dead.[3]

His beliefs too the Jew acquired from both the written and oral laws. They may be summarized as follows:

The universe is governed and controlled by a personal God, all-powerful and all-perfect. Though His spirit permeates the cosmos, He resides in the Heavens. God is One. His will for His children was long ago recorded in the Torah.

The Bible, according to this tradition, contains the literal word of God. Its commandments and ordinances are therefore to be taken literally. Obedience to the commandments or mitzvos, as they are called in Hebrew, brings the reward of life eternal. Disobedience is punishable by extinction. Though God governs the universe, man may induce Him to change His course through prayer and supplication. God is forever concerned with humankind, for men are His children.

God has prescribed certain ways in which man should walk. There are ethical and moral precepts, enjoined not only upon those of His children who are members of "a kingdom of priests and a holy nation," but upon the rest of mankind as well. He has enjoined upon the children of Israel certain ritual and ceremonial practices that must not be neglected. These observances are quite as important in His sight as any other of His precepts. A good Jew is one who fears the Lord and keeps His commandments, moral, ethical, and ritualistic.

These were the basic beliefs and sources of practice of Orthodox Jews the world over.[4] Though there were variations in the practices in different parts of the Old World, these were in the main minor. The Western Jew, living less frequently in an all-Jewish community, usually in closer contact with the larger community, was not quite as observant as the East European, yet all Jews acknowledged the authority of the oral law.

The movement known as Reform Judaism began to develop in Germany during the first half of the nineteenth century. Following upon changes that had already been effected in many of its synagogues — minor changes as we view them now — an effort was made to "reform" Judaism, from the point of view of both doctrine and practice.

The new schism rejected the authority of the oral law. It rewrote the traditional prayers so as to exclude mention of the coming of the Messiah and the hoped-for restoration of Zion. It expressed the belief that the dispersion of the Jews was not a punishment, but rather God's way of making it possible for Jews to spread the teachings of Judaism throughout the world.

Reform Judaism did not accept the Bible as the literal word of God, regarding it rather as "God-inspired," and it held the view that each generation may accept and practice only the laws it believes to be essential. The right to make changes in ritual belonged to the rabbi, who, meeting with other like-minded rabbis, decided the forms of observance and ceremony in Jewish life. Many of the ancient practices of the synagogue and the home were modified or abrogated.[5]

It should be noted, however, that despite the wide difference between Reform and Orthodoxy on matters of ritual and ceremony, there was almost complete accord on such ideas as the belief in a personal God, the efficacy of prayer, immortality, reward and punishment, and the life hereafter.

The German Jews who settled in Minneapolis spoke of themselves as Reform Jews, although there were a few families whose religious tendencies were along traditional lines.

"I do not recall that there were any really Orthodox German Jews among us. One or two of the early settlers may have maintained the dietary laws in their own homes, but for the most part such things were not even considered. The wives of these early settlers prepared delicacies that were regarded as Jewish, but in the main neither they nor their husbands observed Jewish ritual."

Except for the recognition that they were Jews and that there was a Jewish way of worshipping God and that the synagogue or temple was the house of worship for the Jewish people, there are few indications that the early German-Jewish settlers looked with particular favor upon perpetuating the minutiae of Jewish ritual and ceremony in their homes. The changes that have occurred through the years within the German-Jewish community are, therefore, less marked than those of East European Jewry.

The German settlers discarded many of the traditional practices, such as the strict observance of the Sabbath as a day of rest. Most had long before ceased to pray three times daily. There is no evidence that any observed the Orthodox practice of wearing phylacteries during the morning prayers. Indeed, except for two or three of the more pious members of the early community, there is no evidence that morning prayers were recited at all. The knowledge of Hebrew as the language of the prayer book was limited to a mere handful of the old-timers.

BELIEFS AND PRACTICES

The dietary laws were not observed by the majority, though Jewish dishes or delicacies, associated with their people, were dutifully prepared by the wives as a kind of special treat. Businesses were, in most instances, kept open on the Sabbath, although a goodly number regularly attended the house of worship on that day. In dress and general comportment, these people were in no way distinguishable from their non-Jewish neighbors. The process of acculturation had already set in.

As we have observed elsewhere, the early immigrants of the East European group were in almost all instances Orthodox Jews. The traditions they had known in the old country were transplanted to the new land and this community. In their European homes they had observed the dietary laws; they were exceedingly careful about the details of Sabbath observance. Food was prepared for the Sabbath before the Sabbath eve. The home was carefully cleaned in honor of the Sabbath. All business ceased on that holy day. The synagogue was filled with worshippers on the Sabbath, as it was each weekday. Persons who violated any of the traditional precepts and practices were regarded as sinners and as breakers of the morale of the Jewish community.

An early Orthodox settler in Minneapolis describes the religious life of the community in those days as follows:

"We were Fromm (pious) when we came over here. We kept the dietary laws very carefully. We wouldn't think of eating out of our own home, not only because most of us had no money to spend foolishly in the restaurants, but because we really wanted to keep the Jewish law. Those Jews who could, didn't work on the Sabbath. Our wives prepared for the Sabbath very carefully and made the house shine. What little money we had was used to have fine foods for Shabbas.

"No Jew would think of beginning the Sabbath meal without reciting kiddush (sanctification of the wine). No Jewish women would think of beginning the Shabbas without lighting the Shabbas candles. Those of us who hadn't any work, naturally, went to the synagogue to pray, not only on the Sabbath, but every day. Of course, we all put on tefillin (phylacteries) and most of us men wore our arba kanfos (small fringed garments) under our shirts. We all put mezzuzahs on our doorposts in accordance with God's commandment. In the early years most of us wore beards, not long ones, but they were beards nevertheless. Those of us who had been Talmud students in the old country used to meet in the synagogue and study together. Our synagogue was a place of study for us. We really felt that we were Orthodox Jews."

As the years passed there appeared individuals who could not find satisfaction in either the Orthodox or the Reform group. Among younger members of the Orthodox group in particular attitudes about the nature of God and the basic premises of Orthodox Judaism were changing. These people wished to retain the Hebrew language as an integral part of the service, but they believed that the service should not be entirely in Hebrew and certainly that the sermon should be preached in English. There was the feeling too that though Jewish law was necessary for the preservation of the Jewish way of life, certain modifications in the ritual of the synagogue and the home were definitely necessary. This middle group, while anxious to conserve the Jewish heritage, was desirous of living as completely an American life as possible.

Reform had done away with certain ancient forms of the synagogue, such as the required wearing of head covering and shawl by all males in the prayer service, had abbreviated the service to a considerable degree, had permitted men and women to sit together at the services. The newer Conservative group, on the other hand, held fast to certain of the Orthodox practices, such as observance of the dietary laws, although readily accepting certain innovations, notably mixed pews. Conservative Judaism was introduced in Minneapolis in 1912 by members of the Adath Jeshurun Synagogue, formerly an Orthodox congregation, following a course that had been charted by the Jewish Theological Seminary of America in New York City beginning in 1901.[6]

There were many factors at work to produce changes in

the religious practices and concepts of the Jewish immigrants. Primarily, economic factors tended to alter their traditional behavior. None of these people was free from financial pressure. Above all else it was necessary to find some means of earning a livelihood. Men who had come to this country with their wives and children were obliged to take whatever job offered itself. These jobs often necessitated working on the Sabbath for the very first time in their lives. Even single men who had only themselves to support could not afford the luxury of waiting around until they found work which did not require their presence on the Sabbath. The Sabbath was gradually changed from a day of complete rest to one of compromise with the environment.

After a greater degree of financial security had been attained, it was no longer possible to revert to the traditional observance of the Sabbath. New ways had been established. New customs had been substituted for the old.

Nor must we forget that because the financial needs of the family were so great, it was important that children find some means of employment at an early age. It was only natural to expect that the child, once he began to earn his own money, even though he turned all or part of it over to his parents, would no longer feel the same degree of dependency upon his family. As a consequence, parental authority lagged.

The social factor must not be ignored. Early immigrants recall that they compromised with their Orthodox practices because they discovered that old friends who had preceded them to Minneapolis had changed their ways:

"How was I to know that a very dear friend from my home town who had come to Minneapolis just a few years before me had become a freethinker? He used to make fun of me because I prayed every day. His friends did likewise. Before you knew it, I was doing the things they were doing. I still thought they were wrong but I guess I didn't have the strength to keep on doing things the way I was taught."

The process of change was accelerated because these Jewish settlers were now living in a non-Jewish community, in contradistinction to the small East European towns where they had been almost entirely surrounded by fellow Jews. As a consequence each would note the practices of his non-Jewish neighbor, would see differences between the manner in which he had conducted himself in Europe and the way in which the native American was conducting himself. He would then seek to resolve these differences to as great a degree as possible.

It was apparent to him from the very outset that he would be confronted with special difficulties in observing Jewish customs in so far as they were required outside the home. That is why, even though the parent might remain steadfastly loyal to traditional practices, he hardly dared to expect that his children would be able to.

Then too it must be remembered that the father most frequently set the standard for the practices of his children. Because the father was so frequently away from home peddling his wares, the children could no longer look to him for the same kind of guidance and example that had characterized the father in the East European communities. Because the father was a less frequent attendant at the synagogue, his sons would also be seen there less frequently. Because the parent was not at home during the day to have his meals with his children, many religious customs, like the recital of the blessing over the bread and grace after meals, were gradually dropped. When the father was in a great hurry to get to work in the morning, he had less time either to notice or to insist upon a strict observance of morning prayers and other traditional practices.

In the old country most Jewish children attended only Hebrew schools, schools devoted exclusively to study of the Talmud and kindred subjects. In Minneapolis the children attended public schools and they were certain to seek to emulate those whom they regarded as more American than themselves. The teachers were non-Jewish and what they had to say, and the manner in which they said it, often influenced the children far more than anything their parents said.

BELIEFS AND PRACTICES

America was a free country. Freedom implied the right to think for one's self and the lack of authoritarianism. The whole spirit of America ran counter to the idea of strict parental and religious authority. As a consequence neither parents nor children felt the need to accept the patterns that had been set for them in the old country.

"I came from a small town where practically everybody was Jewish. It never occurred to me that anyone would ever break the Sabbath. But when I got here, I began to think, 'This is America. Everyone can do what he likes. He doesn't have to ask questions of anybody.' So I worked on the Sabbath and I stopped praying every day and I did a great number of things that must have made my father turn in his grave. I wanted to be an American, like all other real Americans."

People generally wish to avoid being different, and they seek to resolve their differences to the point where they will be able to fit into society with the least degree of friction. These immigrants were, after all, no different from all other immigrants in this respect. The Americanization process involved not only the adoption of modern garb, but an inner change as well, an acceptance of a new approach to a new environment.

We may also question whether the tendency toward ritual observance among East Europeans was due to great personal piety or to a desire to be socially acceptable. The fact that changes in the practices of these Jews occurred in many instances so swiftly leads to the conclusion the personal piety was more apparent than real.

"Frankly, as I look back upon my father's generation and stop to think how quickly he made the changes from the old Orthodox ways to which he was accustomed to the new ways that were American, I began to think he really had never been quite as pious or religious as he had professed to be. I think that he and the vast majority of the people of this generation were rather following the convention of the society in which they lived. Because it had been expected of them in Europe that their actions would be traditional in character, they followed that procedure. Here in America the majority of people no longer expected that sort of thing. Hence they changed very quickly."

Besides marked changes in the degree of ritual observance, there were changes in the attitudes of the sons and grandsons of the early immigrants with respect to Judaism's basic beliefs. The ideas of many Jews about God, immortality, belief in a life hereafter, and the attitude with respect to prayer appear to have undergone a not inconsiderable transformation.

"I believe in God but I must say that my ideas about God are not the same as they were when I was a child. In fact my father's ideas seem to have changed in this respect too. I think of God not as a Person, but rather as a Force — the First Cause, if you will. I believe that this Force who rules the universe by His own laws, which we speak of as the laws of nature, cannot be cajoled into changing His will just because I or any other person may pray to Him. I believe that this God has a will but that His will has been manifested in these laws."

It is this observer's belief that the vast majority of Jews in Minneapolis would insist that they are believers in a personal God. They would also express their conviction that God rewards the doer of good and punishes the evildoer, that man's soul lives on after death — they would indeed express indignant denials of their acceptance of other than the traditional views. There is, however, an ever-growing minority opinion that must be recorded. The members of this minority, who are to be found particularly in the Conservative and Reform congregations, speak of God as a Force, a Cause, a Power, rather than as a Person.

Ideas about a life hereafter and immortality have changed also.

"I don't believe in bodily resurrection. My body shall not live on after I die. Nor do I believe that any part of my physical being shall survive the grave. When I die I'm through. The grave will be the end for me. But I do believe in a kind of immortality. I feel that if those who survive me think of me or recall anything I may have done or said during my lifetime that will be all the immortality I have a right to expect. I do not believe in Heaven or Hell. Men have both in this world."

The scientific attitude acquired in the schools and universities by the children and grandchildren of the immigrant has tended to reduce the number of believers in a purely personal God. This is not to say that *all* Jews have accepted this approach any more than this is true of all Christians. It is rather to remark that the number of Jews in Minneapolis who have been affected by the scientific attitude of this age is far greater than is generally supposed.

Then too the marked increase in anti-Semitism through the world, the advent of Hitlerism, the gas chambers, the crematoria — these have left their mark upon Jews, both young and old.

"How can I believe in a God who permits such terrible things to happen to any people? It must be that the kind of a God in whom I was taught to believe is not God at all. God must be found in the laws which have been set up for the world to follow. I think that I am worshipping God when I try to understand the laws that exist in this world and live by them. These laws are ethical and moral. If I follow them, I am worshipping God."

There appears to be a positive correlation between reduced attendance in synagogues for prayer services and the increase of bigotry and bloodshed in the world.

There are many Jews in Minneapolis who speak of themselves as "not religious." Association with such persons over a period of many years leads to the conclusion that these people really mean to say they do not observe as much of the Jewish ritual as their fathers did. These persons are definitely not Orthodox, yet in many instances they fulfill the prophet's definition of the religious man.

> It hath been told thee, O man, what is good,
> And what the Lord doth require of thee!
> Only to do justly, and to love mercy, and to
> walk humbly with thy God.[7]

81

The traditional definition of the good Jew appears to have been modified. There is less emphasis upon ritual and observance, less concern for the theological concepts and basic beliefs. The good Jew is generally regarded as the man who is charitable, who has a sense of social sympathy which prompts him to look upon all men as his brothers. The good Jew is one who has a highly developed ethical and moral sense, who practices these virtues in his home and in the market place, as well as in the synagogue. Finally, the good Jew is one who despite any personal denominational predilections works with and for a united Jewish community.

Chapter 5   The Dietary Laws

❧ If we find it hard to understand how holiness can have anything to do with eating and drinking, it is because we fail to grasp the exact meaning which the Hebrew word "kadosh," usually translated "holy," bears in Leviticus. If for "holy" we substitute the term "consecrated," we shall get much nearer to its significance.[1]

THE changes that have occurred in the practices of the Jewish people of Minneapolis can best be noted by describing the norms of Orthodox practice and then seeing how far from this norm the Jews of Minneapolis have moved.

The dietary laws have always played an important, if not the central, role in the Orthodox Jewish household.

A salient feature in the orthodox household consists of the arrangements in the kitchen, which are subject to special dietary laws. All meat foods must be kept strictly separate from milk foods, as the contact of one with the other — such as meat with milk, butter, or cheese — would render both unfit for consumption. This regulation involves the use of two sets of utensils, both for cooking and eating, the one set being reserved for meat dishes and the other for milk or butter dishes, and the crockery and cutlery of the one set being kept rigorously apart from those of the other. This separation of things *fleischig* (meaty) from things *milchig* (milky) is observed by the strict housewife in every conceivable direction: there are separate tablecloths and napkins, separate cruets, separate basins for washing the crockery and separate towels for drying; and in more elaborate kitchens, there are even separate cooking-ranges, dressers, and sinks. There is a special utensil for the preparation of meat, from which the blood must be drained in accordance with the Biblical command (Gen. ix. 4; Lev. iii. 17). It is a slanting board or piece of wicker-work upon which the meat, after having been soaked in water half an hour, is besprinkled with salt; after another hour, the salt is rinsed away, and the meat is ready for cooking. On the Feast of Passover, special crockery and cutlery must be used, and as separate sets are necessary for meat and milk, the orthodox household must be provided in all with four sets of cooking and eating vessels. The Passover sets are usually stored in some out-of-the-way place, where they are safe from contamination by anything "leavened," i.e. the customary food of the rest of the year.[2]

In East European communities it was unthinkable that any Jew would, either within or outside his home, violate the dietary laws. However, times have changed in so far as the Jews of Minneapolis are concerned. Although it is impossible to obtain exact information on the number of persons observing the dietary laws, certain facts have been ascertained by discussing the matter with kosher butchers and meat packers and by studying lists of persons who purchase their meat from the kosher butcher shops. From these sources it seems fair to assume that no more than 20 percent of the Jews in Minneapolis purchase kosher meats for home use. For example, although two thousand Jewish families live on the West Side, there is in this district only one kosher meat market with about three hundred regular customers. It appears, therefore, that only about 15 percent of the West Side Jewish population uses kosher meat, though of course some of them may purchase it from North Side markets.

The number who insist upon eating only kosher meats outside their homes is still smaller, so that the net number of Jews who may be said to observe the dietary laws, from the point of view of using kosher meat exclusively within their homes and eating only kosher foods outside their homes, is no more than 10 percent.

In a random sampling of the pupils of the Minneapolis Talmud Torah, the central Hebrew school system, a series of questions was asked about the observance of various forms of the dietary laws. The responses are given in Table IV. Pupils of the Talmud Torah included those from North Side families who attend either Conservative or Orthodox synagogues and those from West Side families who attend the Conservative synagogue. The figures do not include children attending the Reform temple, because they are not pupils of the Talmud Torah. In examining these figures we must keep in mind, first, that the random sample represents approximately 15 percent of the total student body, and second, that the North Side Jewish com-

TABLE IV. OBSERVANCE OF CERTAIN PHASES OF THE DIETARY LAWS
IN MINNEAPOLIS, 1946

	West Side		Total	
	Yes	No	Yes	No
1. In our home we eat our meat meals without butter, milk, or cream......................	8	31	116	50
2. In our home we have separate meat and milk dishes	10	29	114	55
3. My mother buys meat in a kosher meat market	13	20	138	22
4. My mother makes meat kosher before cooking it	8	19	126	23

munity is more Orthodox and far more observant than the West Side community. It is interesting to note the lesser degree of observance reported by the children of the Conservative synagogue on the West Side.

The number of Jewish housewives who take the trouble to salt and wash the meat in accordance with Jewish ritual is being rapidly reduced.

"I remember that my mother used to salt the meat and wash the salt off before she cooked her dinner. She would never have thought that it was kosher had the butcher salted or washed it. Today, however, I do not follow the practice of salting the meat. I ask my butcher to do so, and I know that he does so for a good number of people. At least, I think he does for he has told me that he does. I do not think it would really make any difference to me if he did not salt the meat. At least I know that I am buying my meat in a kosher butcher shop and that it is kosher."

Thus this detail of the dietary laws is now placed in the hands of the various kosher butchers. It is doubtful that more than 10 percent of the housewives who purchase kosher meat observe the ritual of salting and washing.

Most of the Jewish affairs held in the community are non-kosher, unless they occur in Orthodox or Conservative synagogue buildings. There is seldom any objection raised, except by some of the rabbis, in regard to serving nonkosher meat at public gatherings. At official Jewish dinner meetings fish is usually served in order to avoid offending those few persons who feel the importance of observing the dietary laws. However, the fish is served in nonkosher dishes, that is, dishes that have been used for nonkosher meats. Silverware, definitely not kosher in the Orthodox sense, is also used. Still, little complaint is heard about these matters.

Marriage ceremonies often take place in the large hotels of the city and on these occasions kosher food is seldom served. Although the bride's family may regard itself as Orthodox, there is no relationship between the Orthodox nature of the ceremony and the adherence to Orthodox ritual from point of view of food. Indeed, at these affairs it is considered quite appropriate to serve nonkosher meat or fowl to all the guests and fish to the rabbi. It is considered appropriate — in fact, there are seldom any questions asked or raised about the matter — to serve nonkosher shellfish. It has been noted that members of Orthodox synagogues — even some who are officers and active participants in the affairs of the Orthodox synagogues — are not hesitant about eating nonkosher meat and other foods outside their homes.

In 1946 an effort was made to secure the cooperation of one of the large hotels in establishing a kosher kitchen and keeping dishes for this department under lock and key, to be supervised by the rabbis or their representatives. However, nothing has ever come of this project.

There are no strictly kosher restaurants in the city. Obvi-

ously the Jews of the city will not support one, for if the number
of individuals insisting upon kosher food was sufficiently great,
such a restaurant surely would have been established. There
are, however, two "kosher style" restaurants. One is located in
the downtown area and is owned by a Jewish individual. The
other is maintained as a part of the activities of the Standard
Club. A variety of Jewish dishes are served, but the meats are
not kosher and shellfish and other nonkosher foods are on the
menu. No distinction is made between milk and meat dishes,
and one set is used for all foods. Despite this fact many who
regard themselves as kosher eat in the Standard Club's restaurant when they attend meetings and on other occasions, though
they do not eat those foods that are definitely nonkosher. Here
is another instance of the confusion with respect to the dietary
laws and their observance.

There are five or more Jewish delicatessen stores in the community catering particularly to Jewish clientele. These stores
sell, among other things, the smoked meats such as corned beef,
salami, and frankfurters that are kosher. It is difficult to say
whether these foods, which Jewish people seem to enjoy, are
purchased because they are kosher or because they are commonly supposed to be more tasty than nonkosher varieties.

The double standard in observing the dietary laws — using
kosher foods within the home and paying no attention to the
rules outside the home — results (1) from a desire to respect
the opinions of one's parents, who may on occasion come into the
home of their children and eat with them, or (2) from a certain
nostalgia which prevents a complete and utter break with habits
and traditions acquired in childhood. The dietary laws are certainly not adhered to by the younger generation of Jews even
though their parents may still maintain some degree of respect
or regard for them.

Though it appears that the dietary laws will be reduced in
importance and effectiveness as time goes on, there is a retention
of the special Jewish delicacies and dishes which were associated

with the parents' home. Many housewives take particular pride in being able to prepare these delicacies. They like to speak of their special culinary arts as helping to carry on, in some degree, the domestic skills as their mothers practiced them.

"We don't have those typical Jewish dishes in my own home that we used to have in our home when I was a kid. Only on rare occasions does my wife make gefilte fish and things like that. I guess it's because my mother had more time for preparing those things than my wife has. I remember that my mother used to spend hours working in the kitchen, making those things. I can still recall the bother she would go to to prepare the thin noodles which she used to put into the chicken soup. Today we buy all that sort of thing if we have it at all.

"I think that things began to change when we kids began growing up and when we stayed out late or weren't able to get home for supper or dinner. Then I think my mother stopped making these things quite as often, because she never knew just when we would be home. Our family gatherings for all the children were really something. Mother would prepare all the foods we loved so much. She would be up early working all day long in order to prepare those extra special things for Friday night dinners for the family, when we were all sure to be together."

What factors have tended to produce these changes in attitude toward the importance of the dietary laws? The following statements will in some degree serve to answer this question:

"Most Jewish people of our younger set certainly don't eat kosher food or keep the dietary laws. They may on occasion buy meat from a kosher butcher, but not because of any principle involved. I remember that in my own home we used to buy meat from a kosher butcher as long as it was delivered to us. We never bothered about salting it or concerned ourselves about two sets of dishes. But we kept on buying from the kosher butcher until he couldn't deliver meat to our home because we lived so far out. We never tried to get it from another kosher butcher. Rather, we just purchased it from any butcher shop where we could get it."

"I can see the great changes that have taken place in my own family. When I was a kid, my mother kept a strictly kosher home. She would buy only kosher meat and would salt it and prepare it just exactly according to Jewish law. But after my grandmother (my mother's mother, who used to live at our house) died, she gradually began to change. She kept on buying meat from a kosher butcher shop but she didn't salt it as she used to do. Then gradually we began having other things that would not be regarded as kosher in our home. Finally, our home became in many respects nonkosher, that is, we just didn't pay much attention to kashrus (the dietary laws).

"As far as my home is concerned, now that I am married, we do not buy kosher meat and we have only one set of dishes for milk and meat foods and kashrus doesn't mean very much to us. Of course, I still do not like to eat pork products very much. I have a kind of natural objection to them. Yet every once in a while, I eat these things too. But we definitely do not use these pork products in my home. When we do eat them, we eat them out."

"My parents' home was definitely kosher. We followed Jewish ritual in so far as kosher meat was concerned very exactly. But I never had a kosher home when I got married and I do not feel its importance in any respect. I still do not eat ham or things like that out. I just don't like it. I don't know why. But I certainly eat nonkosher meat out as I do in my own home."

"Nobody pays any attention to the dietary laws in these days. I used to, as a kid, but I got over that when I started going out. In fact, it was during my high school days that I first tasted trefoh (nonkosher) food. At first I rather expected that something would happen to me, but nothing did. So I just kept on. My folks never asked any questions. I don't know whether they really didn't know what I was doing or whether they just kept quiet about it in order to keep things peaceful around the house. But I have kept on eating nonkosher foods since then."

"After all the whole business about kosher meat was just to keep things clean and there really is no need for that today seeing that we have meat inspection and all. My friends all like kosher meals every once in a while. We like our kosher corned beef and all the other Jewish dishes, the kind my mother used to make, but I don't have a kosher kitchen in our home and none of my friends do either."

"I would buy kosher meat, if only the prices that the kosher butchers charged were not so high. I cannot understand why I should be obliged to pay so much more for kosher meat than I pay in any other meat market. The high prices are driving Jews away from keeping kosher. They just can't afford it."

"God didn't write those laws. Man did. What was good or right for one generation isn't necessarily right for us. I don't want to be different in this respect from the rest of the community."

"We're told that the dietary laws have helped the Jews to survive. I would rather place my trust in other things that really matter. I want to survive, but I don't need so many reminders that I am a Jew."

Observance of the dietary laws has dropped because, even though they are biblical in origin, there is little feeling that these are "God-ordained" injunctions. They are not regarded as vital or necessary for the preservation or survival of the Jewish people. Observance is difficult for persons who eat out. It is easier to follow the practices of one's friends. Kosher meats are no longer regarded as cleaner or more hygienic than nonkosher. Finally, it is "right" to follow the majority of Americans in such matters.

Chapter 6   Feast and Fast Days

❧ CEREMONIES *are beautiful for others; they are* vital, *as well as beautiful, for us. Ceremonies, for others, are a luxury; for us they are essential to our very existence.*[1]

THE SABBATH

THE Sabbath, with all its traditional sanctity and beauty, has ceased to exist as a vital factor in the lives of most Jews in Minneapolis. Not only has synagogue attendance been materially reduced on the Sabbath eve and the Sabbath morning, but the traditional practices that were associated with the observance of the day are being neglected if not totally ignored.[2]

As we have already observed, it was customary for all Jewish housewives to make special preparations for the Sabbath. The house was cleaned in anticipation of the Day of Delight which was the Sabbath. All the culinary skills of the housewife were employed in order to provide special dishes for the Sabbath meals. Gefilte fish, chicken noodle soup, chicken, roasted or boiled, home-made Sabbath challos (twists of bread), and innumerable other foods were lovingly prepared.

All was in readiness before sundown on Friday evening, when the Sabbath was officially ushered in with the kindling of the Sabbath candles which had been placed upon the white tablecloth. The traditional Hebrew blessings were recited by the housewife as she lit the candles. The children had all been bathed and freshly dressed. The father would return to his home in sufficient time to cleanse himself for the Sabbath. He and the other male members of the family would then recite the Sabbath eve prayers, either in the home or in the neighborhood synagogue. Then as all the members of the household stood at their places near the dining room table, the traditional kiddush (sanctification of the wine) would be recited, the blessing over the bread was made, and the Sabbath meal was begun.

At the conclusion of the meal, and even between courses, zemiros (songs of a religious nature) were sung by all the members of the family. The grace after meals was recited. The biblical portion for the week, which was to be read in the synagogue on the Sabbath morning, was usually reviewed, or some other portion of Hebraic literature or lore was studied. So, in the quiet and peace of the Sabbath eve, as the candles slowly burned themselves out, the evening would be spent.

But all that has changed! The majority of Jewish husbands return to their homes on the Sabbath eve at about the same time they do on any other business day. The meal is prepared, to be sure, yet few of the old time culinary delicacies are in evidence. As likely as not the gefilte fish is purchased in the delicatessen store around the corner. Though there are in most cases special Sabbath breads on the table, they are no longer homemade.

The number of housewives who light the Sabbath candles in their homes is still large, though around the 1930's the number was diminishing rapidly. Concerted effort on the part of the rabbis in the community has had some effect in increasing the number.

"I never used to light the Sabbath candles and recite the blessing because I thought that it was old-fashioned. I wanted to be a real American. Most of my friends felt the same way about it. But I began to follow the old practice when my children began coming home from Sunday school and asked me why I didn't light the candles or why my husband didn't chant the kiddush. We looked at each other in astonishment. In fact I was rather angry about the whole thing. I even went to the rabbi and told him that I planned to withdraw my children from the school because he was teaching them things in which I didn't believe. He told me if I felt that way to withdraw them. But somehow I couldn't quite do it. Imagine my surprise one Friday when I came home and found that my daughter had purchased candles with her spending money and that she had lighted them herself. I was embarrassed about it, of course. If it meant so much to her, I felt I ought to start the practice again. So since then I have kindled the Sabbath candles. And frankly I am glad I did. It changes the whole Sabbath for us. Now we know it is Sabbath. Before it was just another meal."

The kiddush (sanctification of the wine) is recited by less than 50 percent of the heads of the Jewish households in the community. If he is a son of an immigrant, he may have forgotten the words and the traditional chant years ago, or he may feel no urge to continue the practice. In many instances it is the grandson who chants the blessings because he has had the benefit of training in the Hebrew school or the synagogue. Children of Reform parents seldom know these traditional chants unless they have received private tutoring, for most do not attend the Hebrew school. The traditional Sabbath zemiros are seldom chanted, and the grace after meals is not usually recited.

The number of housewives who are to be found in their homes on Friday, busily at work in preparation for the Sabbath, is surprisingly small. Instead they may be found at meetings, gatherings, or in the downtown shops.

"Yes, I go out on Friday afternoons. I don't stay around the house and work in preparation for the Sabbath as my mother did. Yet I do have a nice Sabbath meal and I always kindle the Sabbath candles and I think that I am no worse a Jewess than my mother was. My home is clean every day in the week. It doesn't require extra special cleaning for the Sabbath. I do not bake bread at home. But I don't bake bread any day of the week. Why should I when any good Jewish bakery can prepare it and save me not only the time but money. Then too I have 'help' in my home. I leave the orders as to what to prepare. I show her how to prepare it and it's done very well. I don't see that my going out on Friday afternoon indicates any lack of regard for the Sabbath. I'm a modern woman. I just use modern methods in my housework, and as a consequence I have more time for the things I want to do."

A comparatively limited number of persons attend the traditional synagogue service which inaugurates the Sabbath at the hour of dusk on Friday evening. Women seldom attended such services. Economic factors have made it almost impossible for most men to be present at the early Friday evening service, except the few who either are strong-willed or possess leisure or wealth.

About three decades ago the practice of conducting a late Friday evening service was instituted in the Conservative and Reform synagogues. With the service beginning about 8 P.M., it was predicted that the synagogue would be filled with worshippers who would come after concluding their Sabbath meals. Whatever the cause, this has not proved to be the case.

In one Conservative synagogue, with a membership of four hundred families, the average attendance at the late service over a period of two decades was about one hundred and fifty adults. At another Conservative synagogue, with about the same number of members, located in the very center of the Jewish community, the average attendance was about two hundred and fifty adults. In the Reform temple, again with about four hundred families, the average attendance was about one hundred adults. It is true of course that at special services the numbers increased greatly, yet the average as stated takes these occasions into consideration.

Until 1941 none of the nine Orthodox synagogues had established late Friday evening services. In that year two of these congregations, located in the very center of the more Orthodox Jewish community on the North Side, established such a service. In the first few years attendance was heavy and it was not uncommon to find the synagogues filled to capacity. But the novelty of the services soon wore off and the numbers in attendance dwindled until today only about one hundred and fifty persons are to be found at each service.

How do the Jews of Minneapolis spend their Friday evenings? If they do not come to the synagogue in large numbers, what do they do with their evenings?

"I just stay home with my family. I come home from work tired. The whole family is together at dinner. We enjoy each other's company. After we finish dinner there are dishes to wash and before you know it, it's already eight o'clock. Unless we rush through the meal, we can't get to services in time. So we just stay home and visit."

"I like to go to the Minneapolis symphony concerts which take place on Friday nights. I always relax when I listen to good music. To me it's a religious act to listen to such music, so my wife and I go to the symphony. Of course, I would like to go to synagogue, and in fact I do when the concerts aren't available, but I really enjoy those concerts, so I go."

"All the sporting events in town take place on Friday nights. I like boxing and I see no reason why I shouldn't go to them, even if it is Friday night."

"When I go to the synagogue I always get home late and I need my rest, so I stay home or we visit with friends."

"Somehow people always drop over to the house on Friday evening. It's a kind of social night. I like these visits. In this town people drop over to each other's homes frequently. I think it's fun."

"At my fraternity Friday night is always a big night. Either it's a celebration before a football game or it's something else that keeps us busy. In fact a lot of the boys don't go to the synagogue because Friday night is one of the few nights they can go out on dates."

"Somehow it doesn't seem right to break away from Orthodoxy by having these late Friday evening services. Sabbath services should take place at sundown and not later. If the people can't come then it's their loss. Besides I don't like the innovations at these services. They are not Orthodox enough for me."

"I just don't believe in prayer, so whether the service takes place on Friday night or any other time, I just don't go. The only exception I make is on Yom Kippur (the Day of Atonement)."

Even before the introduction of late Friday evening services, many of the Jewish youth were using Friday evenings for dancing parties and socials. Apparently the situation proved vexing to the more traditionally minded members of the Jewish community for in 1917 there appeared the following editorial in the *American Jewish World*:

Attendance by our Jewish young people at Friday evening dances is an offense to Jewish sentiment, an affront to the religious element of the community. Many of these young people probably are children of strictly Orthodox parents, or at least of parents who still have a good deal of old-time Jewish feeling and Jewish loyalty in them. How can they be so thoughtless as to offend the sensibilities of their own kindred and of the older element in the community is beyond our understanding.

Attendance at synagogue services on the Sabbath morning is on the whole not very marked. The Orthodox synagogues located on the North Side of the city average about one hundred people each Sabbath morning. The several smaller Orthodox synagogues on the South Side can boast of not more than ten or twelve males. The Conservative synagogue on the North Side averages about two hundred but includes in its figures children who come with their parents or attend as a part of the junior congregation, which is composed of children who attend the religious school. In addition there are those persons who come to the synagogue as guests of the Bar Mitzvah (confirmant) of that Sabbath. At the Conservative synagogue on the West Side the average attendance is about one hundred and fifty persons, including Bar Mitzvahs and members of the junior congregation. At the Reform temple, which is also located on the West Side, the number of worshippers is far less.

The economic factor is by far the most important reason for small attendance on Sabbath mornings. The Sabbath day cannot be hallowed when the business establishments of the community are all open. The day of rest and leisure is, in reality, Sunday, because as competition grows keener most men feel that they cannot afford to close their places of business while others remain open. There are, of course, some businessmen who keep their establishments open on the Sabbath and entrust their affairs to others for several hours while they attend the synagogue. But their number is rapidly diminishing.

FEAST AND FAST DAYS

The Sabbath has become more a day of recreation than a day of prayer and rest. Children use the day for parties, movie-going, shopping, dancing, music, and other special lessons, eating out, and in general having a good time. Mothers in ever-increasing numbers do their shopping, attend theaters and parties and the like. Fathers go out to the golf clubs, attend football games, indulge in a friendly game of cards, or take the family on an outing.

The sampling study of Talmud Torah students which was discussed earlier may serve to provide an over-all picture of Orthodox and Conservative Jewry of Minneapolis with respect to Sabbath observance. (See Table V.) It must be borne in mind that these figures are representative only of the Conservative and Orthodox families whose children attend the Hebrew school and do not indicate the practices of the Reform members of the community. Though no figures are available for the Reform group, which numbers about four hundred and fifty families, it is safe to assume that the number who observe the orthodox traditions is considerably less than for the Orthodox and Conservative groups.

TABLE V. RELIGIOUS PRACTICES OBSERVED BY FAMILIES OF HEBREW SCHOOL PUPILS, MINNEAPOLIS, 1946

1. Do the following attend synagogue on Friday night?

	Attend Regularly	Attend Sometimes	Never Attend
I (Talmud Torah pupil)....	9	93	48
Father	20	84	40
Mother	7	76	59
Older brother(s)	3	31	32
Older sister(s)	0	32	36

2. Do the following attend synagogue on Saturday morning?

	Attend Regularly	Attend Sometimes	Never Attend
I (Talmud Torah pupil)....	71	60	24
Father	12	69	74
Mother	1	62	93
Older brother(s)	5	22	32
Older sister(s)	2	26	41

TABLE V — *Continued*

3. My father does not go to work on
Saturday 24
Passover 35
Shavuot 30
Rosh Hashonah.......131
Yom Kippur 132
Sukkot 28

4. On Saturday my mother

	Never Cooks	Warms Up Cooked Food	Cooks Regularly
	20	90	49

5. We play our radio on Saturdays

	Yes	No
	117	11

6. a. We have musical instruments in our home
Yes
92

   b. We play violin, piano, etc. on Saturdays
Yes
62

7. Riding on Saturdays in our family

	Do Not Ride	Do Ride
I (Talmud Torah pupil).................	17	152
Father	17	145
Mother	26	139
Older brother(s)	7	49
Older sister(s)	8	48

8. Writing on Saturday

	Do Not Write	Do Write
I (Talmud Torah pupil).................	62	107
Father	47	112
Mother	58	100
Older brother(s)	18	40
Older sister(s)	18	47

9. Smoking on Saturday

	Do Not Smoke	Do Smoke
Father	29	85
Mother	26	51
Older brother(s)	14	18
Older sister(s)	9	12

10. Shopping on Saturday

	Do Not Shop	Do Shop
I (Talmud Torah pupil).................	28	137
Father	53	88
Mother	23	140
Older brother(s)	13	30
Older sister(s)	10	39

TABLE V — *Continued*

11. Putting on lights in our family

	Do Not Put on Lights	Do Put on Lights
I (Talmud Torah pupil)	15	146
Father	20	130
Mother	19	136
Older brother(s)	8	40
Older sister(s)	4	50

	Regularly	Sometimes	Never
12. a. Mother lights candles on Friday night	116	35	13
b. Mother lights candles on holiday nights	113	36	16
c. My father lights candles on Chanukah	113	22	18
d. My father recites kiddush on Friday nights	42	44	63
e. My father recites kiddush on holiday nights	68	48	38

13. My father says a prayer before meals on

	Regularly	Sometimes	Never
Weekdays	10	25	115
Saturdays	23	26	102
Holidays	63	45	51

14. My father says grace [prayers] after meals on

	Regularly	Sometimes	Never
Weekdays	8	19	103
Saturdays	15	18	113
Holidays	36	37	56

These figures, though not intended to present an infallible record of the religious practices of the Minneapolis Jewish community, support the belief that religious observance is definitely weakening. When we consider that of the 184 parents whose country of origin was given only 16 fathers and 25 mothers were native born, it becomes evident that the religious practice and observance, even of the foreign-born parents, is definitely waning.

ROSH HASHONAH

The Jewish New Year, which occurs about the middle of September, begins the most solemn season of the Jewish year. Starting with the traditional two-day observance of the New Year and concluding ten days later with the Day of Atonement (Yom

Kippur), Jews enter their houses of worship to ask forgiveness for their offenses against God and man. Jewish tradition has it that during these ten days God judges man and signs His decree concerning him. "On the Rosh Hashonah it is inscribed and on the Yom Kippur it is sealed who shall live and who shall die." [3]

For the average Jew no holy days have such sanctity or solemnity as this season. In preparation the home is carefully cleaned, the candles are kindled, and the appropriate blessings are recited. The holy day meal is begun with the blessing over the wine (kiddush) and the grace before the meal (motzi). The meal is very much like that prepared for the Sabbath. In keeping with the nature of the prayers that are shortly to be uttered in the synagogues and temples for a year of life, the meal is traditionally begun by eating a slice of apple dipped in honey, symbolic of the year of sweetness for which all the members of the family will pray.

Among Orthodox and Conservative Jews it was customary to be in the synagogue before sundown, so that the evening prayers might be chanted at the proper hour. Services began on the following mornings at about seven o'clock and continued until one or even two in the afternoon. The cantor and his specially trained holy day choir performed the traditional heart-rending melodies and the rabbi would sermonize. Though these were solemn days, they were not days of sadness. Men and women dressed in their best and newest clothes. If prayers were recited in cursory fashion throughout the rest of the year, there was a new heart and a new spirit on the New Year.

In the Reform temple the same spirit of devotion and piety manifested itself. There was, however, a choir composed of both men and women and there was organ music. The Reform prayer book contained more English than Hebrew and the service was abbreviated in length. But whether the service was Orthodox or Reform, the same feeling of awe and an awareness of God's impending judgment of His children was ever present.

From the earliest days of the community until the present

friends have continued to greet each other with the Hebrew phrase *LeShonah Tovah TiKosayvu* (May you be inscribed in the Book of Life for a good year).

The sanctuaries of the synagogues in the city were built with due regard for the number of pews required to seat the large holy day congregations. Thus synagogues that can hold 1000 or more are usual. They are filled to overflowing only on the high holy days of Rosh Hashonah and Yom Kippur. So large, in fact, have the holy day congregations become that in three of the Conservative and Orthodox synagogues it has become necessary to establish auxiliary services.

The traditional ram's horn is blown on Rosh Hashonah in all synagogues except the Reform. In the latter a trumpet is used to simulate the sound of this ancient instrument.

The Orthodox and Conservative congregations observe the traditional two-day festival. Members of the Reform congregation observe but one day. Except for the Sabbath and the Day of Atonement all festivals are observed traditionally for a two-day period in Orthodox and Conservative synagogues. Despite this the vast majority of Jews who call themselves Conservative and many who regard themselves as Orthodox actually observe most festivals on one day only. Most Jews still observe the Jewish New Year for two days.

The number of Jewish children who attend school on the second day of any festival, except the New Year, is increasing rapidly. The Jewish child on the West Side of the city who does not go to school on the second day of the festival is a rarity.

SHABBAS SHUVAH

The Sabbath between the New Year and the Day of Atonement is known as Shabbas Shuvah (the Sabbath of Return or the Sabbath of Repentance). Though this particular Sabbath has as its theme the need for men to repent their misdeeds and is basically at one with the other holy days, attendance in the synagogue falls off very sharply. To most of the Jews of Minneapolis it is not just another Sabbath, but rather just another work day.

YOM KIPPUR

Yom Kippur, the Day of Atonement, is also known as the Sabbath of Sabbaths. It begins at sundown on the eve of Yom Kippur, known as Kol Nidre Eve from the prayer which begins with the words "Kol Nidre" and known best because of the traditional, haunting melody which has been sung to these words for unknown generations. The following twenty-four hours are hours of judgment. God's decree concerning man is to be signed. What the future holds in store no man may know. One can therefore well understand the mood and temper of the worshippers at this season.

On the day before Yom Kippur traditional practice required that men expiate their sins by pouring them out upon a goat and sending it into the wilderness. Jews of a later age were to transfer their sins upon a chicken or rooster, depending upon the sex of the sinner. As the fowl was lifted over his head, the penitent prayed that it would constitute an appropriate substitute for himself. The fowl was then slaughtered in accordance with Jewish ritual by the shochet (ritual slaughterer) and was used as food.

This custom prevailed in the homes of those who called themselves Orthodox and Conservative until two decades ago. Then a marked falling off in this practice was noticeable. It has gradually become the practice to contribute to some charitable cause as a means of expiating one's sins. In Reform homes of Minneapolis the earlier custom was never observed. However, the practice of contributing to some philanthropy has generally not taken hold, perhaps because it is far less dramatic, and because philanthropy happens to be an everyday matter in the lives of great numbers of Jews in Minneapolis.

Services on Kol Nidre night are, according to tradition, to begin at sundown. However this custom may have been observed in the past, it became apparent that men were unable to reach the synagogue in time without forfeiting the right to enjoy a meal before the beginning of the Great White Fast. The Conservative congregations have therefore arranged matters so that services now begin as late as 7:30. The service in the Reform congregation begins at 8 o'clock.

Every synagogue and temple in Minneapolis is crowded to the doors on Kol Nidre Eve. Seats for the high holy days are assigned to all dues-paying members in the Reform and Conservative congregations without charge. In the Orthodox synagogues, where the membership dues are usually low or where men and women may worship without assuming the financial obligations of membership, a separate charge is made for high holy day seats. The many persons who have no direct synagogal affiliation, but who want to attend the services, are accommodated as well as possible.

In the Orthodox synagogues the men sit on the main floor, while their wives and daughters occupy seats in the women's gallery. In one of the Orthodox synagogues men and women sit together on the main floor at the Friday evening service, but on Sabbath morning and on the high holy days, the women are seated in the balcony. There is no synagogue in this community where women sit in an elevated section on the main floor. In the Conservative and Reform synagogues men and women sit side by side in family pews. Sons and daughters sit with their parents, all except those of public school age. For them a special service is arranged for both Rosh Hashonah and Yom Kippur.

Why are the synagogues and temples so crowded on the high holy days? Why do practically all Jews come to the synagogue on these days and yet refrain from coming in large numbers during the rest of the year? The following reasons are suggested:

"I really don't believe in prayer. That's why I can't make a regular practice of going to a synagogue. But on the high holy days I like to be where my parents are. I like to feel that we are all one family. I don't want my children to think I am not religious because, despite my feeling about prayer, I really would

103

say that I am religious. I believe in a God. But He is not the same personal God to whom I paid my respects as a child. Whether the prayers mean something as they are written or not, the fact is that even if these days were arbitrarily chosen (and I feel that they were), it is a good thing for man to take time off to stop and figure out where he's going and sort of get a hold on himself once again. In other words the holy days mean something to me even if I don't think of God as actually checking me off in the Book of Life. I keep saying to myself 'Will I be here next year? Have I really been living properly?' Whether one is religious or not, there is a lot of good that comes to me from the holy days. I rather feel cleansed by the experience of fasting and sitting in the synagogue and praying."

"I am a religious Jew. God has meaning for me. I believe somehow that men are judged for their deeds. I pray because I feel that I want Life for myself and my family. I feel closer to my God because of the holy days."

"I believe in the Jewish people. I get a thrill out of being with my fellow Jews in the synagogue. I feel the history of my people affecting me very directly. The prayer book for me is a book about my people more than it is a book of prayer. It tells me what the Jew has felt, how he has thought, what his ideals are, how he wants to live. I don't take everything in the prayer book too literally. I find enough, however, of really great value that I want to hold onto it. So I come to the synagogue and listen to the Kol Nidre. I don't believe there is anything to the Kol Nidre that cannot be eliminated without harm. But I know that in so doing I would lose an important chapter in my people's life. I would forget about the Spanish Inquisition. I would forget how Jews suffered just to perpetuate their way of life. So I come to the synagogue and I join with my fellow Jews. I fast too. All because I want to feel part of the Jewish people and its history."

The number of Jews who fast on the Day of Atonement, from sundown of Kol Nidre Eve to sundown the following day, though not as large as it was a decade ago, is still surprisingly great. The number, though not obtainable with any degree of statistical accuracy, is assumed to be large because of the apologetic attitude of those who do break fast. While violations of the dietary laws are made openly and often aggressively, persons who eat or drink on the Day of Atonement either refrain from doing so in public or apologize for their actions by claiming "a splitting headache" or "doctor's orders."

In the Orthodox synagogue services continue on Yom Kippur without interruption from about seven o'clock in the morning till sundown. In the two Conservative synagogues and in the Reform temple there is an intermission of about an hour in the early afternoon. The intermission is possible because certain changes have been effected in the service. Some prayers have been abbreviated, others have been eliminated, all of which has reduced the length of the service.

From time to time congregants leave the synagogue for short periods. Men and women may take brief walks; conversations about such purely secular matters as the baseball or football scores or new styles are known to take place. Not all Jews who enter the synagogue keep their minds on their prayers through the service. But they are there and for reasons best known to themselves they continue to fill the Minneapolis synagogues to overflowing on the high holy days.

At the conclusion of the services families return to their homes and break the fast together. There are Yom Kippur dances conducted by synagogal and other groups, which many younger couples attend.

It is not considered in good taste for Jewish-owned places of business to remain open on Rosh Hashonah and especially on Yom Kippur. Yet the number which do so is increasing rapidly. That accounts for the fact that in many cases synagogue seats which have been assigned to various families are occupied by all members of the family except the breadwinner. He may drop in sometime during the day or attend the evening service.

The high holy days occupy a unique place in the lives of the Jews of Minneapolis. Though the degree of piety that characterized their fathers and grandfathers may not be as high, there is little question but that the high holy days represent one of the pivotal points around which the people build their lives as Jews.

Each Jew and Jewess may find his or her own reasons for observing these days in a traditional manner. What matters most is that the importance they attach to these days makes it clear that ties to their past, though loosened in many ways, will not soon be broken.

The Three Pilgrimage Festivals [4]

PESACH

Pesach or the festival of Passover, the first of the pilgrimage festivals, which occurs in the spring of the year, recounts the story of the great Exodus from Egyptian bondage which took place about 1200 B.C.E.[5] The festival is greatly loved by the Jewish people not only because it tells the story of how Israel attained its freedom, but also because it has associated with it the Seder, the service in which Jewish families gather around the table to recount the tale of the Exodus from Egypt and Israel's redemption from slavery.

During the eight days in which the Passover is traditionally celebrated, it is expected that no leaven will be used in the home. As a consequence Jews traditionally eat only unleavened bread (matsoh) during this period. They are required too to use separate sets of dishes and cutlery for the week of Passover in accordance with Orthodox ritual. Any food or food product that has come in contact with leaven is prohibited. A great variety of the articles used in the home for food must be specially prepared for the Passover. These foods are labeled in order that they may be recognized as "kosher le Pesach," ritually fit for use on the Passover.

The traditional Seder service is still observed to a very large degree. There are few families in the Minneapolis Jewish community who do not either prepare their own Seder or participate with other members of their family or friends.

It is true that whereas the traditional practice was to celebrate the Seder on the first two nights of Passover, now a larger number of families celebrate the Seder on only one night. The ritual is not as closely adhered to as in former years, for the abil-

106

ity to read Hebrew fluently is less marked than it was. The long traditional service is often abbreviated by omitting certain portions or substituting other reading. However, additional activities which help to hold the interest of all the members of the family, both young and old, are sought for and utilized. Even though many of the practices associated with the Seder are somewhat strange to members of the younger generation, there are available today a variety of manuals and aids and modified Seder services. As a consequence the Seder retains its hold and often gains in beauty because of the variations and additions that have been made. It remains a strong unifying force because it is basically built around the family.

Seldom is a Seder conducted without the foods that are particularly associated with the Passover cuisine: gefilte fish, chicken soup with knädlach (dumplings), roast chicken, and a variety of other delicacies.

When we examine the matter of other ritual observance on the Passover, the situation is not quite the same. Though it is true that the vast majority of Jews, Reform, Conservative, and Orthodox, eat matsoh on the Passover, they do not do so to the exclusion of bread and other leavened foods. One may find the kosher-style restaurants crowded with Jewish businessmen during the Passover week. The matsoh will be on the table and men will eat it to the exclusion of bread. However, they will eat other products that are traditionally forbidden on the Passover.

About two decades ago there were very few products available for Passover use. Such items as candy and soda water were not to be found within homes that wished to keep the Passover in accordance with Orthodox practice. All that, however, has changed. Today these products, with labels affirming their ritual correctness, are to be found in most Jewish homes. The approval for these items is usually provided by a local Orthodox rabbi. This includes such foods as milk, cream, and butter, which it was almost impossible to find on the Passover table several decades ago. Now one may find them regularly and there is little question concerning the correctness of their use. As a result of the gradual accretion of the number of products that are to be regarded as kosher for the Passover, there has developed a tendency on the part of the children and grandchildren of the early Orthodox settlers to become skeptical about the idea of requiring special labels on any foods that are to be used for this festival.

"When I realize that the rabbis who give their approval for these Pesach foods are receiving pay for each such approval, I begin to question the reason for trying to keep up this sort of thing. It seems to me that we have cheapened the whole Passover idea and I, for one, am not as careful now about the foods I use in my home on Passover as I used to be. Nor am I as much concerned with making complete changes in my home with respect to dishes and other things as I used to be or as my mother was. Inasmuch as I really don't keep a very kosher home throughout the year, it seems to me rather silly to do so on the Passover alone. My mother used to put boards over the regular table and cover the kitchen sink with boards in order that the food used for Passover might not come in contact with any leaven.

"It seems to me that this sort of thing doesn't add very much to the whole idea of keeping Passover, and so I ignore it. The vast majority of my friends pay no attention to that sort of thing. They do keep matsohs in their homes and they do prepare the special Passover foods that we all like so well, and we try to buy those foods that are definitely associated with the Passover festival, but I don't think that we are anywhere near as careful about the whole thing as our mothers were."

The Reform element in the Minneapolis Jewish community also purchases matsoh and other Passover items for their homes. But since the vast majority, if not all of them, do not maintain kosher homes throughout the year, they do not change their practices for the Passover.

It was Orthodox practice to make a fictional "sale" of all the leavened products in the home to the rabbi before the Passover. He in turn disposed of these items to some non-Jew. The reason for this was to avoid legal possession of anything that might be regarded as nonkosher for Passover. Today only a limited number of persons come to the rabbi or to his home for the purpose of "selling" their leavened products.

It was the practice in the traditional Jewish home to combine the spring cleaning season with the Passover season, and in preparation for the Passover the whole household was carefully gone over and anything that might in any way be associated with foods that were leavened was stored in the basement or in other parts of the home. Today there is far less of this kind of cleaning of the home in preparation for the Passover.

"My home is kept very clean. I see to it that there isn't a speck of dust in my home at any time. I not only work myself but I call in extra help whenever I need it, so it isn't necessary for me to go through that trying period of preparing my home for Passover in the same way that my mother used to do."

Although preparation for the Passover is still in most instances regarded as a "labor of love," it is a chore and an inconvenience to many others. This may in some measure help to explain the tendency to eliminate the fine distinctions that used to exist in the Jewish home between the Passover season and the rest of the year.

"As one of the oldest Jewish physicians in the city, I can remember the time when any Jewish woman who was in the hospital, having given birth to a child sometime before Passover, would appeal to me frantically in an effort to be released from the hospital so that she might be with her family some time before Passover and at least supervise in the matter of preparing for the Passover week. Today, however, all that has changed. I have had Jewish women who, being in the hospital after childbirth, would instead plead with me to remain in the hospital over Passover so that they might not have all the work involved in preparing for the Passover."

There is still evident a great love for the Passover season, or at least for the Seder service. People like to meet together, they like to have the various members of the family assemble around the family table, and, as is characteristic of this midwestern community, they like to invite their friends to join them in a

109

friendly evening. If the Passover provides this opportunity, then it is so much to the good, and Passover itself benefits from the point of view of the degree of observance.

SHAVUOT

Shavuot, the feast of Pentecost and the second pilgrimage festival, is traditionally a two-day festival which occurs fifty days after the feast of Passover.[6] Reform Jews observe it for one day. Originally the first of two harvest festivals in Palestine — the second, Sukkot, occurring in the autumn — Shavuot was known as the Season of the Giving of the Torah. It was at this season, according to tradition, that the Ten Commandments were given through Moses to the children of Israel as they stood at the foot of Mount Sinai.

"Shavuot never had any special meaning for us as children. I remember the holiday mainly because my mother used to make wonderful blintzes (cheese wrapped in paper-thin egg dough). My father used to go to synagogue on Shavuot. My mother always went on the second day of the holiday because the yizkor (memorial) services on behalf of the dead took place on that day. But I do not recall going to the synagogue. In fact, because the holiday usually occurred during school days, I used to go to school.

"My folks never really objected, though every once in a while my father would get rather angry and denounce America because it was taking his children away from him. At least that's the way he used to put it. What he really meant was that we just had to go to school and later on to work, and we didn't attend synagogue services with him. But we always would have the family dinners, special for the holiday, on the eve before the first day of Shavuot. Father made kiddush (sanctification of the wine) and the dinner was very much like the kind mother used to prepare for Sabbath. When I got married, and this holds true for my brothers and sisters as well, we really didn't have very much of a holiday on Shavuot. If the children hadn't all gathered for dinner on the holiday night at my folks' home, I think we would not even have known that it was a holiday. My husband always has gone downtown and shopped without thinking twice about it."

FEAST AND FAST DAYS

Attendance in the Orthodox and Conservative synagogues had been decreasing on Shavuot over a period of years. Attendance in the Reform temple had been even smaller. However, it was the Reform movement which helped to revitalize the Shavuot festival by introducing the confirmation ceremony for boys and girls in the graduating class of the Sunday school.

"At first we used to regard the confirmation service, which was conducted by the Reform temple on the first day of Shavuot, as something non-Jewish in form and content. We all connected it with the Christian confirmation services. But we found that the service seemed to mean something to the children. They loved the pageantry. They learned something about their own people, its history, and its ideals; they gave public affirmation of their faith and what is more, because all this took place on Shavuot as a part of the service, it brought their fathers and mothers and friends into the synagogue. The Conservative synagogues began to copy the idea, gradually adopting the ceremony, making changes to suit their own ritual. Today confirmation is an accepted fact.

"Both Conservative synagogues conduct confirmation services. Adath Jeshurun has it on the first day of the holiday, as does the Reform Temple Israel. Beth El, the other Conservative congregation on the North Side, conducts the service in the evening of the first day. There are about an equal number of boys and girls in the confirmation classes at Temple Israel and Adath Jeshurun. Their classes have from twenty to thirty in them each year. Beth El includes in its ceremony of confirmation only girls, although it presents certificates of Bar Mitzvah to the boys who were Bar Mitzvah during the year at the same time. There are usually about twenty girls in the class. The Orthodox synagogues do not conduct confirmation services, and the Minneapolis Talmud Torah does not conduct such a service, because even if it wanted to the ceremony certainly belongs in the synagogue."

The confirmation service usually brings five hundred or more worshippers into the Conservative and Reform synagogues on Shavuot. Were these confirmation services omitted, the number of persons attending services on the first day of Shavuot would be materially reduced.

The confirmation service has grown in importance in the eyes of both the congregants and the children who participate. The reason may be partly because parties and receptions are arranged in honor of the confirmants and their parents at the conclusion of the service. These receptions usually take place in the vestry rooms of the synagogue and temple buildings. The party-like atmosphere, the beauty of the floral decorations, the new dresses, and the many gifts which are showered up- on the confirmants by their parents, relatives, and friends help to give even greater significance to the occasion.

"I'm not sure that the confirmation service has too much meaning for the children from a religious point of view, though I know that the rabbis and teachers try hard enough to make it a real experience. I think that if the parents stopped holding these parties and receptions, and if instead of gifts the children and their friends would learn to give real contributions to worth- while causes it would be of greater value."

But there is another point of view:

"Confirmation was a really wonderful experience to me. Al- though I was excited and pleased by the presents and the recep- tion and all that, I think that I shall always remember the beauty of the confirmation and its solemnity. I shall never for- get the rabbi's blessing of me and the few words he said to me in whispered tones as he stood before the Holy Ark. With that ceremony, the synagogue became *my* synagogue and the rabbi became *my* rabbi."

On the second day of Shavuot the yizkor (memorial) services are conducted in the Conservative and Orthodox synagogues. Attendance at these services is marked by the large proportion of women. About a decade ago it became noticeable that fewer men were coming into the synagogue to recite their memorial prayers. At Adath Jeshurun (Conservative, West Side) the ratio of women to men at this service is two to one. At the Reform temple it is three to one. At Beth El, located on the North Side, it is about one and a half to one. At the Orthodox synagogues the ratio is about that of Beth El.

FEAST AND FAST DAYS

Though the service begins at approximately nine o'clock in the morning, the number of worshippers is always very limited until around ten o'clock, when a large number come for the sole purpose of reciting the yizkor prayers. It was common practice until the 1930's for these worshippers to leave almost immediately upon the conclusion of the special yizkor service. Now as a result of the pleading and insistence of the rabbis most worshippers remain in the synagogue until the conclusion of the service.

SUKKOT

Sukkot, the third of the pilgrimage festivals recorded in the Bible, is known as the Feast of Tabernacles or the Feast of Booths.[7] The children of Israel had been commanded to live in tabernacles or booths for seven days in commemoration of the frail structures in which they dwelt during their years of wandering in the wilderness. This festival, which occurs around the end of September, just five days after Yom Kippur, was traditionally a joyous experience. The second harvest of the year had been gathered in Palestine. Prayers of thanksgiving to the Lord were to be offered at this season for God's bounties.

The frail succah or booth, covered by rushes, leafy branches, or corn stalks and decorated with fruits of the harvest season, was erected by each household. During the festival all meals were eaten in the succah. It was lighted at night by candles over which the traditional blessing had been recited by the housewife. The kiddush (sanctification of the wine) was recited before each meal by the head of the household. It was not only a mitzvah (religious duty) in the sense of a commandment issued by God to dwell in booths; it was as well a joy which no Jew would think of foregoing.

The early East European immigrants in Minneapolis not only were mindful of this mitzvah, but saw to it that it was performed. Most families on the North Side spent a major portion of the five-day interval between Yom Kippur and Sukkot building and decorating the succah.

JEWS IN TRANSITION

"We always enjoyed Sukkot because we had our own succah in our own yard. It was wonderful, sitting there, having our meals in the succah, looking up through the corn stalks on the roof at the star-studded sky above. We children loved it all. We kept up the custom for many years, until the youngest of us was about fifteen, I guess. Then we moved and we didn't have a yard and things became crowded. Dad was troubled with money matters. In the meantime, the synagogue built a large succah in the synagogue yard. It wasn't anywhere near as pretty as ours. But people used to congregate there after services on Sukkot. Most of the Orthodox and Conservative synagogues built their own succahs and there were, somehow, fewer private succahs. My children wouldn't even know what a succah is supposed to look like if the synagogue didn't have one.

"It was a special mitzvah for us to recite the blessing over the esrog and lulav (citron and palm branch). At one time my father used to order these from Palestine. We would get it from the Holy Land shortly before Sukkot. How we used to enjoy its beauty! The wonderful odor of the citron and the green palm branch, around which the myrtle and willow branches entwined! Later my father stopped buying his own esrog and lulav, even though he used to enjoy the privilege of carrying them with him in the synagogue procession during the Hallel (Psalms) prayers. I can still remember the beautiful sight of about thirty or forty men, each wearing his tallis (prayer shawl) and holding his prayer book in one hand and the esrog and lulav in the other, walking slowly in the procession around the synagogue, led by the cantor who chanted the prayers. The rabbi of the Orthodox synagogue used to carry his esrog and lulav with such dignity. The sexton used to buy a good number of them and each morning before we left for school he would appear at our house and each of us children would recite the blessings, flick the palm branch lightly, and be off for school.

"But my children have never had an esrog and lulav in their home. The sexton of the synagogue to which I go does not come over to my home or to any other home so that we may offer the proper blessings. And if he did I'm sure we would all be embarrassed because we really don't know the blessings. Neither I, my husband, nor my children go to services on the days of Sukkot. The children are at school. My husband is at work and I just don't get around to it. Now my children see the syna-

114

gogue succah and the esrog and lulav on Sunday as a part of their Sunday school lessons around Sukkot. They participate in the new consecration service for new pupils in the religious school and see a beautifully decorated succah on the pulpit. I belong to the women's league and we have a Sukkot program of some kind, as does my husband in the men's club of the synagogue. But it is really far different from the way it was when I was a child."

Minor Feasts and Fasts

CHANUKAH

The Feast of Lights or Chanukah commemorates the victory of the Maccabees over the Hellenized Syrians in 165 B.C.E. and the rededication of the temple in Jerusalem to the worship of God.[8] This festival has traditionally been symbolized by the lighting of the eight-branched candelabra. The eight-day festival is observed by kindling one light on the first night and adding another light on each succeeding night until on the last night eight candles stand lighted on a row.

Special blessings of thanksgiving to the Almighty for having performed miracles "in those days as well as in these days" are recited, usually by the head of the household and the male members of his family. Special Chanukah songs are sung after the candle-lighting ceremony. Each of the children receives "Chanukah gelt," a gift of money in honor of the festival. The special Jewish delicacy of the Chanukah season, potato latkes (pancakes) made by the housewife, served further to bring the festival to the attention of the entire family.

Chanukah occurs at approximately the same time as Christmas. As a consequence the two solstice festivals, both utilizing lights and gift-giving, have vied with each other for the attention of the American-Jewish child.

"When I was a child, I remember that we always had a Chanukah menorah (candelabrum) in the house. When Chanukah came, my father would call us together around the menorah, just as it got dark outside. He would light the little candles, one more on each night, recite the berochos (blessings), and sing something which most of us really didn't understand. We children didn't participate in the ceremony to any real extent. We all loved the little candle lights to be sure. It was beautiful to see those tiny lights in the darkened room. Then my mother would give us little gifts, most of the time little things which she knew we needed. We were all so happy with that part of the holiday, as we were with the latkes which my mother served at dinner on the first night of Chanukah.

"But I can't say that the holiday of Chanukah was really very important to me or to my brothers and sisters. We really never got all the details of the story of Chanukah as we should have. We knew the story of the Maccabees and the miracle of the cruse of oil that burned for eight days only in a general sort of way. Then my father and brothers were usually very busy at this season of the year with the Christian business. Business was always better at this time of the year, so it happened that on many of the nights of the Chanukah somehow the candles weren't lighted by my father. He came home too late. Also we children had been hearing all about Christmas in the public school from our teachers as well as from other children. We heard all about the wonderful gifts they were going to receive. We knew every detail about the Christmas tree they were going to decorate. By comparison our Chanukah seemed more drab and less important. I remember that around this time of the year I used to say to myself 'I wish I were a Christian.' It wasn't a matter of theology. It was just a matter of fun. And I missed what the Christian children had.

"When I grew up, married, and had a family of my own, I always worried about this situation. I saw my children and the children of my friends looking enviously upon their Christian friends. I used to send my children to Sunday school and to Talmud Torah. They knew much more about the story of Chanukah than I ever did. To them the Maccabees were great heroes, but somehow I used to hear them too say the very same thing I used to think at this season: 'I wish I were a Christian.' They said it. I had only thought it.

"But something has happened which has changed things considerably within the past ten or fifteen years. I can't say exactly what it was, but I think I know some of the facts. In the first place, we attended a synagogue that no longer ignored the problem of how to keep Jewish children happy on Chanukah. Sunday schools and Talmud Torah classes really made Chanukah an exciting holiday. They gave Chanukah plays. They beautified the festival in the eyes of the children. Several of the rabbis even worked out an arrangement with several schools on both ends of town, so that in addition to the annual Christmas play given by the children the story of Chanukah, in some phase, was presented as well. This made the children feel that their holiday was important too. They felt like equals. Teachers were singing Christmas hymns in their classes. But they added some of the Chanukah songs which the children had learned in their Sunday schools, in the synagogue, and in the Hebrew school. In addition the rabbis of the two Conservative synagogues in the city began to urge a greater degree of special home decoration for Chanukah and actually conducted home lighting and home decoration contests for which special prizes were awarded.

"Then too one of the rabbis issued special pamphlets on 'How to observe Chanukah in the Home.' We women got this material through our sisterhoods in our congregations. Instead of making it a holiday on one night, a great number of my friends make each night of Chanukah 'partyish' and the children get really beautiful gifts from all the members of the family, not on one night but on each of the eight nights. And we have family dinners and general good times during that season. The candles are lighted and the songs are sung and I think that there is a greater awareness of the beauty and meaning of Chanukah today than when I was a girl. It just goes to show that if you work away at it, you can revive a holiday.

"Of course, there are still a great number of Jews who do not observe Chanukah; there are some who light the Chanukah candles and yet decorate their homes with Christmas trees 'for the children.' They argue that the fir tree isn't really a Christmas tree at all, that it does not belong to Christmas exclusively, and that if it helps to make the holiday beautiful, that's all that matters. There are still others who dress up in some costume and call themselves the 'Chanukah Man' in imitation of Santa Claus. And there are many who do not even bother to light the Chanukah candles on the festival. But I think that despite all these things I have just mentioned, conditions are really better here in Minneapolis than they used to be."

PURIM

The Feast of Purim (Lots), which commemorates the victory of the Jews over Haman, as recorded in the Book of Esther, no longer attracts the attention of as many Jews in Minneapolis as it did up to the 1920's. Perhaps it is more accurate to say that the *form* of the Purim observance has changed.

Formerly the recital of the Book of Esther in the synagogue, in the presence of a large congregation of adults and children, was the customary practice. As the name of Haman, the villain of the Purim story, was read, the children would whirl their greggers (noisemakers) and stamp their feet in order to drown out his name. The night was one of merrymaking and parties intended especially for adults. Refreshments were served to the children in the synagogue. On the following morning the Megillah, a scroll consisting of the Book of Esther, was read once again. The synagogue attendance was not as great as it had been the night before, yet it was still considerable.

Currently the number of children and adults who attend the reading of the Book of Esther in the synagogue is greatly reduced, even though refreshments are still served in all the Orthodox and Conservative synagogues. As a social inducement to the parents Purim parties on a grand scale are usually conducted immediately after the synagogue service. Orchestras are engaged for dancing. Buffet suppers are served; entertainment, either amateur or professional, is provided.

Formerly the Megillah was read in the Hebrew language alone, but today, even in several of the Orthodox synagogues, there are English interpolations and explanatory notes intended to give greater meaning to the Purim story.

Purim is celebrated elaborately in the Sunday and Hebrew schools and in all synagogues and temples. The two Conservative synagogues and the Reform temple prepare special programs in their Sunday schools with Purim masquerades and carnivals for children. The Minneapolis Talmud Torah does likewise. Whereas in former years the emphasis was placed upon the reading of the Megillah alone, there is today a far greater emphasis upon the social aspect of the holiday.

The Reform temple does not conduct a special service for the reading of the Megillah on Purim as do the Conservative and Orthodox congregations. Instead the sermon preached by the rabbi on the preceding Sabbath eve is usually devoted to the theme of anti-Semitism as a problem to be reckoned with. The appropriateness of this theme, which is also used by the rabbis of the other synagogues at this season, derives from the fact that Haman is traditionally regarded as a prototype of anti-Semitic feeling and action.

TISHAH B'AV

The ninth day of the Hebrew month Av, known in Hebrew as Tishah B'Av, is the anniversary of the destruction of the ancient Temple in Jerusalem. Orthodox Jews would assemble in their synagogues to read and chant the Book of Lamentations, in which the prophet Jeremiah describes the desolation and heartbreak resulting from the fall of Jerusalem. The national life of the Jewish people ceased in 586 B.C.E. with the conquest of Jerusalem by the Babylonians. Later the Jews were permitted to return to the Holy Land and they carried on their national existence until the year 70 C.E., when they were conquered by the Romans. Both these conquests are said to have occurred on the ninth day of Av. The Jewish people have through the centuries regarded this day as a day of mourning.

Not only in the East European Jewish communities, but in the Western world as well, even in the city of Minneapolis, from the coming of the first East European Jew until the 1920's, the synagogues were always crowded with worshippers who came to listen and to join in the traditional mournful chant of the Book of Lamentations. But conditions have changed.

"When I was out peddling, in the middle of August, on Tishah B'Av, I was really beside myself. It was as if I were cutting myself off from my people. I shall never forget the first time that happened. It was during the first year I was in Minneapolis. Even though I was peddling, carrying a pack on my back, and it weighed about seventy pounds, I always carried my Hebrew s'forim (books) along. I was not near any town. There were no

Jews around. All I could do was to get a copy of Eicha (the Book of Lamentations) from my pack, climb onto a wooden fence along the road, and in that desolate place chant the Book of Eicha. I think I understood the meaning of galus (exile) bettei that day than I ever did before."

The custom of reading the Book of Lamentations is still observed in the Orthodox and Conservative synagogues. But the number of persons who attend these services has been sharply diminished. Except for the few old-timers and the mourners who come to the synagogue daily during the first eleven months of their period of mourning, or those who attend on that day because it happens to be the anniversary of the death of a parent, the synagogues are rather empty.

To those in attendance, however, an appeal is usually made to contribute sums of money toward the rebuilding of the Jewish national home in Palestine. Thus this day of mourning and fasting is converted to a higher purpose. Still, the number of persons affected by the message of Tishah B'Av is small.

The major feast and fast days of the Jewish people are important in the life of contemporary Jews in Minneapolis in varying degree. The high holy days retain their hold upon the people. The festival of Passover, though its traditional observance is not strictly followed, plays an important role. The Seder service, with its family convocation, remains a strong tie to the ancient tradition. The Sabbath is gradually losing its central position in the ceremonial life of the people. The Feast of Lights is in the process of becoming once again a vital home, family, and synagogal festival. The Feast of Lots and the pilgrimage festivals of Pentecost and Tabernacles become meaningful and are observed only to the degree that new ceremonies such as confirmation and consecration services are added to the ritual of the synagogue. Minor fast days such as the Ninth of Av seem to have lost their position of prominence and importance.

Chapter 7   From the Cradle to the Grave

❧ ALTHOUGH the Jewish tradition is formally repudiated by a comparatively small section of Jewry, in practice most Jews, with the exception of the strictly Orthodox, treat it as though they had repudiated it.[1]

Whether Orthodox, Conservative, or Reform, the Jews of Minneapolis make it clear by their practices that they no longer regulate their lives by the traditional code, the Shulchan Aruch. Reform Jews have seldom, if ever, claimed adherence to the code. Orthodox and Conservative Jews, though they pay lip service to its provisions, have changed, modified, or abrogated a goodly portion of the traditional code.

The preceding chapters, dealing with the religious beliefs and practices of the Jewish community, indicate certain of the changes that have taken place. In this chapter we shall point out further modifications and changes that have occurred in the practices associated with major events in the life cycle.

THE RITE OF CIRCUMCISION

Jewish law requires that for a male child the rite of circumcision should take place on the eighth day after birth. This ceremony is called Brith (covenant), recalling the covenant that God made with the Patriarch Abraham.

Until the beginning of the 1910's most births took place in the home. On the eighth day the ceremony of circumcision was performed at home. The child was carried by its godmother, who placed it in the lap of the godfather. There the circumcision rite was performed by the mohel, a pious Jew, possessing ecclesiastical license, with no medical training other than that acquired by experience. After the operation, and as part of the ceremony, the child was given a Hebrew name such as "Abraham, son of Joshua," usually the name of a deceased parent or relative. The child was then returned to its mother. There followed a brief celebration, with wine and cake and even a bit of speechmaking in which the good wishes of those in attendance were expressed.

It is important to note that in former years it would have been unthinkable for the parents of any male child to ignore this rite. To do so would mean that the parents wished to read both themselves and their child out of the Jewish community. This rite was as binding upon the Reform Jews as it was upon the Orthodox and Conservative.

Though circumcision is still regarded as a religious necessity, there is an ever-increasing tendency to have Jewish doctors perform the operation instead of the mohel. In so doing the doctor combines within himself both medical and religious duties. Though this tendency is frowned upon by the Orthodox and Conservative rabbis of the community, it nevertheless persists.

"When my son was born, I had our doctor circumcise him because I don't like these old-fashioned mohels. I'm not too sure about their methods, whether they are as clean in their practices as the doctors. Besides the doctor was a Jew and he could read Hebrew, so if he said the Hebrew lines, which none of us could understand anyway, I saw no reason why it wasn't just as good."

Despite this growing tendency, there are four mohelim in the community. Two are young men who are recognized, even by Jewish physicians, as skilled and capable.

Today nearly all circumcision ceremonies take place in hospitals, because all births now take place there. Because the ceremony is observed in the hospital, the number of persons who may attend is limited by the hospital management. Seldom does one find a minyan, the required number of ten males, at such ceremonies. The mohel or the doctor, as well as those in attendance, wear white hospital garb and the ceremony, despite the Hebrew prayers, is coldly scientific. What little celebration occurs takes place in the mother's hospital room to which the invited guests come after the ceremony.

New methods are being employed in the circumcision rite itself. Where once a sharp surgical knife was the only instrument used, today at least one mohel uses a modern type of clamp, which is regarded by some as superior to the older instrument. It is said to meet the requirements of Jewish ritual law.

PIDYON HA-BEN

If the son is the first child Jewish law prescribes an additional ceremony, Pidyon Ha-Ben, "Redemption of the First-Born" (Exodus 13:2; Numbers 18:16). It is required that the child be redeemed from the service of God by payment of five *selaim* or silver coins by the child's father to the cohen or priest. The money thus received is devoted to charity. Though this practice was firmly established in Minneapolis up to the 1920's, it has largely disappeared.

NAMING THE CHILD

The traditional practice of giving the male child a Hebrew name at the time of the circumcision ceremony is still observed. All children are, however, given English names and it is by these that they are always called. There is often no direct relationship between the English and Hebrew names other than that both begin with the same phonetic sound.

In the case of a female child the Hebrew name is formally given in the synagogue at a regular service on any day when the Bible is read. On the Sabbath following the birth, or even on Monday or Thursday when the Torah (Five Books of Moses) is read, or perhaps on a holy day, the father of the child is called up to the Torah. He recites the blessings and listens to the special reading of the day; then a special blessing is recited for the newborn child, its mother, and its father. The child is named in the presence of the congregation with a name such as "Sarah, daughter of Jacob." It should be noted that it is always the

123

father's Hebrew name that is used, not the mother's. In some synagogues the rabbi may read a special English prayer.

If, as occasionally happens, the father of a newborn child finds himself unable to attend the synagogue service, one of the grandfathers takes over. He is called up to the reading of the Torah, the special blessings are recited, and the baby is officially named.

It is considered proper to name the child, either male or female, after some deceased member of the family. If the deceased happens to have been a female and the newborn child is male, the root of the name is often used, modified by masculine or feminine ending as the case may be. For example, if the name of the deceased female was "Yente," a male child acquiring the name would be called "Yonah."

Traditional practice is not in favor of giving the child the name of a living person, especially his own father or mother. One hears today only infrequently of parents naming their son "Jacob, Jr." This custom is observed less for reasons of respect for Jewish law (which does not really forbid it) than for reasons of superstition.

"I wouldn't think of naming my son after my father or even after myself. Each name has something holy about it. I was told that if I did such a thing I would be helping to shorten the number of years of my father or myself."

Though most parents give their children ceremonial Hebrew names, there are a few Reform Jews who give their children only English names.

Of special interest is the fact that the English names often appear in forms so far removed in form and spirit from the original Hebrew names as to appear unrecognizable. Biblical names are definitely not very popular among Jews of the present generation. The following list of English names of children and their parents, culled from two issues of the *American Jewish World*, will illustrate the newer mode:

FROM THE CRADLE TO THE GRAVE

Name of child	Name of parent
Judith Joyce	Edward
Joel Miles	Maurice
Dennis	Paul
Howard	Benjamin
Lewis	Sylvan
Richard Bruce	Ben
Marlene	Hyman
Stephen Bruce	Manuel
Steven	Irving
Robert David	Sol
Fern Linda	Harry
Ronald Michael	Prentice
Joan Lee	Bernard

If it were possible to ascertain the name of the grandfathers of these children, the change away from biblical names would be even more evident.

Parents, as well as children, are less familiar with their Hebrew names than was true a generation ago. Except for the children who attend the Minneapolis Talmud Torah, where they are addressed in class by their Hebrew names, there is an ever-increasing tendency to forget the Hebrew name. The greatest loss of awareness of one's Hebrew name is to be found among the children of the Reform temple.

BAR MITZVAH

The rite of Bar Mitzvah (Son of the Commandment), observed when a boy reaches his thirteenth birthday, has always enjoyed an important role in the life of the Jewish people. According to Jewish tradition the boy must assume his religious majority at this age. He is deemed to be responsible for his acts in God's sight and he may henceforth be counted as a member of a minyan, the minimum of ten males thirteen years of age and over necessary for public worship. The rite of Bar Mitzvah has been universally observed by Jews.

In East European Jewish communities, where male children

began their Hebraic studies at a very early age, the ceremony of Bar Mitzvah involved little, if any, special preparation. On the Sabbath nearest his birthday the boy was called up to the reading of the Torah and accorded the privilege of reading the prophetic portion. The youth would in many cases be responsible for his own preparation. He even prepared a special Talmudic discourse which he delivered on the Sabbath of his Bar Mitzvah as a demonstration of his erudition and learning. Following the synagogue ceremony parents would invite friends who had witnessed the public ceremony to their home for kiddush (the blessing of the wine) and a repast. The child received few special presents or gifts. He knew, however, that he had acquired a new and important status in the eyes of the Jewish community.

The sons of the early immigrants in Minneapolis, both Orthodox and Reform, were Bar Mitzvah. In Orthodox families sons would be given private tutoring, often for no more than several months before the thirteenth birthday. Of course there were some fathers who saw to it that their sons were provided with longer periods of study. Bar Mitzvah boys were given set speeches to memorize, either in Hebrew or Yiddish, seldom in English. English speeches would have been unintelligible to many of the congregants. Members of the family and friends were invited to the synagogue for the occasion. After the service friends were invited to the home, where a meal was served, brief congratulatory addresses were delivered, and good wishes exchanged. The Bar Mitzvah was given gifts by his family and friends. He was almost sure to receive a gold watch from his parents.

The sons of Reform parents were Bar Mitzvah too, though a goodly number of the Reform element regarded the ceremony as unimportant, especially since the confirmation ceremony, which included both boys and girls, was intended to take its place. Bar Mitzvah ceremonies have gradually decreased in number in the

Reform temple. In the decade from 1930 to 1940 there were no more than ten Bar Mitzvahs in the temple.

In the Orthodox and Conservative synagogues Bar Mitzvah ceremonies take place about twenty times a year. These ceremonies have become esthetically more satisfying and more enriching both spiritually and materially. Children are showered with a variety of gifts, often costly, that please the boys greatly. Spiritually there is a gain because the standards for Bar Mitzvah have gradually been elevated. In the Conservative congregations, for example, no boy may be Bar Mitzvah in the presence of the Sabbath congregation unless he has attended Hebrew school classes for a minimum of three years. In addition he receives special instruction so that he may chant most of the service on the Sabbath of his Bar Mitzvah. Also, on the Friday evening of his Bar Mitzvah he chants the blessings over the wine in the presence of the congregation. The Bar Mitzvah boy is no longer required to deliver a formal address before the congregation. Rather, his time is devoted to Hebrew training which it is believed will benefit him throughout the year.

In the Orthodox synagogues little is required of the Bar Mitzvah other than the ability to chant the special blessings over the Torah and to read the prophetic portion of the week. The boy may or may not deliver an address, depending upon his own Hebraic knowledge and the wishes of his parents. He receives numerous gifts and his parents arrange for a reception either in the synagogue immediately after the conclusion of the Sabbath morning service or on Saturday or Sunday evening in the parents' home.

In preparation for the Bar Mitzvah all boys are taught how to wear the tefillin (phylacteries) and the tallis (prayer shawl). In the Orthodox synagogues Tallis and Tefillin clubs have been formed. Following the Bar Mitzvah boys of Bar Mitzvah age are invited by the club to a special Sunday morning prayer service, after which breakfast is served and a brief social program takes place.

The parent has little to do with the actual preparation of his son for the Bar Mitzvah. All the duties are assumed by the Hebrew school, the synagogue, and the private tutor. And it frequently happens that the Bar Mitzvah boy of today is far better trained than was his father at the same age. In many instances the fathers of these boys seem to know less of Jewish ritual or how to recite the blessings over the Torah or to chant the Sabbath morning prayers or the blessings over the wine on Friday evenings than do their sons.

"It's a real heartbreaking experience to come into the synagogue on a Shabbas morning and see a fine youngster being Bar Mitzvah, and then to see his father get up, fine man that he may be otherwise, and be unable even to recite the berochos (blessings) over the Torah without stumbling all over himself. I get embarrassed for these fathers. Why they don't prepare themselves for the occasion is more than I can understand. Their sons actually know more about things Jewish than they do."

A father, aware of the problem, explains the situation this way:

"I never had a chance to go to Talmud Torah when I was a child. I worked hard. My family needed every cent and I helped to support them. When I was young the Talmud Torah was just beginning. All I had for a very short time before my Bar Mitzvah was a private rebbi (tutor) who wasn't very good and from whom I learned next to nothing. I haven't been able to come into the synagogue on Shabbas. I work. I am one of the 'lost generation.' But I'm very happy and proud that my son knows more than I do. That's why I am a member of this synagogue. That's why I support the Talmud Torah. I feel that we're raising a far better generation of young people than was true in the past. I'm proud I can give my son advantages I didn't have when I was his age."

No more than five Bas Mitzvah ceremonies (the equivalent of the Bar Mitzvah ceremony for girls) have taken place in Minneapolis. The privilege of being a Bas Mitzvah is accorded only to a girl who has passed her thirteenth birthday and who has attended Talmud Torah classes for a minimum of three years. The ceremony, only recently introduced by the Reconstructionist movement (the left wing of the Conservative movement) in

FROM THE CRADLE TO THE GRAVE

New York City utilizes the Friday evening or Sabbath morning service in the synagogue as the setting. The girl reads and chants various portions of the service in the Hebrew and may read and translate portions of the Bible, recite the kiddush, and deliver an address. Though no objection has been voiced to this ceremony in Minneapolis, it has not taken much of a hold.

The confirmation ceremony, another comparatively recent addition to the religious life of the Jewish community, has been described in Chapter 6.

COURTSHIP AND MARRIAGE

Marriage is traditionally regarded as a religious duty. The biblical commandment, "Be fruitful and multiply," is taken quite literally. Hence marriage is invested with deep significance in the life of the Jewish community. According to tradition marriage should take place by the eighteenth year. If the youth was a scholar, devoting himself to the study of the Talmud, he might postpone marriage until a later age. However, the unmarried youth was regarded as unfortunate and even as sinful.

The Jew of Eastern Europe accepted and followed this tradition quite literally. Marriage took place at an early age. Large families were the rule. Not only was family life important and beautiful in itself, but it constituted the fulfillment of a religious duty. The Jews of Western Europe were less inclined to marry at quite so early an age, but marriage itself was highly desired.

Girls might be betrothed at any time after they had reached the age of puberty; they were often promised in marriage long before they had reached their teens.

In East European countries the shadchen (marriage broker) was much in evidence. He performed the valuable service of assisting families in the arrangement of proper matches for their children. Whether these marriages were always "love affairs" is questionable. The facts seem to point to another and entirely different standard, based upon the qualities of the respective families, their scholastic attainments and heritage, even more

129

than upon the particular attainments of either groom or bride. Sometimes the couples whose marriage had been agreed upon by the parents hardly knew each other until the wedding day. In the smaller communities of Europe, where the families knew each other very well, it was customary for marriage agreements to be entered into between the parents on behalf of their growing children.

On the Sabbath before the marriage the groom was honored by being called up to the reading of the Torah in the synagogue. All the members of the two families would assemble in the synagogue. From the women's gallery would come a shower of raisins as the groom ascended the pulpit. Following the service the congregation was invited to partake of the kiddush (sanctification of the wine) and refreshments and goodies.

The marriage, always a religious ceremony, usually took place in the synagogue or its courtyard. The bride took the prescribed ritual bath on the day preceding the marriage. Both bride and groom fasted on their wedding day in expiation of their sins. The ceremony took place under the chupa, the wedding canopy. The rabbi pronounced the traditional blessings and gave the bride and groom a cup of wine. The kesubah (marriage contract) was read in Aramaic, the vernacular of the Jews of ancient Babylonia, in the presence of the parties to the marriage. Over the second cup of wine the seven concluding blessings of the service were chanted. The glass was crushed under the foot of the groom to symbolize Israel's grief over the loss of Jerusalem. Then came the cry "Mazel Tov, Mazel Tov" ("Good Luck, Good Luck"). The marriage ceremony was thus concluded.

Children of the early immigrants were protected with the same concern that had characterized European parents. Parents sought to check most carefully upon the young men who called on their daughters.

"I was very careful about telling my children the kind of persons they should marry. We came from a good, learned family. I felt that it would be disgraceful if in my family which boasted of having rabbis and scholars for generations back, we should have a son-in-law who knew nothing or whose parents knew nothing about Hebrew learning. 'Yichus' (pedigree) mattered with us. We always wanted to know: 'Who is the boy? Who is his family? Does he come from a religious family?'"

These questions were of great importance to the early immigrants, whether of German or East European stock. The German, though paying less attention to Hebraic learning, regarded himself as a more aristocratic member of the Jewish community and was anxious to have his children marry into those families whose background was West European.

The training of the girls centered in the home. Young girls were seldom to be found as employees in the downtown stores.

"It wasn't considered 'right' for girls to be working. Much as I needed whatever money my children could earn, I never wanted my daughters to go to work. I think I felt that it might affect their marriageability in some way."

Before the turn of the century, it must be remembered, the general attitude toward work for women was no different from that of the Jewish community. Sons were not as carefully watched as the daughters. It was assumed that as men they would take care of themselves. What is more, the sons of these immigrants, particularly the East Europeans, had from a very early age contributed to the family income by selling newspapers, running errands, and doing a variety of other jobs. As a result they had acquired an independence that was far different from that attained by sons in the European villages. They could, with perfect equanimity, maintain their independence and do that which seemed right in their own eyes.

In the early days, young couples went to the various social clubs or to dances and parties arranged by these clubs or by various benevolent societies and lodges in the community. Boys and girls had the opportunity to meet at the public hall and at weddings and parties to which they were invited. There was always music. No one objected to dancing. There were buggy rides and later street car rides, hay rides, outings, and picnics. Home parties were frequent. In the small community there was ample opportunity to meet everyone else. Relations were never too formal, despite the watchful eyes of parents over their daughters.

Though the shadchen still had his uses in the community, he was completely and utterly despised by the younger people who had been born or reared in America. It was expected that the girl's parents would have the opportunity to meet the young man with whom their daughter kept company. It was further assumed that the father had every right to inquire about the "intentions" of any young man who had dated his daughter more than twice. Mothers and fathers were, nevertheless, no longer in a position to arrange matches without regard to the wishes of their children. Love began to play an important role in the marriage plans.

"When I was a girl, I was very much in love with a boy who happened to come from a very fine family in Europe. He was also a good Hebrew scholar. But he had to earn his living and work very hard and he didn't have the chance to keep on with his studies here in Minneapolis. My parents happened to meet a young man who was a scholar; he earned what little money he could as a teacher. Even though they knew that I was very much in love with the other one, they insisted that I marry the man of their choice. I did, because what my parents said to me was law. I always tried to honor my father and my mother. But I must say that I was a very unhappy girl. It happened that about a year later my husband became very ill and died. It was only then that my parents felt that I should marry the man I had really loved all this time. We are married and have lived very happily together."

Most young American girls in Minneapolis, however, would have refused to obey their parents under similar circumstances.

In the European communities it was usual to receive some form of dowry from the bride or her family, but in Minneapolis this custom gradually disappeared. Marriages based on love were not predisposed to wait for dowries. Nevertheless, sons-in-law were often taken into the business establishments of their fathers-in-law or helped financially to start their own businesses.

For the most part these young people were poor as the proverbial church mouse. They would rent one or two rooms in the neighborhood, buy inexpensive furniture on credit, and borrow a few dollars, if necessary, to go into business peddling or selling fruit. Inasmuch as few of these people lived in elegant homes, there was no problem of keeping up with the Joneses. Frugality was a virtue, living within one's income a necessity.

The first marriages in Minneapolis usually took place in the home of the bride. There the Orthodox ritual was followed. A minyan (ten males) was required for a wedding service. This rule was strictly adhered to. The rabbi's sermon was usually in Yiddish. Heads were always covered. The marriage contract was read in the Aramaic, the groom always pronounced the *Harey at Mekudeshet Li* . . . ("Behold Thou art consecrated unto me, with this ring, in accordance with the Laws of Moses and of Israel"). The blessings were recited over the two cups of wine, the little glass was placed and crushed under the heel of the groom. Everyone wished the happy bride and groom "Mazel Tov." Refreshments were served in the home, or the family and friends might be invited to a public hall where all the food (kosher, of course) had been prepared by the bride's family.

If a Reform rabbi officiated, the sermon would be in English, no hats would be worn, no chupa would be used, no marriage contract would be issued, no minyan was required.

"When I got married, I don't think that I understood very much about the religious ceremony. All I knew was that it was expected that I be married according to the way in which my parents had been married. I knew the *Harey at* . . . I did not understand the contents of the kesubah (marriage contract) and I never did understand why they broke the glass at the end of the marriage service."

The wedding gifts were most practical:

"I remember that we got a great number of things for the kitchen, much crockery of various kinds, a few decorative things like pitchers, and even a few pictures, but for the most part there was never anything really grand or truly beautiful. The fact is that most people didn't have beautiful or valuable things in their own homes, so they certainly wouldn't give them to us."

There were very few elopements in the Jewish community of Minneapolis. Parents would have regarded such an arrangement as an affront. The young people saw no reason for such procedure, for it would have deprived them of the social aspects of the wedding to which everyone looked forward and there would certainly have been fewer wedding gifts.

"I recall only one elopement in my early days here. That was because a Jewish girl married a Gentile boy. So they ran away and got married. They didn't come back here to live."

Since 1917 many changes have occurred in the marriage customs of the Minneapolis Jewish community. Gradually, almost imperceptibly, these changes have tended to reduce the degree of Orthodox ritualism, though the community would insist that it is thoroughly Jewish in character.

During World War I a greater number of Jewish girls were working as stenographers, saleswomen, bookkeepers, and so on. They were earning their own money and spending more time away from their homes. The younger children of the early immigrants had gone to elementary and high school. Many had gone on to the universities.

Girls were meeting boys under far different circumstances. There was a much greater degree of informality about dating. Dating was not only more frequent, but less directly associated with marriage. Girls did not regard every boy with whom they were friendly as a possible husband. Less attention was paid to whether the youth came from learned or unlearned stock and more to the financial status of the boy and his family. Though parents expected their future son-in-law to ask for their daughter's hand in a formal way, there was less of that sort of thing and far more of a joint announcement by the young people of their betrothal. Engagement parties were formally arranged.

Showers were given for the brides. The prospective grooms were invited to "stags" and parties by their friends. Young people saw much more of each other during their engagement period than had been true of an earlier age.

The day for the marriage ceremony was chosen with little regard to the matter of "lucky" or "unlucky" days. Marriages took place any day on which the rabbi said it was possible to officiate without violating Jewish law. The custom of reciting the viddui (confessional) before the marriage ceremony, the ritual bath, fasting on the day of the marriage — all these were less frequently observed. It is the writer's belief that today less than 5 percent of the Jewish community follow any of these traditional practices.

The Shulchan Aruch has given way to Emily Post in the matter of marriage customs.

"Parents used to ask the rabbi for specific information about the manner in which the bride and groom and their attendants should conduct themselves at the marriage service. Today the rabbi will discover, much to his surprise, that either the bride or her mother is carrying a copy of Emily Post's rules of etiquette in much the same manner as if it were a Bible."

As a result Conservative and Orthodox rabbis are often obliged to make last-minute requests for changes so that the ceremony will be in keeping with Jewish tradition. The most usual of such changes are having the groom stand at the left of the bride and asking the bride to wear her wedding ring on the forefinger of her right hand. Even at marriages at which Conservative and Orthodox rabbis officiate, the bride or groom or both often suggest that the ceremony take place without head covering for the groom and male attendants, a request which is never granted. About one of every ten couples requests a double-ring ceremony. Despite the fact that this practice is not traditional, it is added to the ceremony without question.

Conservative rabbis dispense with the ritual of having the groom crush the little glass at the conclusion of the service, explaining that they do so "because it is better to make a contribution toward the rebuilding of the ancient homeland than merely to mourn its loss in this symbolic fashion." Conservative rabbis often perform marriages without the traditional minyan present. A floral canopy is used even more frequently than the traditional cloth chupa. The Reform marriage service does not require the wearing of head coverings by the groom and his attendants, and the traditional ritual is not followed except when it is specially requested.

Young couples invite the rabbi of the synagogue to which they and their families belong to perform the marriage ceremony. In the event that the families are members of different congregations, it is not unusual to see two rabbis officiating. Orthodox rabbis will officiate with Conservative or Reform rabbis. On these occasions the ritual usually follows the pattern of the more orthodox rabbi. The children of Orthodox parents often invite Conservative rabbis to officiate at their marriages, because "there are going to be many Gentiles present and we want the rabbi to speak English and make the ceremony as nice as possible." Even the older Orthodox rabbis, to whom English is more difficult, try to use it whenever possible. The Hebrew benedictions and other traditional phases of the ceremony remain the same.

According to one rabbi's experience, during the 1940's about 60 percent of the marriage ceremonies took place in hotels and public places, about 30 percent in the rabbi's study, and the remainder in either the synagogue or the home of the bride's family. Recently, however, all the rabbis of Minneapolis and St. Paul announced that after March 1949 they would not officiate at weddings in hotels. All weddings must now be performed in the home, the synagogue, or the rabbi's study. No objection was made to dinners or receptions at hotels after the ceremony.

Music is regarded as essential at all weddings except those taking place in the rabbi's study. Vocalists, violinists, organists, pianists, cellists, or harpists are engaged to perform such ballads as "I Love You Truly" and "At Dawning." "Lohengrin" is almost required music for the processional, with Mendelssohn a poor second.

A wedding dinner usually follows the ceremony. If the service takes place at a hotel, the meal is always catered, usually a nonkosher chicken or turkey dinner. Should the rabbi or his wife remain for dinner, fish is served to them. No thought is given to this incongruity. It is traditional practice for the Sheva Berochos (Seven Benedictions) to be chanted at the wedding dinner. This ceremony is no longer observed at a vast majority of weddings.

Customarily a reception takes place, either at the hotel or at the home of the bride. There is always an ample supply of food, prepared by the bride's family with the assistance of special helpers and waitresses. Drinks, both hard and soft, are always available. A local orchestra provides dance music.

The hotel and synagogue weddings are often costly affairs, but they are usually in good taste. On occasion a lavish display of foods, floral decorations, and clothes is observed, though in most instances sanity prevails.

Young married couples usually receive many gifts, not only from the members of their families, but from friends as well.

"Practically all the young brides choose their own sterling silver pattern at one of the several exclusive stores and their friends try to get as many pieces of the set as possible. Most of my girl friends like to get sterling pieces and cut-glassware."

Parents, when they are able, furnish anywhere from one room to a houseful of furniture as their wedding gift.

The young married couple usually lives in rented quarters of their own choosing. Until the war years created a housing shortage, few of the couples lived with their parents.

"I think that it's best for young people to live by themselves. I don't want my daughter-in-law to feel that I am running her affairs or guiding her husband. Of course, I'm hoping they will visit us as often as possible. I'd like especially to have them to dinner on Friday evening, for Shabbas. But they can be their own bosses. It's better that way."

OLD AGE

The aged of the Jewish community are regarded with respect by their children. Every effort is made to satisfy the desires and needs of fathers and mothers who are no longer able to earn their own living.

"My parents were never very well off financially. They barely got by, but we children always contributed toward the upkeep of the home and regarded it as our duty to do so. When my father was taken ill, I saw that he was given every medical attention and I know that both my parents feel that all of us children would do all we can for them. I have been maintaining the home for them. They live alone because it's better for them. That's what they want."

When children are unable to provide for their parents, they are assisted by the Jewish Family Service Society. However, in the majority of cases children make every effort to provide adequate care for their parents.

The Jewish Home for the Aged of the Northwest, organized in 1907 in St. Paul, is now a Twin City institution. Its officers and board members are elected from both cities. The home, located on Midway Parkway in St. Paul, provides facilities for aged men and women, including medical care. Children usually contribute to the limit of their ability toward the maintenance of the home. In both Minneapolis and St. Paul there are ladies' auxiliaries that raise funds for the organization. The main sources of revenue, however, are the community funds of both St. Paul and Minneapolis.

DEATH AND BURIAL RITES

Death claims an average of 185 Jewish persons in Minneapolis annually.[2] Until the second decade of the 1900's, most deaths occurred in the residences. As was true of the rest of the community, there was a fear of hospitals and hospitalization: "I used to be told that one never left a hospital alive." Such sentiments were expressed by many people and there was a considerable amount of truth to the statement, because only those dangerously ill would permit themselves to be removed to a hospital and, of these, very few returned to their homes.

According to Jewish traditional practice, when death was near, the person was expected to recite the Viddui (confession of sins). If possible, he was to say the Shema ("Hear, O Israel, the Lord our God, the Lord is One"). After all signs of life had ceased, the eyes were closed, and the corpse was washed and prepared for burial by the chevra kaddisha (burial society), which regarded it as a religious duty to serve in this capacity. Autopsies and embalming were forbidden by Jewish law. The body was placed upon a board on the floor; candles were lighted and a pious Jew was expected to "watch" the body until the time for the funeral. The tachrichim (linen burial shrouds) covered the body. It was not permitted to dress the body in a business suit or dress, in accordance with the rabbinic decree that "all must be uniform in death." If the deceased was a male, a tallis (prayer shawl) was placed across the shoulders. Burial was required within twenty-four hours after death.

The funeral service usually took place in the home. Not until 1914 was there a Jewish undertaking establishment in Minneapolis. Even then most funerals continued to take place in the homes because funeral establishments were looked upon askance. A plain pine coffin was always used. Flowers were prohibited, as was music other than the chant of the cantor as he recited the memorial prayer.

It was forbidden to place the casket in a vault of concrete or any other material. A little bag of sand from the Holy Land was placed under the head of the deceased just before burial. The rabbi delivered a eulogy as the members of the family and friends sat in closely crowded quarters. Rabbis were prone to deliver sermons which would bring tears to the eyes of the mourners, and their wailing was something to be reckoned with.

Before the funeral service and at its conclusion a member of the chevra kaddisha would be seen holding a tzedokoh box (charity box) into which the mourners, mindful of the Hebrew phrase *Tzedokoh Tatzil MiMaves* ("the giving of charity saves one from death") placed a small contribution. The mourners would make a rent in their outer garment as a symbol of their mourning and recite the traditional phrase.

Carriages hired from the undertaker took the mourners to the cemetery where the body was to be interred. When the funeral procession reached the burial ground, the casket was removed from the carriage and carried to the grave by the six pallbearers, usually relatives or close friends of the deceased. As the distance from the carriage to the grave was traversed, seven momentary stops were made while a psalm was recited.

No attempt was made to make the grave appear less gruesome to the living. No one saw any reason for hiding the stark reality of death. Before the casket was lowered into the grave, the handles, usually of metal, were removed. The casket was opened for a "last look," the body was adjusted, a small piece of broken china was placed over each closed eye, and the coffin was lowered into the grave. The grave was then quickly covered with dirt. It was a duty to place a shovelful of dirt on the coffin. After the coffin had been covered so that it was no longer visible, the burial service was read. After the reading of several psalms, the mourner's kaddish (memorial prayer) was recited by the male children of the deceased, or if there were no descendants by a brother or father or friends. The service was concluded by the *El Moley Rachamim*, the traditional Hebrew memorial prayer.

After the service the friends in attendance formed two parallel lines through which the immediate family passed as they listened to the traditional Hebrew words of consolation, "May the Lord comfort you and all other mourners in Israel." The mourners and their friends then went to the small chapel on the cemetery grounds where afternoon prayers were recited. The chapel service was concluded with the mourner's kaddish, said by the mourners alone. Before entering the chapel, all persons were expected to pour water over their hands as a symbol of their cleansing from the "uncleanliness" associated with the dead. The mourners then entered their carriages and were driven to their home, where the neighbors had in the meantime prepared some food.

The traditional practice of covering all the mirrors with cloth was invariably observed. The period of shiva, mourning for seven days from the time of burial, was then begun. Mourners were expected to remove their shoes and wear sandals or slippers, to sit on low chairs or boxes, and to refrain from any occupational duties during the entire period. It was not permitted to shave or cut the hair during this period. Morning and evening services were conducted daily in the mourner's home. This required the traditional minyan of ten males. Usually a study period devoted to some Hebrew text of the Bible or Talmud was arranged for. This preceded the evening prayers. During this period friends of the family and of the deceased would visit the home to express their sympathies. Such visiting was carried on quietly. People spoke in hushed tones and soft voices.

The yahrtzeit (memorial) light was kindled in the home. Either candles or a small glass containing oil and a wick was used. The period of mourning continued in modified form for thirty days from the time of burial, and male mourners, after the period of shiva, were expected to attend services in the synagogue thrice daily for eleven months and one day. After this period they were no longer regarded as avelim (mourners). Every year on the anniversary of the day of death, the mourners came to the synagogue to recite the memorial prayer and on the same day and the eve preceding, the yahrtzeit lamp was kindled in the home and in the synagogue.

This detailed account of the traditional practices associated with death, burial, and mourning is recorded in order that the changes which have occurred since 1930 may stand out more clearly. For changes there have been, marked in many respects by their sharp contrast with the past.

A composite of the statements of the two Jewish undertakers in Minneapolis will serve to make these changes more clear.

"I went into business as an undertaker in Minneapolis in 1914. When I began, on the North Side, where most of the Jewish people lived, there was much opposition, which came principally from the chevra kaddishas (burial societies). I think their objections arose not from the fact that I was not Orthodox enough, although that is what they told people, but from the fact that these people came to me first and asked me to make the funeral arrangements instead of coming to the chevras as they used to.

"When I came into the business, all funerals in town were conducted by non-Jewish undertakers. Heinrichs, on the North Side, had about 40 percent of the Jewish funerals. Practically all the funerals of the Reform temple and of Adath Jeshurun Synagogue (Conservative) went to the non-Jewish undertakers. The Reform still turn over practically all their funerals to non-Jewish undertakers.

"It was not until 1926 that I was accepted by all elements in the community and I had about all the Jewish funerals. Up to that time all the funerals were from the home of the deceased. The undertaker sold only the coffin, and provided whatever carriages were needed to take the mourners to the cemetery. The bodies were washed and dressed in the homes. Until 1930 about 50 percent of all the funerals were from the homes.

"In the old days I never saw a funeral service take place in the synagogue; it was always in the home. The honor of having a funeral service in the synagogue was only accorded to an outstandingly pious Jew. Today synagogue services are frequent because the funeral parlors aren't large enough, for one thing, and because so many families ask for it that synagogues can't refuse. How can you say to people: 'Your father wasn't as good or pious a man as Mr. X?' In order to avoid embarrassment the new practice is followed.

"Until 1940 most people insisted that the bodies be dressed in the traditional tachrichim (linen garments) only. After that time only about 50 percent wore tachrichim only. The others insisted that the traditional tachrichim be placed under the regular clothes, so that one sees only the regular clothes and not the linen garment. In the early days all people objected to having any cosmetics used on the body or having it fixed up in any way. Today they no longer object. In fact they would, I am sure, re-

142

mark if I didn't do these things as a matter of course. Embalming takes place in about 75 percent of the cases. That's because there is a state law which requires it, unless the body is buried within twenty-four hours. Even when we bury the body within that period, there are requests for embalming. And the rabbis, even the most Orthodox, do not say anything about it. There is no objection at all to flowers in practically 90 percent of the funerals. People send them and they are used in the funeral home and in the cemetery. Very few of the people cry out as they used to at these funerals. I remember when it was really something to hear the wailing at the funerals.

"The tzedokoh boxes (charity boxes) were stopped in 1933 at my funeral home. I objected to it and I called a meeting of the chevras and they stopped it almost completely. About 10 percent of the people use metal caskets today instead of the plain pine caskets. About 20 percent of the people buy metal vaults in which they place the casket in the grave. Today about 85 percent of the funerals which I conduct take place from the funeral home. Practically all the others take place from the auditoriums of the synagogues, Orthodox and Conservative. That's because there is no chapel in town large enough to seat five hundred or more people, and if a man is well known, his friends all come to the funeral. There is still a great objection to autopsies, though the Conservative rabbis do not object to it, while the Orthodox rabbis do. Of course, the Reform rabbi has no objections to it.

"There is a great difference too in the sermons delivered by the rabbis. Today, instead of trying to make the people cry more, the rabbis try to lighten their burdens. The sermons are much shorter than they used to be. The *El Moley Rachamim* prayer used to be a difficult thing to listen to because people insisted on making this prayer for all their dead relatives at the funeral. But today, owing to the insistence of one of the Conservative rabbis, this practice has been cut out. We do not use music at the funeral parlor — most of my people would object — but music is used at the other funeral home on occasion.

"Coffins are rather expensive. People have spent an average of two hundred and fifty dollars for coffins for about ten years. And that is only about 60 percent of the total cost of the funeral.

"No one takes the handles off the caskets any more when they are about to be lowered into the grave. The grave is usually covered with a kind of grass rug so that it doesn't look as horrible as it used to. Then too the grave is no longer covered with dirt in the presence of the family. The chevra waits until the family and others have gone on to the chapel for the afternoon prayers. The little sack of Palestinian sand is seldom placed under the head, although the body is still adjusted in the coffin just before burial.

"Immediately after a death occurs, the undertaker is notified. We take charge immediately, the body is washed, and all the ritual is followed in the undertaking parlor.

"We used to provide horse-drawn carriages until the automobile became standard equipment. Today we rent cars, including the hearse, to the families.

"The traditional period of shiva is observed, but only in a formal fashion. In well over 75 percent of the cases only three days of mourning is actually observed. Men then go about their business affairs. In about the same number of cases men shave during the period of shiva. Of course these people are in their homes in the evening when friends call to pay their respects. Less than 5 percent of the mourners still sit on low boxes and wear only sandals or slippers on their feet. The others retain their regular garb.

"Few people wash their hands after the funeral service. Most still come into the chapel to hear the afternoon prayers chanted. Traditional prayers are recited at the grave by the Orthodox and Conservative rabbis. But both use more English in order to make the service more understandable. The sermon is usually preached in English."

Mourners are to be seen in the house of worship reciting the kaddish (traditional mourner's prayer) at least once each day during the period of mourning. Yet within the past two decades the number has gradually been reduced. For example, all sons of a deceased parent would in former decades attend each service faithfully. Of late the sons take turns in attending the services. The Orthodox practice of observing the yahrtzeit (anniversary of date of death) for one's parents is still followed to a greater degree than almost any other Jewish practice.

Special memorial (yizkor) services are conducted in the synagogue on the Day of Atonement, the Feast of Solemn Assembly (Shemini Atzereth), Passover, and Pentecost. About a decade ago men and women would fill all houses of worship to over-flowing at these services. Today the number of persons at such services has been considerably reduced. What is more, if these holy days happen to fall on a weekday — that is, a work day — the service is attended largely by women. Here too the tendency to give up a traditional practice, even if associated directly with one's own parents, is marked.

There are eight Jewish cemeteries in Minneapolis. The first in Minneapolis, the Montefiore Cemetery, was established by German Jews in 1876, two years before the organization of the first temple. Until that year Jewish burials had always taken place in the older Jewish cemetery in St. Paul. However, on one occasion a child passed away in mid-winter and the funeral procession was lost in a blinding snowstorm. It was night before the party found its way into St. Paul and the hour was too late to obtain a burial certificate or inter the body. After this incident the members of the Minneapolis community decided that a cemetery was needed at once. A small tract of land located about four miles from the center of the city was purchased by a group of individuals known as the Minneapolis Burial Association.

It is worthy of note that the Montefiore Cemetery was a separate organization, in no way affiliated with any congregation, and all members of the community, whether of German-Jewish origin or not, were permitted to bury their dead there.

The growth of Adath Jeshurun Congregation in its early days caused a group of members to decide that the congregation ought to have its own burial ground, and in 1887 a tract of land was purchased on the southwestern outskirts of the city. This was the second Jewish cemetery in Minneapolis. Whereas in the case of the German-Jewish community the burial ground was purchased first, in this instance it will be noted that the congregation was established first and the cemetery purchased later.

In 1889 the fraternal Order Brith Abraham, with seven lodges established in north Minneapolis, purchased two acres of land far beyond the southwest city limits as a burial ground for their deceased members and their families. In 1904 one of these lodges purchased its own cemetery and provided burial plots not only for its members, but for the general Jewish public. The name of United Hebrew Brotherhood was assumed. Since most of its members were of Russian origin, it was known as the Russian Cemetery. The earlier O. B. A. cemetery came to be known as the Lithuanian Cemetery. Actually no fine line of distinction was ever drawn on the basis of country of origin when death took some member of the community.

The Rumanian congregation, B'nai Abram, purchased a tract of land in 1917 and established a cemetery for the use of its own membership and others. This cemetery is immediately adjacent to the Adath Jeshurun Cemetery on the southwest outskirts of Minneapolis. Several years ago B'nai Abram purchased a new tract of land adjacent to the Russian Cemetery.

The Gemilas Chesed (Bestowal of Loving Kindness) Society also owns a tract of land which is used for burial purposes. This land became the property of the society in 1936, and about twelve burials took place in the following decade. Two other Jewish cemeteries are located in the town of Robbinsdale on the northwestern border of Minneapolis. One is owned by the Chesed Shel Emes Society (True Loving Kindness), a dues-paying organization, and the other by the local branch of the International Workers' Order, the left-wing element of the Jewish labor movement.

All the cemetery associations are nonprofit organizations. Receipts from the sale of graves and family plots accrue to the organization which owns the cemetery.

Each cemetery association has appointed a special committee known as a chevra (brotherhood), whose duty it is to take charge of all funerals and preparations for burial in accordance with Jewish ritual. If, for example, a deceased person were to be buried in the Rumanian cemetery, the chevra of that cemetery association would arrange for the digging of the grave. It would also have a representative at the undertaker's establishment, where the religious rites associated with preparation for burial would be observed. The shrouds are provided by the chevra. The chevra accompanies the funeral procession to the cemetery and seeks in a general sort of a way to be helpful.

The rules of the cemetery associations, based upon traditional practice, require that only Jews may be buried in a Jewish cemetery. In the case of intermarriage, if one of the parties to the marriage was not formally converted to Judaism, he or she may not be buried in the cemetery. This rule is still adhered to. No more than one Jew is buried annually in a nonsectarian cemetery. Most Jews regard it as wrong and do not hesitate to say so.

Cremation has always been considered contrary to Jewish law and is still a very rare practice among Jews of Minneapolis.

Burial plots and graves are sold by the Jewish burial societies. The size and kind of tombstones and grave markers are strictly regulated in order to avoid the chaotic appearance of many cemeteries. Until 1930 not much care and attention was given to most cemeteries because people were little concerned about appearances. Today, however, there is a marked improvement in the appearance. New chapels have been erected to take the place of the shanties which passed for chapels in an earlier day. Landscape artists are employed to keep the cemeteries in good condition. The two best maintained cemeteries in the city are the Adath Jeshurun (Conservative) and Montefiore (Reform).

In contrast to the practice in larger cities, such as Chicago and New York, the Jews of Minneapolis do not arrange for the formal dedication of tombstones over the graves of their deceased. The practice in Minneapolis is to place a tombstone over the grave on or about the first anniversary of death. After the stone has been erected, the members of the family gather around the stone and a Hebrew memorial prayer is recited. In most cases this rite is performed by the sexton of the synagogue with which the family is associated. On occasion the rabbi is invited to conduct the service, which is then a bit more formal and includes a brief commemoration of the deceased.

147

Chapter 8   The Changing Synagogue

ود THE *Synagogue is the one unfailing well-spring of Jewish feeling. There we pray together with our brethren, and in the act become participators in the common sentiment, the collective conscience, of Israel. There we pray with a mightier company still, with the whole House of Israel. We become members of a far greater congregation than that of which we form a physical part. We join in spirit our brethren in their homage to the God of our people.*[1]

THE synagogue through the centuries has made for the survival of the Jewish way of life. In European towns and cities the synagogue was the center of Jewish life. To it the Jew repaired when he wished to join his fellow Jews in public prayer. Within its walls he could listen to the traditional, heart-warming chants of the cantor and the erudite sermons of the rabbi. To it he came when he wished to study his ancient literature and lore. In it he made his bed when, as a student of the Talmud, there was no other place for him to live. He met his friends within its precincts and with them shared the gossip of the town.[2] Particularly in Eastern Europe the synagogue was the Jew's second home. He loved it as he loved his people. He could no more imagine himself without benefit of the synagogue than he could conceive of life without his holy Torah.

The rabbi too was a unique personality. It was not expected that he should be a leader in communal affairs, nor was he to be an "ambassador of Good-will to the Gentiles." He was rather the scholar, the teacher, the arbiter on religious matters. He was to decide all matters concerning ritual law. He was the symbol of Jewish piety. As a consequence, he was highly respected and revered.

148

THE CHANGING SYNAGOGUE

The synagogues of Eastern Europe, whether large or small, did not, perhaps, provide the very best examples of congregational orderliness and organization, but they did offer a sense of "at homeness." They managed to fulfill with distinction their three-fold ancient functions, as house of prayer, house of study, and house of assembly.

The synagogues of Western Europe were usually larger in size, perhaps better organized, and usually more decorous than those of Eastern Europe. The rabbi here too was an honored member of the Jewish community, which turned to him for its knowledge, understanding, and interpretation of Jewish law. He was also the spokesman for the Jewish community in the eyes of the larger community. Though the great academies of study of the Talmud were not directly associated with the synagogue, they did derive their spiritual sustenance from the synagogue and the rabbi.

Though the first Jewish settler came to Minneapolis in 1866, it was not until 1878 that a permanent congregation was established. Before that German-Jewish settlers, rather than attempting to organize a congregation of their own, worshipped in St. Paul, where the older community had started Mount Zion Synagogue. The start of synagogal organization in Minneapolis was made in 1876, when the city had grown considerably by the influx of about a dozen West European Jewish families. A hall was hired for worship on the high holy days and a minister was engaged.[3] This was by no means a permanent congregation but it was the forerunner of the Shaarei Tov Congregation (Reform), which was incorporated in 1878.

It should be noted that had the early German settlers been as close to synagogal life as East European Jews were, they would most certainly have discovered a great void in their lives without a synagogue close at hand. For public worship takes place not only on the high holy days, but daily and on the Sabbath as well. A local correspondent, writing in the *American Israelite*, in 1882, made the following comment on the situation:

JEWS IN TRANSITION

Till 1878, Minneapolis, then 23 years old, had a few Hebrew families, but no Minyan. On the most solemn festivals the few Hebrews met together in some rented room and worshipped God according to the very old fashion, that is everyone singing "Hallelujah" to his heart's delight,— a circumstance which scared away the progressively inclined families and induced several Jewish young men to marry beyond their denomination.[4]

Shaarei Tov synagogue was established through the efforts of a Mr. Edward Bernstein, who had lived in Pittsburgh before coming to Minneapolis. "Deeply religious and anxious to perpetuate Judaism, he made a canvass among the first Jewish citizens and persuaded them to unite in organizing a congregation and establishing a regular place of worship." Services were held in a centrally located hall until a temple was built in 1880. The first service in the new building was held on Rosh Hashonah, September 5, 1880. The Minneapolis *Journal* gave an account of that service which is of interest because it indicates not only the type of service conducted, but something of the thinking of the congregation's rabbinical leadership.

On Sunday evening, at 7 o'clock, the first Service was held in the new Temple of the Hebrew Reform Congregation, on 5th Street South, the occasion being the beginning of the Jewish New Year 5884. Every seat in the Synagogue was occupied, quite a number of those present being Gentiles. The pews were sold by auction by G. L. Levi, who undertook to animate his fellow co-religionists to the tune of $500.00. The first choices were bought by Messrs. Rees, Bernstein and Rosenband, and nearly all the members responded, paying liberally for the choice of their seats, besides contributing largely for the yearly support of the minister and for the building fund. The Services were conducted by Rev. Mr. Stemple, Mr. Bernstein, the president, Mr. Schreiber, the former pastor, being on the rostrum. The Services consisted of the regular ceremonies of their Holiday, the New Year.

Professor Larsen accompanied the choir on an organ from Mr. Penfield's Music Store. The solos and duets were sung by the Misses Jacobs, who formerly belonged to the Synagogue Choir at Oil City, Pennsylvania, and deserve the greatest praise.

The sermon, a short one, was truly interesting, and ex-

150

pounded the doctrines of Judaism which, though not despising the doctrines of other religions, claims for itself the first place. He said: "We have erected a House of Worship of Israel, not only to show that the mother of Christianity is not to be despised although she is old. The mother remembers well her duty to all her daughters, inviting them to the universal shrine of worship." The Services were impressive and the beautiful prayers of the Philadelphia Prayer Book were rendered with due solemnity. Praises are due to such a small congregation for their grand effort in erecting and sustaining such a place of worship, which is a pride to themselves and the city.

From this account we may gather that in a formal sense at least the relationship of the members of this congregation to their non-Jewish neighbors was a healthy one.

Religious services were conducted by the congregation on Friday evenings and Sabbath mornings. Even before the temple was built, the congregation maintained its Sunday school classes in the home of a member, Leopold Ehrlich.

By 1895 Temple Shaarei Tov had a membership of seventy-five, and sermons were being preached in English and German. Something of the activities and interests of the congregation may be gathered from the following item:

The only event of any interest recently was the Concert held by the Temple and Sabbath School. The affair was given through the efforts of Mr. Stromberg, our worthy president of the Congregation, who, ever since he made his home here, has striven to advance the cause of Judaism. The proceeds of the evening are to be used toward purchasing a pipe-organ. Quite a neat sum was realized there and the affair will probably be repeated at no distant date.[5]

Temple Shaarei Tov was the center of the spiritual as well as social life of these first Jewish citizens of Minneapolis. To it the people came for their Jewish education and for the religious training of their children. Through the activities conducted by the men and women of the temple, there developed a greater sense of cohesiveness as well as a greater awareness of their Jewishness.

Not until the coming of Rabbi Samuel N. Deinard in 1901 did the congregation have leadership in the highest sense of the word. A man of personal charm and spiritual quality, Dr. Deinard soon became the recognized leader of his congregation and one of the strongest forces for good in the city of Minneapolis.

With the death of Rabbi Deinard in 1921, the congregation, which had meanwhile changed its name to Temple Israel, invited Rabbi Albert G. Minda, ordained at Hebrew Union College in Cincinnati, to become its leader. He has served his congregation for more than twenty-five years. During his period of service Temple Israel has continued its growth and has maintained its position of leadership. Rabbi Minda has served not only his own congregants but the community as a whole with distinction. Among his many contributions to the development of the Jewish community is the notable achievement of founding the Minneapolis Federation for Jewish Service.

Temple Israel during the years has expanded its program of activities and interests. In addition to services conducted regularly on the Sabbath and on holy days, numerous opportunities have been provided for the cultural and social interests of the whole congregation. For the young there are the Sunday school and a program of club activities. The teen-agers have their junior congregation and socials. There are the sisterhood and the men's club, which provide for the special interests of all members of the temple. Housed in the finest synagogal structure in Minneapolis, with outstanding facilities, the temple and its membership have played a prominent role in Jewish community life.

THE SOUTH SIDE

The first Orthodox synagogue in Minneapolis was founded in 1884 by several of the better established merchants of East European origin. Adath Jeshurun (Congregation of Israel) soon came to be regarded as the leading Orthodox synagogue of the community. Russians and Rumanians were among its first members. Here we find evidence that a change in financial status of the early settlers helped in some degree to overcome the tendency to establish congregations exclusively on the basis of country of origin.

The affairs of the Adath Jeshurun Congregation depended in a large measure upon the financial success of several merchants in the community who acted as sponsors and financial guardians:

"They conducted practically everything about that synagogue. When their business disintegrated, the synagogue went to pieces." After seven years the congregation was dissolved, only to be immediately reorganized.

Aided by several public-spirited men, as well as by a number of social affairs given by a committee of ladies of the congregation, a frame building was purchased by the congregation in 1900. It was located on the South Side, where a large proportion of the city's Rumanian Jews lived. The congregation continued its activities and moved from one edifice to another on the South Side. For the next decade the rabbis and teachers who were engaged used Yiddish as the language of conversation and instruction. Then the younger element, dissatisfied with the arrangement, asserted itself and in 1911 elected a new group of officers. The congregation proceeded to elect its first English-speaking rabbi, C. David Matt.

With the coming of Rabbi Matt, who was ordained at the Jewish Theological Seminary of America in New York City, a new era began in the life of the congregation. A young folks' society was organized. The Deborah Society, for young girls, and the ladies' auxiliary played an important role in the development of the congregation and its gradual change from Orthodoxy to Conservatism. Hebrew classes were conducted daily for younger pupils and the Sunday school was reorganized.

When the movement from the South Side to the West Side of the city began, the congregation decided to purchase and erect a new synagogue building, and in 1927 it dedicated the new Adath Jeshurun Synagogue building, at Dupont Avenue South and Thirty-fourth Street.

Rabbi Matt had resigned his pulpit after fifteen years of service, and in 1930 the author, who was also a graduate of the Jewish Theological Seminary of America, arrived in the community and assumed the spiritual leadership of the congregation. He continued to serve in that capacity for sixteen years.

The congregation was in the process of change. The members, though anxious to retain their loyalty to their Hebraic traditions, were no longer as orthodox as were their parents. In the following years the congregation proceeded to modernize the service, establish study classes for young and old, develop a strong women's league and men's club, inaugurate a public lecture forum, in which important public issues were discussed, and develop a program of youth activities which gave the synagogue a renewed vigor and strength.

The oldest congregation composed exclusively of Rumanian Jews was the B'nai Abram Congregation, established in 1896. Its members were for the most part peddlers, small shopkeepers, and artisans. It was strictly Orthodox in its religious philosophy. It never engaged a rabbi, but instead relied upon the more learned of its members to conduct services. From time to time it engaged preachers and cantors to conduct services on the high holy days. The congregation always maintained a daily minyan (ten or more males) for worship. It also conducted various chevros (brotherhoods) for the study of the Talmud and other Hebraic literature. As late as 1922 B'nai Abram had a weekday Hebrew school with an attendance of eighty-five pupils, but by 1937 the enrollment had dropped to thirty-five pupils. These children then became pupils of the South Side Talmud Torah, which was housed for a time in the B'nai Abram building. B'nai Abram has always been located in the heart of the South Side Jewish community.

The third congregation on the South Side, which included in its membership not only Jews of Rumanian origin but others as well, was the Agudas Achim Congregation (Assembly of Brothers). This small congregation, organized in 1902, has never

154

had more than a hundred members on its rolls. Its present building was erected in 1903 and has a capacity of about three hundred and fifty persons. When the Jewish community of the South Side was still growing, this congregation was able to maintain itself, after a fashion. Since 1927, when the South Side Jewish community began to shift to other sections of the city, this congregation too has almost ceased to function. In 1945, according to the report of its president, it still retained some twenty members. The status of the congregation may be judged by the following comment:

"For a period of twenty-eight years, until 1939, not even a fresh coat of paint had been put on the synagogue building. We have a few dollars in our treasury, but not much."

The congregation never maintained its own Hebrew educational system for its children. For a time it sent its children over to the North Side by bus to attend the Minneapolis Talmud Torah.

THE NORTH SIDE

The need for a synagogue on the near North Side was apparent from the arrival of the first East Europeans, but for some years none of the immigrants was financially able to make a real synagogue structure possible. Yet almost from the day of their arrival they sought out their fellow countrymen and established minyanim for public worship.

The first regularly organized Orthodox synagogue on the North Side was established in 1888. It was named Ohel Jacob (Tent of Jacob) and met for worship daily as well as on holy days above a store at 605 Second Street North. Early records of the congregation indicate that it paid a monthly rental of twelve dollars for its quarters. The cantor received sixteen dollars a month and the sexton was paid the munificent sum of five dollars a month.

The Ohel Jacob Synagogue became the headquarters for the majority of the newly arrived immigrants. Many of these newcomers had been yeshivoh bochurim (Talmudical students) in Europe. They found this congregation to approximate most closely the kind of religious service with which they were familiar. They found too other former students of the Talmud with whom they would spend time and study on the old tractates of the Talmud in the synagogue proper. In a real sense it was the very heart of the Orthodox Jewish community. Ohel Jacob Congregation dissolved in 1891, to be succeeded by another and larger Orthodox synagogue, the Kenesseth Israel, which was to become the leading Orthodox congregation of the community.

In 1890 there was yet another congregation, the Bes Ha Midrash Ha Gadol, consisting entirely of Russian Jewish immigrants. According to early accounts, it was located on Washington Avenue North and Eighth Avenue North above a store. It served the same function for many of the Russian Jews as the Ohel Jacob Synagogue did for the Lithuanians and Poles. This congregation, however, dissolved after a few years.

Still another congregation whose membership was composed entirely of Russian immigrant Jews was the Anshei Russia (Men of Russia), founded in 1890. Rabbi I. Jaffa, who was serving as the spiritual leader of the Ohel Jacob Synagogue, was invited to minister to this congregation as well.

Originally the congregation conducted services on the Sabbath only, for most of its members were away during the week, peddling their wares in the country areas. In 1895 the congregation changed its name to Mikro Kodesh Synagogue. As related by one of the members who was present at the meeting called by the president, the reasons given for the change in name were as follows:

"First, we have no reason to perpetuate the name of a foreign land in a synagogue which has been established by Jews who are living in America; second, of all countries that ought not to be memorialized by the Jew, certainly Russia is that country. Its treatment of the Jewish people does not warrant such recognition."

THE CHANGING SYNAGOGUE

It was not until 1936 that a regularly ordained young rabbi was invited to occupy the pulpit of Mikro Kodesh. Since 1942, when another young "modern" Orthodox rabbi was invited to the pulpit, the congregation has taken a new lease on life. Activities for the young people as well as for adult members have been carefully planned. This congregation too is gradually veering away from strict Orthodoxy to a position which borders on Conservatism. The ritual of the synagogue, however, remains Orthodox in character even though the members are today far less strict in their observances than were the early members of the congregation.

The Kenesseth Israel Synagogue was organized on December 22, 1891. In 1892 the officers of the Ohel Jacob Congregation "surrendered and gave up their cash and property" to the new congregation, and Rabbi I. Jaffa became its spiritual leader. In 1894 the congregation established a Hebrew free school for the children of its members, as well as for others in the community. It also granted the use of its Hebrew school building to the Reform synagogue, Shaarei Tov (now Temple Israel), which proposed to establish a Sunday school for children on the North Side. The teachers for this venture were all volunteers from the ladies' auxiliary of the temple and the Council of Jewish Women.

In January 1902, Rabbi S. M. Silber, from Kroz, Lithuania, was invited to accept the pulpit of Kenesseth Israel. A fine gentleman and Hebrew scholar, he became the acknowledged leader of the Orthodox Jews of Minneapolis. He broke with precedent when, contrary to the general practice among Orthodox rabbis, he participated in the affairs of the community and helped to plan and guide its destiny. Until his death in 1925 he was the foremost Orthodox religious leader in the community.

Almost from its beginning Kenesseth Israel was the center of Jewish activity on the North Side. Its membership consisted for the most part of peddlers, and those who had advanced to the stage of owning small businesses in the community. They were

157

zealously concerned with the perpetuation of their Orthodox traditions.

Not until 1913 was there any indication that there might ever be changes in the ritual or in the manner of conducting the services. Apparently, however, the younger generation felt the need for bringing into the community a more modern Orthodox rabbi. It may well be that the example set by Adath Jeshurun Synagogue in electing Rabbi Matt as its first English-speaking rabbi proved to be a deciding factor. In 1913 a young English-speaking rabbi was invited to assist Rabbi Silber in officiating at the services and to preach to the congregants in English. However, he was not destined to remain more than a few years in the community. According to all accounts, he was a young man who enjoyed outdoor sports, such as horseback riding and ice-skating, and, so it is said, he even went out on "dates" occasionally. These unheard-of acts so aroused certain members of the Kenesseth Israel Synagogue that the rabbi severed his connection with the congregation and returned to New York City. The congregation remained strictly Orthodox in its ritual and practice.

Though the women sat in the balcony of the synagogue building at public services, as was true of all Orthodox congregations, they played a very important role in the development of the morale as well as in the financial support of the congregation. In 1912 they organized a ladies' auxiliary and helped to meet many of the pressing bills.

The youth of the synagogue were not neglected. Not only were there Hebrew classes, but the young women of the congregation were organized for social activities. The fact that many of the dances and socials undertaken by this group proved of financial benefit to the congregation is only incidental.

The congregation played an important role in the development of the Minneapolis Talmud Torah. From 1894 when Hebrew school classes were first conducted in the synagogue building, members of the congregation worked actively in the development of a modern Hebrew school for Jewish youth.

In recent years the Jewish community of the North Side has moved away from the neighborhood of Kenesseth Israel. Other synagogue buildings have been erected. Orthodoxy is no longer being adhered to with the degree of loyalty which characterized an earlier generation. Though the beautiful synagogue structure on Lyndale Avenue remains, it is now only a symbol of the glory that was once associated with traditional Orthodoxy. Today the few active members of the congregation plan to erect a new and more modern building in the Homewood district. What the future holds in store for Kenesseth Israel Synagogue only time will tell.

One of the most interesting aspects of the history of the early community is the variety of ways by which congregations came into being. An example is the Anshei Tavrig Synagogue (Men of the Town of Tavrig), which was founded in 1902. When the Kenesseth Israel Congregation brought Rabbi S. M. Silber from Lithuania to occupy its pulpit, certain members of the congregation believed that the former rabbi, I. Jaffa, had not been well treated, and they decided to organize another congregation with Rabbi Jaffa as its head. These dissidents happened to come from the town of Tavrig in Lithuania. Hence the name and the origin of a congregation which continued its precarious existence until 1913.

When Anshei Tavrig was about to dissolve because of inadequate financial support, it discovered that a group of Jews were conducting services in a home on Girard Avenue North between Sixth and Eighth avenues. This minyan was known as the Gemilas Chesed Synagogue. An influential member of the Anshei Tavrig Synagogue, recognizing that his congregation could not continue to exist, invited the members of the Gemilas Chesed Synagogue to take over the old synagogue. In 1915 the new group literally moved the old synagogue building to Girard Avenue North. The officers of the Gemilas Chesed Society, which was then a free loan society, conducted the affairs of the congregation in the strict Orthodox tradition.

The synagogue, which has few actual members, has remained at its same site all these years. The congregation conducts no activities other than the traditional worship service each weekday morning and evening. In 1946 the attendance at the Sabbath service, according to its rabbi, was sparse: "most people can't come on Shabbas." The congregation maintains a Chevra Mishna and Shass (brotherhood for the study of the Talmud) in which about fifteen persons participate daily. There are no young people associated with the congregation other than its rabbi, who is also a shochet (ritual slaughterer of meat and fowl). Though individuals within the congregation participate in the affairs of the Jewish community from time to time, the congregation as such never has been active.

In the 1890's some ten to fifteen Jewish families had moved to what was then the far end of the North Side, Thirty-second Street and Emerson Avenue North. They were also of East European origin. The Jewish residents in the Washington Avenue district spoke of these persons as residents of the "Vald" (the woods), because they lived so far out in the country. These Jews too established their own minyan. It was, however, never formally organized as a congregation and never was given a special Hebrew designation.

Another congregation, organized about 1890, was the Tiferes B'nai Israel. This too originated as a landsman synagogue; that is, all the original members came from the town of Fileshter in Bessarabia. In its early days it was known as the Fileshter Shul (synagogue). In 1920 the congregation took the name of Tiferes B'nai Jacob. It too maintained various study classes for its male adult members in Talmud and other Hebraic literature. However, it never carried on any program of activities that was likely to attract the younger sons and daughters of its members.

Only in recent years did the congregation engage a "modern" Orthodox rabbi, one who during his student days at an American university had "actually played and enjoyed football." Not long ago the congregation, which had always been strictly Orthodox, revised its service and became a Conservative synagogue. Its members, though interested in maintaining certain of the traditional practices in their homes, as well as the traditional ritual in the synagogue, are less Orthodox in their practices and tendencies than their fathers were. Many members of the younger group are assuming positions of leadership in the congregation and in the Jewish community.

Another instance of unusual congregational organization is the Sharei Zedeck Synagogue, which has always been located on the near North Side. This account is told by one of the members of the early community.

"The Lyndale synagogue (Kenesseth Israel) had been built many years before and it was beyond question the leading Orthodox congregation of the city. When the father of one of the members passed away, that member felt that he wanted to have the funeral service conducted in a synagogue. It was not customary in those days to bring other than the body of a very pious man into the synagogue for a hespod (eulogy). The president refused to grant permission to this family for such a service because he felt that the deceased had never been a great student of the Talmud nor was he particularly learned in the law.

"The family of the deceased became incensed at what they regarded as highhanded action on the part of the president. So they decided to secure the help of certain of their 'landsleute' (countrymen) from Neustadt, Lithuania, and with their help they built a small synagogue at Aldrich Avenue and Eighth Avenue North. In honor of the deceased they called the synagogue by that man's first name, which was Aaron. The synagogue was known as Bes Ahron (House of Aaron). When they painted their new building, they used green paint. Everyone forgot the original name of the synagogue and instead called it the 'Greener Shul' (Green Synagogue). This building was erected in 1916. Later they moved the synagogue to another location. Even though the new synagogue was painted a different color, the name Greener Shul stuck."

This congregation, also strictly Orthodox, became well known in the life of the community when Rabbi S. I. Levin became its spiritual leader. In 1948 he was recognized as the dean of rabbis in the community from the viewpoint of years of service. However, the congregation has never played very much of a role in the affairs of the Jewish community, though it has sought from time to time to win back the younger members of the community to Orthodoxy.

The largest congregation on the North Side was dedicated March 14, 1926. It is known as Beth El Synagogue and has since its beginning been located at Fourteenth and Penn Avenues North, in the heart of the new district to which the wealthier Jews had moved about that time. The synagogue actually began to take form in 1921 when the alumni association of the Talmud Torah established its Young People's Synagogue in the Talmud Torah building. These young people, dissatisfied with the synagogues in which they had been brought up, established this service of their own, hoping to make it modern, decorous, and meaningful to young members.

Impressed by this service and sensing the need for the creation of a more modern synagogue which would still retain a traditional adherence to Jewish custom and ritual, these young people, aided by some of the more forward-looking and progressive elders of the community, decided in 1922 to erect a new synagogue. After many meetings and long delays one hundred and fifty families organized Beth El. Since its founding Rabbi David Aronson, a graduate of the Jewish Theological Seminary of America and one of the foremost Jewish leaders in the community, has been its spiritual leader. It is today the leading synagogue on the North Side.

In the 1940's a little congregation, Orthodox in tradition, was organized with Rabbi Chaim Ginzberg as its leader. Although it is believed that this congregation has fewer than twenty-five members, it exerts considerable influence upon its members and friends inasmuch as the rabbi is known to be a Chasid (Pious One) and a descendant of a famous Chasidic rabbi. Excepting for those affairs that helped to maintain the rabbi and his family in the community, the congregation has not had much influence upon the life of the Jewish community as a whole.

There were in 1948 eleven congregations in Minneapolis. Of these, seven were Orthodox, three Conservative, and one Reform. The leading congregations, from the point of view of membership and status in the community, are Conservative and Reform.

Practically all the synagogues grew in membership during the decade from 1935 to 1945, in spite of the high cost of membership in Conservative and Reform congregations (about eighty dollars a family on the average). The Conservative congregations more than doubled their memberships between 1930 and 1945. Table VI gives the membership of each synagogue in 1945, based on membership rolls where available and authoritative reports of congregational officers in other cases.

TABLE VI. SYNAGOGUE MEMBERSHIP IN MINNEAPOLIS, 1945

Synagogue	Membership (in families)
Adath Jeshurun (Conservative)	388
Agudas Achim (Orthodox)	20*
Ahavath Achim (Orthodox)	20*
Beth El (Conservative)	376
B'nai Abram (Orthodox)	40*
Gemilas Chesed (Orthodox)	65
Kenesseth Israel (Orthodox)	200*
Mikro Kodesh (Orthodox)	300
Sharei Zedeck (Orthodox)	125*
Temple Israel (Reform)	450
Tiferes B'nai Jacob (Conservative)	185
Total	2169

* This is an approximation.

These figures do not include at least an equal number of families who avail themselves of any or all of the facilities of the congregations, except that of having assigned seats on the high holy days. Little wonder that in the official survey made by the

Jewish community in 1936, we find the statement: "Judged by congregational affiliation, religious interests occupy a dominant position in the organized life of Minneapolis Jewry." [6]

The aggregate cost of these synagogal structures as of 1936 was $862,292. The total annual budget for the maintenance of the congregations and their activities is now estimated to be approximately $150,000.

The program of the congregations varies with the point of view of its leadership, rabbinic and lay. Yet practically all have the following: religious services on the Sabbath and holy days; study classes for all age groups; religious schools that meet Sundays or daily; youth activities, such as clubs; women's societies; men's clubs; socials for young and old.

"If you don't belong to some synagogue, you're practically out of everything around this town. Less than a week after I moved to Minneapolis, a committee from one of the synagogues was calling on me and asking me to join. And they really give you a salestalk. They tell you all about their activities. They tell you the important people of the community who belong and make it appear that unless you join you'll be practically a nobody. The very first thing people want to know in this town is 'Where do you belong?' And they don't mean some club, they mean the synagogue."

So blatant has this approach been that the president of one congregation finally wrote a letter of protest which was published in the *American Jewish World*:

It seems that certain supposedly responsible people in their desire to increase the membership of their respective synagogues have started a campaign to entice members from other synagogues. They omit the fertile field of unaffiliated Jews, but concentrate their efforts on the more wealthy members of other synagogues.

The reason for such action is obvious. Holding such bait as meeting your social equals or climbing to a seemingly high social level, or "you don't belong where you are, you belong to us," the zealous ones fall all over themselves in their misguided efforts, to increase their membership rolls.

THE CHANGING SYNAGOGUE

It seems to me that membership in a synagogue is not to be haggled over, as fishwives haggle and bargain over a pushcart. It seems to me that there is plenty of missionary work (if they are sincere in their roles as missionaries) to be done among the non-affiliated Jews of the community, regardless of their financial status, rather than attempt to snare the financial cream of sister institutions.[7]

As is true of all church affiliation, membership in any congregation does not necessarily indicate a high degree of piety. It may, rather, indicate a desire to attain social status which would otherwise be impossible. Because the synagogal programs are so varied, the reasons for affiliation with a synagogue are also varied:

"I want my children to get the benefit of a kind of training that I never got. The Hebrew school and the Sunday school are modern. That's what I want for my children. As long as they are happy there that's all I want. I didn't join the synagogue until my children were old enough to go to Sunday school."

"I like the rabbi. He's active in the community. He's our good-will ambassador. I think I ought to support a man who helps me by giving Jews a better name in the community."

"I go to the synagogue because my friends go. If they stopped going, I think I would stop too."

"Every Jew ought to belong to a synagogue. It doesn't matter whether I go to services or not. It's the right thing to do. I believe in Religion."

"I was interested in the Rumanian synagogue because I grew up there. My father went there and I had gone along with him. I did object to the disorder, but it never occurred to me to leave because of that. Rather I wanted to overcome the disorder. I took my going to the Rumanian synagogue as an accepted fact, the same as I took my height or the color of my hair."

"I joined the temple in 1904 because the services at the Rumanian synagogue meant nothing to me. I couldn't read Hebrew. All I did there was to usher. I tried to help in whatever I could. When I went to the temple I read the prayers for the first time in English. I could actually understand them and I couldn't do that at the other place."

Many marked changes are to be noted in the Orthodox and Conservative synagogues of today as compared with these same institutions two decades ago. With only few exceptions these changes were gradual and almost invisible. Yet even the most Orthodox Jew acknowledges the fact that there has been a change in the nature of the service, in decorum, and in the general program of activities that are conducted by the congregations. The change within the Reform congregation is less marked only because so great a change was effected in ritual and general conduct from its very inception.

"I belong to the Conservative synagogue. Years ago all the men wore their own hats. There was no such thing as uniformity. I remember that I objected when the rabbi urged us to check our hats and wear skull caps that were uniform in appearance. Today I look back and wonder how I could possibly have objected. We all had our own prayer books, of whatever kind we liked. Today all the prayer books, even on the high holy days, are the same. The rabbi can announce the page and we all follow. There is more English reading in the service. That helps us to understand the service better.

"It was considered wrong for women to sing in the choir. Today it's done in both Conservative synagogues and nobody thinks anything of it. Why, we even have an organ in our synagogue which we play on the Sabbath. That would have been regarded as a great sin. But today nobody objects.

"There used to be a lot of talking while the services were being conducted. Today it's really quiet and orderly. People used to get up and walk out at any time but the rabbi made them stop that, and it's really so much better now. We have ushers and they watch you pretty carefully so there is no disturbance of any kind. We all get up together at specified points in the service and we all sit down together. We even used to think that it was wrong for women to sit in the same pews with the men, but today even in some of the Orthodox synagogues that's all right."

But the change is even more marked than that! Today there is a far greater sense of the need for participation in the affairs of the community, both Jewish and non-Jewish, and the synagogues constitute the nucleus around which community campaigns for relief and rehabilitation are built. An organization or cause which wants to get its message to the Jewish community seeks to do so through the congregation and its rabbi.

Membership on the board of a congregation is today regarded as an honor. The number of young people who are participating in the affairs of each congregation is definitely increasing. Of the five chief officers of the Adath Jeshurun Congregation (Conservative), two are not yet forty years old and two others are less than fifty. The officers and board members of the other congregations are, by and large, equally young.

Despite these healthy signs attendance at synagogue services is not very large, though it is no smaller in proportion to the Jewish population than in New York City or Chicago. If anything, it may even be larger. More significant is the fact that the number of young people who participate in the affairs of the congregations in Minneapolis appears to be proportionately greater than it is in the large centers of Jewish population.

Prayer, both public and private, is apparently becoming a lost art. The Jewish tradition always emphasized the importance of prayer. In the Orthodox home it was always customary to wash the hands before the beginning of the meal, to recite the motzi (grace before meals), and to conclude with a recital of grace. These traditional practices are no longer observed by at least 95 percent of the Jewish people of Minneapolis.

The number of male persons who pray either at home or at the synagogue is limited. Most children do not recite the morning prayers, nor do the boys of Bar Mitzvah age wear the phylacteries, except perhaps for several months following the Bar Mitzvah service. Although most boys of Bar Mitzvah age receive a prayer shawl, few bring it to the synagogue or use it in connection with their daily prayers. The number of adult Jews who attend daily services in the synagogue, either morning, late afternoon, or evening, is extremely limited. In most synagogues there is difficulty in securing the daily minyan.

In the Reform temple there is no daily service. Members of

the temple usually recite their annual memorial prayers for deceased parents in a Conservative or Orthodox synagogue.

There is a marked difference in the three generations of Minneapolis Jews in the ability to read Hebrew and to understand the Hebrew prayers. A good number of the older generation, the original settlers, are able to read Hebrew and they often pray at a rapid pace. This does not indicate a detailed knowledge of the meaning of the Hebrew words, but the older people do have a general knowledge of the prayers they recite. Their grandchildren, the third generation, are also fairly well acquainted with the Hebrew language and Hebrew prayers, owing in no small degree to the training they have received at the Minneapolis Talmud Torah. But their fathers are not at all well versed in Hebrew. Indeed, at least 50 percent of them are unable to read Hebrew, let alone translate it. There is similarly, a difference in attitude toward prayer.

"When my father prays, he knows what he is saying, in a general way. I don't think that he himself understands every word of his Hebrew prayers, but he certainly understands the spirit of the prayer and he feels like praying. But I am altogether different. Not only don't I know the meaning of the words that I use in the prayer book, but I can hardly read the Hebrew. It is very difficult for me. What is more, when I pray, I really am doing what is expected of me more than I am doing what I really care about. The fact is that except for a belief in a God whom I cannot describe, I don't happen to believe that prayers have any special meaning or value. They certainly don't affect the world in any degree as far as I can see."

Then too there is the type which regards itself as "scientific" in its viewpoint. Such persons are to be found in rather large numbers among the younger professional men, men who have had the benefit of college training. They look upon prayer as unscientific and as a consequence seldom enter a house of worship to offer their prayers. Here too we find many paradoxes.

"I'm a scientist. When I was a child, I used to pray three times every day. My father took great pride in the fact that even while I was attending the university, I used to put on my phylacteries each morning and pray the real Orthodox way. One day I just found that I couldn't continue to do so. I could not reconcile my scientific training and knowledge with the whole idea of prayer. In fact I think that I simply stopped believing in a God, in the sense that my father believed in a very personal God who was concerned with each human being. During my youth I had received good Hebrew training. I went to Hebrew school. In addition my father taught me. I really knew not only how to read Hebrew but I could translate it as well. I could translate whole sections of the Bible from the Hebrew, without any difficulty. All of a sudden the whole thing seemed useless and meaningless to me.

"I still remember how to pray. In fact I can recite whole sections of the prayers by heart. Yet not until my father passed away did I really come back to the synagogue and to prayer. Here once again I found myself changing, almost overnight. I wanted to pray. Not because by the recital of these prayers I expected the world to be changed one bit, but rather because I knew that my father would have been happy to know that I was praying once again. So, out of respect to his memory, I am attending daily services at the synagogue and praying once again. Now I have children. I have tried to teach them something of the Hebrew language, but it is a far cry from the kind of training that my father gave me and I am sure that the God to whom they may pray is far different from the One to whom my father prayed."

The synagogue in Minneapolis has become the center of Jewish life and activity. It is definitely the house of assembly of the Jewish people. It is becoming more and more a house of study in that the number of study courses for young people and adults is increasing rapidly. It is, however, less of a house of worship than it was around the turn of the century.

The program of adult Jewish education is the present responsibility of the synagogue. Many of them sponsor regular courses for adults which include classes in elementary and advanced Hebrew, both as a spoken language and as the language of the prayer book; Bible classes, in which the ideals and social values of the Bible are taught from a higher critical viewpoint; and classes in Jewish current events and contemporary problems. In Adath Jeshurun a course was offered on the subject "Know Your Neighbor," in which representatives of various non-Jewish denominations presented their philosophies, which were compared with Judaism. Courses in child psychology have also been given.

Three of the synagogues — Adath Jeshurun and Beth El (both Conservative) and Temple Israel (Reform) — have offered lecture courses on subjects of general interest such as politics and world affairs. These lectures are attended by audiences of five hundred and more persons, many of whom are non-Jewish.

The men's clubs, sisterhoods, and women's leagues of the congregations introduce Jewish educational materials into their programs. There are Bible readings and presentation of Jewish current events which use materials provided by the national organizations with which the synagogues are affiliated. Original plays and music are regularly prepared and presented at these meetings. In several synagogues discussions based upon problems and issues of interest to Jews take place immediately after the conclusion of the late Friday evening service.

"Though a great deal is being done in the field of adult education, it's a shame that more people do not take advantage of their opportunities. The average study class has about twenty-five students which of course isn't bad. But when you stop to think how much we need to know and how many there are who don't come, it hurts."

The functions and duties of the modern rabbi have changed through the years. Today he is not alone the preacher and teacher but the administrator as well. He is active not only in the affairs of the Jewish community, but also in the general community.

Kenesseth Israel Synagogue (Orthodox) in 1892 defined the duties of its rabbi as follows:

"First, to deliver an address to the congregation at their Synagogue, every second Saturday. Second, to answer all questions relating to religion to every member and their families." [8]

Were the present rabbis of the community to perform only these duties, they would find themselves without pulpits in short order.

"Our rabbi has to know about business methods. He has to keep up with modern educational techniques. He should be a good teacher, be friendly with people, help the men and women to work out the programs for their monthly meetings, and be ready and willing to raise funds for the synagogue when necessary. He should be a 'good fellow.' We rather like to see the rabbi at the golf club and we don't mind if he dances or goes to football games or attends the theater. There is no reason to believe that doing these things make him a poorer rabbi. We like it too when the rabbi is called upon to address public meetings and gets appointed to serve on city or state commissions. He is our representative and we look up to him for these talents. Personally, I prefer a rabbi who can do these things as against one who confines his activities exclusively to his congregation."

Rabbis serve on all boards in the Jewish community. Their advice is sought, even if it is not always followed. Laymen often object to the "rabbinical bloc" which occasionally opposes the opinions and actions of the laymen. Despite this two rabbis have at various times been elected to serve as president of the Minneapolis Federation for Jewish Service, the fund-raising and over-all planning body of the Jewish community.

Though the number of persons in Minneapolis who seek the rabbi's guidance in matters of Jewish law is rapidly diminishing, the rabbi has become increasingly important as counselor and guide in the personal lives of his congregants. What is more, even those who are not directly affiliated with a congregation seek the rabbi's advice in practically all matters pertaining to family life and even in business affairs.

Most of the rabbis are regarded as personal friends by their congregants. Few congregants would consider it proper to arrange any joyous occasion in the household, such as a marriage anniversary party, without inviting the rabbi and his wife to be present.

The rabbis of all congregations are well paid. Congregants expect their rabbis to live well. While the rabbi is not revered in the sense that he is placed upon a pedestal to be worshipped, the religious leader is an honored member of the Jewish community.

In the early days there were many persons in the Jewish community who might be termed "antireligious," as there were and still are some who are nonreligious. The antireligionists were, in the main, youthful radicals who had come out of Eastern Europe believing that religion is "an opiate of the people." They defied the conventions of the society in which they lived by arranging for meetings and socials on Friday evening, the beginning of the Sabbath. They smoked on the Sabbath and otherwise acted so as to offend the sensibilities of the majority. However, this group, never large, has already disappeared. Strangely, many of the children of these rebels are members of synagogues and are neither more nor less radical in their views than most Jews in the community.

There were some Jews too who became great admirers of the liberal Christian preachers in the community and subsequently joined the Unitarian and other liberal churches. Others, a handful, became members of the Christian Science Church, divorcing themselves entirely from the Jewish community.

At present one finds Jewish religionists, culturists, and nationalists, and some antinationalists, within the synagogue fold. Though there are many varieties of Jewish opinion and belief, somehow the synagogue in Minneapolis manages to attract and hold them all.

Chapter 9   The Educational Process

⧉ THE *mastery of Torah is not a matter of mere knowledge. It must express itself in the growth of one's character and in the development of one's personality.*[1]

THE early immigrants had little time for formal education. From the very first day of their arrival in Minneapolis, they were obliged to concern themselves with the all-important matter of earning a living. What little education they could acquire came indirectly from their contacts with the general public and their fellow Jews, through conversation, and through the Yiddish newspapers which were published in New York. In addition the synagogue helped to provide a background of knowledge about what was expected of them in their new environment. Perhaps of greatest importance as an Americanizing aid for these early immigrants were the various lodges. They helped to give these immigrants a more properly focused picture of American life.

FRATERNAL ORGANIZATION

The fraternal orders, which were popular before the turn of the century and shortly thereafter, helped to meet the social needs of these people and became, as well, powerful Americanization agencies.

In 1885 the first lodge of the Order Brith Abraham was organized in Minneapolis. This national order, which offered its members certain insurance protection, attracted many of the East European Jews. By 1900 there were seven lodges meeting on the North Side. Some of the lodges were established by individuals who believed they had not received sufficient honor and distinction in the lodge to which they already belonged. Hence they had withdrawn and organized another lodge.

JEWS IN TRANSITION

The membership, consisting of Russian, Lithuanian, Polish, and Rumanian Jews, paid dues of approximately four dollars a month and received assurance that three hundred dollars would be paid to their families upon their death.[2]

These lodges were of tremendous importance to their members not only because of their insurance features, but because they, next to the synagogue, provided the basic social organization which these people sorely needed. The lodges conducted annual balls, picnics, and socials, all of which helped round out the lives of their members.

In addition the lodges helped their respective members to meet financial and other crises in their personal lives. Funds were always being gathered in order to aid some indigent brother. One of the early members of the O. B. A. related the following incident:

"Just a few weeks before I got married I had invested all my savings, which amounted to about a hundred and fifty dollars, in a horse and wagon, which I planned to use in order to peddle in the country. Just two days after my marriage the barn in which I kept my horse and wagon burned to the ground and I was left with absolutely nothing. I didn't know what I was going to do, but sure enough, my lodge brothers came over to my home and gave me fifty dollars and said: 'See what you can do with this to help you get started again.' Well, that really helped me. Because I was so grateful for what they had done, I became a big worker for the lodge."

There were other lodges and fraternal organizations in the North Side Jewish community. There were two lodges of the Order Sons of Benjamin, a Mendelssohn Camp of Modern Woodmen of America, a Baron de Hirsch Camp of the Woodmen of the World, Modern Samaritans, Knights and Ladies of Security, Loyal Mystic Legion of America, Supreme Court of Honor, Modern Brotherhood of America, and Free Sons of Israel. The latter organization seems to have been the only one supported and actively led by members of the German-Jewish community.[3]

The very names of these organizations give some indication of the desire of these immigrants to attain status. Exactly what these organizations did, aside from the social fellowship and insurance features which many of them offered, is not clear. Yet each played its role and, having lived for a brief span, disintegrated.

By 1920 only the Mendelssohn Camp of the Modern Woodmen of America remained. All the others, including the various lodges of the O. B. A., were dissolved. Members of the older generation passed away and their sons and daughters were finding newer and more exciting interests with which to fill their lives.

THE YIDDISH LANGUAGE

Yiddish was the natural language of conversation of the East European immigrants. The German-Jewish settlers spoke English or German, with the former language predominating. Only the most recent arrivals continued to speak German.

Not until East European children began their public school education did they use conversational English. So great was the use of Yiddish even by 1915 that when the Minneapolis Talmud Torah organized a Hebrew kindergarten for children from four to six years of age, the following advertisement was inserted in the *American Jewish World*:

Wanted — a young lady, high school graduate preferred, to work five days a week, 9 to 4 P.M. as assistant teacher in the Talmud Torah Kindergarten. *Must be able to understand and speak Yiddish.* Knowledge of Hebrew and experience not required.[4]

The children all spoke Yiddish in their homes. Their mothers, at best, spoke a broken English. As late as 1920 5.1 percent of the foreign-born white stock of Minneapolis gave Yiddish and Hebrew as their mother tongue.[5]

The use of Yiddish was, for ideological reasons, fostered by a segment of recently arrived immigrants from Russia. This group was certainly not Orthodox in its tendencies. It was even regarded as antireligious by many persons in the Jewish community. It may, however, be classified as nonreligious. One of

175

the members of this group, who arrived in Minneapolis as a Russian immigrant in 1906, relates his early experiences as follows:

"I found here hundreds of other young men and women, Yiddish-speaking immigrants, also recently arrived from Russia, where the first revolution was raging. We were imbued with the spirit of Socialism; our interests were not in religion. We found our cultural satisfaction in the Yiddish press. We read the *Jewish Daily Forward*, the *Abend Blatt, Die Zukunft,* and the *Frie Arbeiter Stimme*. Yiddish lecturers from New York came to us from time to time. The second year after my arrival, we established a library of our own in the basement of Kistler's Hall. Many friends donated to us Russian and Yiddish books.

"We had a dramatic group that put on Yiddish plays in Finnish Hall on Glenwood Avenue. Traveling theatrical companies from the East came to Minneapolis half a dozen times a year.

"In 1910 the first branch of the Arbeiter Ring (Workman's Circle) was established here. The national office of the Arbeiter Ring, propagandists from the 'Bund' of Poland, and the Yiddish branch of the Socialist party stimulated us in our work.

"We even organized Yiddishist schools, with the emphasis upon the Yiddish language as the carrier of our culture. There was a minimum reference to Hebrew and to religion. We carried on this activity for approximately five years, up to 1920. This project, which at one time had an enrollment of sixty children, was subsidized in part by our national headquarters. The experience with our Yiddish school was short-lived because the Minneapolis Talmud Torah began to wield great influence in the community. We saw in it something we began to want. Gradually we sent our children to that school.

"Most of our group did not long remain proletarian. We continued to speak Yiddish until we learned to speak English. The parents came to live the lives of their children rather than be permanently influenced by European background. We moved from the wage-earning, laboring class to the lower middle class and then to the upper middle class. Most of our members found their way into the synagogue, into the Zionist movement, and into the Labor Zionist movement."

In 1936 the three local Workman's Circle branches made another attempt to establish a Yiddish school, with a registration of forty-five children. The enrollment dwindled to half the original number within a few years.

Though Yiddish is still spoken in Minneapolis, it is not used regularly even by the old-timers in the community. These people are able to speak and read fluently, but their contacts with the general population, in business and otherwise, as well as the continued use of English by their children, has driven Yiddish to a weak secondary position. Yiddish sermons are delivered by several of the Orthodox rabbis, yet even they use English in conversation more frequently than Yiddish.

At the present time many of the children of the early immigrants understand Yiddish, though they speak it haltingly. They grope for the proper Yiddish words when, on occasion, they speak it to their parents. The grandchildren do not speak the language at all. They are, however, familiar with various Yiddish words and expressions which they hear from their parents or grandparents.

The Yiddish press provided contact with the world scene. It served also as a valued aid in the Americanization process. It familiarized the immigrants with the American scene. According to the late Dr. George J. Gordon, until 1917 there were as many as seven hundred subscribers to the Yiddish daily press. Only the oldest members of the East European community continue to read the Yiddish newspapers. The number of local subscribers and purchasers of Yiddish papers, published in New York City, is given in Table VII. The figures, obtained from the publishers and local distributors, take no account of the degree of duplication that exists in these lists. The same family may read several Yiddish papers. It is safe to suggest that there are no more than three hundred families in Minneapolis who subscribe to or read a Yiddish paper. Inasmuch as the children do not read the papers and very few of the wives of subscribers do, it is believed that in 1946 less than five hundred persons actually read Yiddish papers in Minneapolis.

A Yiddish weekly newspaper, *Die Shabbosdige Post,* was published in Minneapolis beginning in 1917. Dr. Israel Markus was the editor and publisher. It continued publication until 1921 when, owing to lack of subscribers, the paper ceased publication.

TABLE VII. NUMBER OF READERS OF YIDDISH NEWSPAPERS, MINNEAPOLIS, 1945

Name of Paper	Subscribers	Purchasers at News Stand
Daily Forward	152	100
Der Tag ("The Day")......	0	10
Daily Journal	114	0
Weekly Journal	0	25
Amerikaner ("American") ...	90	0
Freiheit ("Freedom")	0	10
Total	356	145

There appears to be an emotional bias against the Yiddish language among the children of the immigrants. Often one hears such persons hush up anyone who begins to speak Yiddish or use a Yiddish expression in a public place. They speak of not liking the language because it is so "guttural." On the other hand the children of these self-conscious parents look upon Yiddish as they look upon any other foreign language, utterly without emotional bias. Being secure in their Americanism, they cannot understand the attitude of their parents with respect to the Yiddish language.

Yiddish is waning in importance and usage. Except for the Yiddishisms that are used because no English word or phrase seems to meet the exact need of the moment, the Yiddish language will, unless all signs are misleading, cease to be used at all within another generation in Minneapolis.

THE MINNEAPOLIS TALMUD TORAH

The Hebrew educational system of Minneapolis, acclaimed nationally as one of the very best of its kind in the United States, came into being in 1894. The story of its rise and development is important because it indicates something of the striving for the preservation and transmission of Hebraic cultural ideals which characterized this midwestern community. Hebrew education in Minneapolis owes much to the inspired leadership and zeal of one man, Dr. George J. Gordon.

Dr. Gordon, born in Neustadt, Lithuania, of Orthodox parentage and educated at the famous academy of higher Jewish learning, the Telz Yeshivoh, came to America alone at the age of eighteen. For a brief period he was employed as a factory worker in New York City. In 1893 he came to Minneapolis, attending the public schools and studying English. A little more than a year after Dr. Gordon arrived in Minneapolis, he became very much concerned about the haphazard and unproductive methods of the old-time cheder or Hebrew school, which was then meeting on the North Side of the city. In the cheder there was little of what we think of as system or efficiency in teaching. The curriculum consisted chiefly of learning to read Hebrew and then studying the five books of Moses and the commentaries on them. Dr. Gordon described the development of the Talmud Torah as follows:

"I was going to North Side High School in 1894. I was then twenty years old, and I was doing my best to make up for the secular training I had missed in Europe. I could not forget how much Hebrew education had done for me, and I felt, as I looked around the North Side community, that the cheder system here, with its very poor teachers and no method worthy of the name and poor classrooms and ungraded classes, was certainly not the kind of school that ought to be developed in an American-Jewish community. I couldn't see how very much knowledge could be acquired under these circumstances. I was sure that the children wouldn't even get very much of Jewish history. I had talked to a good number of people about the situation and they agreed with me that something ought to be done. So I called together a number of people and we held a series of meetings to decide on what it was that we wanted to teach our children.

"In addition to knowing what we didn't like about the existing Hebrew schools, we also had a pretty fair idea of what we really wanted to include in our curriculum. We not only wanted our

179

children to know their Bible and history, but we wanted them to know the Hebrew language, to be able to use it conversationally, to speak it naturally. But of course the times weren't really right for the kind of advanced school that I wanted. All we could do then was to secure a room over on Fifth Street North, and we brought a Hebrew teacher from Fargo, North Dakota, of whom we had heard. We paid him forty dollars a month. He really wasn't too good, but he was certainly better than what we had had until that time.

"In 1898 we decided to transfer the school to the Kenesseth Israel Synagogue. We secured a new teacher and with the help of the synagogue officials, who were very much interested and wanted to do something for Hebrew education, we built a four-room building in the back of the synagogue. Then we set ourselves to the task of securing some really good teachers, and we began to have some excellent results. Our classes met from four to eight o'clock in the evening every day in the week. We had about seventy-five pupils. Classes lasted about one and a half hours each session. Still the school was not too good.

"There were too many people who were opposing the kind of ideas I had, and the program for the school was still not good enough. I organized a revolt against the old Talmud Torah and all its inadequacies. One of the teachers in our school had asked for an increase in salary, and because of this his contract was not renewed. I felt people had to understand that if you wanted a good school you had to pay good salaries to good teachers in order to have them work for you and with you, so I just urged everybody whom I knew to refrain from helping the old school. That was how we really got started. The old school simply couldn't keep going without our support.

"In 1910 I got together a group of men on the North Side who were themselves learned Jews. They were convinced that the old cheder of East European origin could not thrive on American soil. We realized how important it was to teach our Jewish youth in accordance with modern methods, and we realized the necessity of integrating Jewish life into American life. We did not want our children to make unfavorable comparisons between the Hebrew school and the public school.

"In February 1911 our new school, consisting of four classrooms, was opened. It was a vast improvement over anything that had ever been offered to Jewish parents and children. We had an enrollment of approximately one hundred and fifteen children. The school was maintained through the efforts of a group of men who personally solicited funds from members of the community in order to keep it going. The school grew. In 1913 there were two hundred and sixty-four students enrolled. Then we changed the name of the school to the Talmud Torah of Minneapolis. By 1914 the school population had grown so that our building became overcrowded.

"On April 17, 1915, we dedicated our new building, which had cost forty-five thousand dollars, and on the same day we graduated our first class of seventeen boys and three girls. Shortly after this graduation an alumni association was formed, and it has grown in size so that there are now over eight hundred members. Many of the graduates of the Talmud Torah have become rabbis. Others of them are active in Jewish community life, both here and throughout the country, and we are very proud of them. In 1916 we organized a high school department, and we graduated six students in that first high school graduation. We also, in 1920, established a college course of study which we called the Beth Hamidrash (house of study). In order to graduate all the departments a child has to attend our school for a period of ten years.

"We were one of the first institutions in the country to teach Hebrew by using it as the language of conversation in the classrooms. All our classes and all our subjects were taught in Hebrew. Our school reached its highest development in 1930 when we had a total enrollment of eight hundred and fifty-six pupils. Thirty-six percent of the pupils enrolled in the Talmud Torah in 1943 actually graduated, as against the national record of Hebrew schools of only 5 percent."

When the Jewish residential areas began to shift, the Talmud Torah established branches: in 1922 in the old Adath Jeshurun Synagogue on the South Side and at Beth El Synagogue on the North Side, and in 1927 in the new Adath Jeshurun Synagogue on the West Side. In 1948 the Talmud Torah was in the process of making plans for the erection of a new school building which would more adequately house its seven hundred pupils.

The Talmud Torah is not a parochial school. Classes meet in approximately two-hour sessions from four to six in the afternoon. It supplements the public school by providing a knowledge of Hebraic culture, both biblical and modern, to its pupils. Although it teaches the customs and traditions of the Jew, it is not a religious school. It does not insist upon uniformity in thought or practice by its pupils.

Great as was Dr. Gordon's desire to establish a modern Hebrew educational school system in Minneapolis, he was no less interested in making the Talmud Torah the important social service center for the North Side Jews. Toward that end, he worked for the establishment of a social service department, which began its activities in 1917. Clubs were started for young and old. Classes were created for foreigners desiring to study the writing and reading of English. Social groups were organized for foreign boys and girls, in order that they might get to know each other and develop friendships. A day school was organized for children under eight years of age, for which the women of the German-Jewish community provided paid supervision. In 1920 the Talmud Torah opened free dental and prenatal clinics for the benefit of the neighborhood. It had a few months earlier established an infant welfare clinic. So important had these activities become that is was necessary to engage a full-time director.

By 1922 a swimming pool and gymnasium had been opened for the children in the Talmud Torah building. The program for both youth and adults was so full by 1923 that there were "fifteen clubs on the waiting list, asking for meeting space. Due to lack of room same cannot be granted them." The attendance at the clinics has constantly increased.

The steps by which the social service department moved to a new building and became the Emanuel Cohen Center have been described in Chapter 2.

PAROCHIALISM

Despite the recognized excellence of the Minneapolis Talmud Torah, there were some persons in the community who felt that it wasn't Orthodox enough. They wanted the Hebrew school to follow more traditional modes of study. Less concerned with having their children speak the Hebrew language and far more interested in inculcating the standards of Orthodoxy they had known in the old country, they established a small Hebrew school on Logan Avenue North, in the heart of the Jewish neighborhood. In association with the Mikro Kodesh Synagogue (Orthodox), this small school, which never had an enrollment of more than a hundred pupils, conducted classes, first in rented quarters and later in a building of its own. The school met vigorous opposition from laymen as well as from Orthodox rabbis, who denied its charge that the Minneapolis Talmud Torah was unorthodox in its teachings. By 1945 attendance and financial support had fallen off to the point where merger of the two institutions was inevitable.

Dissatisfaction with the amount of Hebrew knowledge and religious practice on the part of the children and grandchildren of the immigrant generation led in 1944 to the establishment of another Jewish parochial school, the Torah Academy. This school owed its origin to a New York group of pietists, the Torah VeDaas Academy of Jewish Study. It is supported in part by local contributions. The teachers are young Orthodox rabbis who have been made available to the school by the New York headquarters. Its classes are conducted in the building once used by the Logan Avenue Talmud Torah. It is the Jewish equivalent of the little red schoolhouse of a generation ago.

Every effort is made to teach Hebrew not only as a language but also as the holy tongue. The emphasis is placed upon religious observance and piety, in so far as they are expressed through ritual and ceremony. The school began with a prekindergarten class alone. Each year another class has been added and it is hoped that in the course of time the regular eight classes of the public school will be established. English subjects are included in the curriculum, but the emphasis is definitely upon the introduction of knowledge and habits concerning the Orthodox Jewish way of life.

The larger part of the Minneapolis Jewish community is opposed to parochialism in any form:

"I think that we would be sabotaging America and American principles if we gave up our Hebrew schools, which now meet after school hours, and instead established parochial schools, even though they would include the curriculum of the public schools. It is as much a part of our duty to see to it that Jewish boys and girls get to know their Christian neighbors as it is for us to try to give them a Jewish education."

It seems hardly likely that parochialism will become the accepted standard of the Jew in Minneapolis. The opposition is too strong. The present leadership of the Jewish community will not accept it. Funds for such a purpose are not likely to be granted by the Minneapolis Federation for Jewish Service.

THE SUNDAY SCHOOL

The Jewish Sunday school is essentially an American development, modeled after the Protestant church's Sunday school. Because it was difficult to secure as large an enrollment as was desired in the Minneapolis Talmud Torah, the two Conservative congregations, Adath Jeshurun and Beth El, established Sunday schools similar to the one that had been established almost from the date of its founding by the Reform temple.

In 1944 there were four Sunday schools with the following enrollments: Adath Jeshurun (Conservative), 275, Beth El (Conservative), 250, Temple Israel (Reform), 217, and Mikro Kodesh (Orthodox), 58. Mikro Kodesh includes children of pre-Talmud Torah age only. The total in 1944 was 800; by 1946 the number had increased by about 100.

Classes ranging from kindergarten through the first two years of high school meet in the respective synagogue buildings and are conducted independently of each other. In each case the rabbi supervises the curriculum and the program of the school. In the main the subjects, taught in sessions of approximately two hours, include Jewish history, the Hebrew Bible, customs and ceremonies, appreciation of Jewish holidays, and current events. Religion is not taught as a separate subject.

Whenever possible the teaching staff is recruited among Jewish teachers in the public school system and graduates of the Minneapolis Talmud Torah and other Jewish educational institutions. All teachers receive a salary, in most cases ranging from two and a half to five dollars a week. The majority of the pupils are girls.

Hebrew is a required subject in all the schools. Pupils in the upper grades who have not attended or are not attending Talmud Torah classes are required, in addition, to attend Hebrew classes for at least one afternoon during the week. Children in the upper grades are also expected to attend Sabbath morning services. Programs and assemblies are arranged for holy days and before feast days and other occasions, such as Chanukah and Purim.

Except for Temple Israel none of the schools has adequate facilities. All, however, are at present undertaking building programs in order to correct this situation. These schools cost from twenty-five hundred to three thousand dollars to operate annually, excluding the cost of textbooks and other materials, which is borne by the individual pupil.

Despite the cost and the effort, Sunday schools are not regarded as entirely adequate for the purpose of providing Jewish children with good Jewish training.

"When you stop to consider that Jewish children have to become acquainted with a long history and tradition, and that they should know Hebrew if they are to fit into synagogal life, and if they are to be able to read their Hebrew Bible, let alone the fact that there is the new Palestinian culture to become acquainted with, and if you stop to realize that for all this, children who go to Sunday school only get about seventy hours of instruction annually, you can see how impossible the whole thing is. We are fooling ourselves if we call this an educational system. The job is too big for Sundays alone."

There are others, however, who feel that what with dancing

and music lessons and all the other kind of lessons which parents can think of, and even ignoring the child's need for physical exercise and relaxation, Sunday school is all that can be expected of the American Jewish child.

PRIVATE SCHOOLS

The number of Jewish boys and girls who attend private schools in Minneapolis is limited. It is debatable whether this situation is due to the desire of parents to keep their children in public schools or is rather the result of a conscious effort of the private schools to limit the enrollment of Jewish children. The improved financial status of the Jewish community makes it appear that there will be an increasing number of Jewish parents who will seek admission for their children in these schools. The number of Jewish children attending the private elementary and high schools in and around Minneapolis in 1945 is shown in Table VIII.

TABLE VIII. JEWISH STUDENTS ENROLLED IN PRIVATE SCHOOLS IN MINNEAPOLIS, 1945

School	Total School Population	Number of Jewish Students
University High School	275	85
Northrop School for Girls..........	225	4
Breck School for Boys.............	400	50*
Blake School for Boys.............	314	3
Shattuck (military academy).......	231	2†
Total	1445	144

* This is an estimate.
† Shattuck is located in Faribault, Minnesota. This figure includes only Jewish students who come from Minneapolis.

UNIVERSITY STUDENTS

The number of Minneapolis Jewish youths who attend colleges and universities has increased considerably. It is commonly believed that this increase became marked about the year 1917. Jewish parents have always emphasized the importance of education, but not until the older generation had attained some degree of financial stability was it possible for Jewish youth to continue their schooling beyond high school. In 1936 there were nine hundred Jewish students at the University of Minnesota; in 1946 there were about fifteen hundred.

Before 1917 very few Jewish girls were students at the university. Thereafter the number of female students increased so that there are now about four girls for every six boys on the campus. The girls take courses in the College of Science, Literature, and the Arts as regular procedure. A goodly number take undergraduate and later graduate courses in social work; some take graduate work in education. The number of graduate students in education has never been large because it is the general impression that Jewish girls will find it difficult to secure employment as teachers in the small towns of Minnesota, and, for that matter, in Minneapolis itself.

Male students are to be found in practically every one of the graduate schools of the university. Whereas in former years Jewish youth thought in terms of such professions as medicine, dentistry, and law, today they are to be found also in the school of business, the social sciences, journalism, chemistry, physics, and engineering. Despite an awareness of the difficulties in securing employment in many of the professions because of their Jewishness, there is an ever-increasing insistence upon taking those courses which will bring personal happiness.

The Hillel Foundation was established on the campus of the University of Minnesota in 1940. This organization, sponsored by the National B'nai B'rith and supported in part by the local Jewish Federation, the local chapters of B'nai B'rith, and their women's auxiliary, has become the center of Jewish youth activity on the campus. Cultural, religious, and social activities under the direction of a rabbi who is the professional leader of the foundation are conducted throughout the school year.

Not all college students attend the local university. A small number attend the Presbyterian Macalester College, located in

St. Paul. Several attend the Congregational Carleton College, in Northfield, Minnesota. Jewish students from Minneapolis may be found in many of the eastern universities and colleges, such as Princeton, Harvard, Pennsylvania, Wellesley, and Smith. Every season a few of the girls attend Stephens College in Missouri.

The youth and their parents, especially if they are in the middle class economically, take it for granted that they will attend some university.

Chapter 10 The Family and the Home

ళ**THE** *Jew's home has rarely been his "castle." Throughout the ages it has been something far higher — his Sanctuary.*[1]

THE traditional Jewish home was the center of a strong family life. The values that had meaning for the Jew — a high moral sense, the love of learning, the beauty and sanctity of religious practices, and the importance of strong family ties — were all fostered in the home. Within the home the Jewish parent shed his daily cares, his economic problems. Children both accepted and respected the authority and judgments of their parents. The Jewish mother poured out her love and devotion upon her children. The father was the disciplinarian and over-all guide, setting the desired pattern for the family.

The Jewish symbols of the traditional home were always prominently displayed. The mezzuzah (literally, "doorpost") was always the first distinctive Jewish symbol to be seen as one entered the traditional Jewish home. This small tubular case, made of metal or wood and fixed slantwise on the upper part of the righthand doorpost, contained a rolled piece of parchment on which were written verses from the book of Deuteronomy (6:4–9 and 11:13–21), beginning with the words, "Hear O Israel the Lord our God the Lord is One," and including the commandment to "love God and obey His commandments." It was placed not only upon the outside doorpost in accordance with the command, "Thou shalt write them upon the doorposts of thy house and upon thy gates," but also upon the doorpost of every room in the home.

No Jewish home in Eastern Europe was without at least one Hebrew book. Even the lowliest family treasured a Hebrew text of the Bible, a prayer book with a special Yiddish translation, or the Teitsch-Chumosh, a Yiddish translation of the Pentateuch with the added feature of homilies and legends which were easily understandable and highly entertaining to the Jewish housewife. In many homes there were other Hebrew volumes, including the digest of Jewish law known as the Shulchan Aruch and the numerous volumes of the Talmud.

The traditional Jewish home usually contained some picture of specific Jewish interest. Whether it was a special design placed on the east wall of the living room to remind the Jew that his prayers were to be recited while facing east, a representation of Moses, or perhaps a portrait of the philanthropist Baron Maurice de Hirsch or the Zionist leader Theodor Herzl, these "art objects" were about the only ones that graced the Jewish home. There were, of course, the brass candlesticks used for the Sabbath and holy day candles, the spice box associated with the Havdalah ceremony at the conclusion of the Sabbath, and on occasion, the dried lulav (palm branch) that was used on the Feast of Tabernacles.

Whatever needlework that was done, in the form of sewing or knitting, was associated with the housewife's endeavor to make more decorative the traditional challah cover, used to cover the Sabbath loaves, or the matsoh cover, used on the Passover. Wives took great pains to decorate the velvet bags in which the prayer shawls or phylacteries of their husbands or sons were carried.

The charity box was a characteristic of the Jewish home in the East European communities. In these boxes were deposited small sums of money in aid of causes, both local and Palestinian. It was unthinkable that a housewife would not at least once a week drop a few coins into one or all of the charity boxes. These boxes or pushkes, as they were commonly called, were collected at least once a year by the representatives of their respective institutions. The receipts were signed and turned over to the housewife, and the process of collecting funds was begun all over again.[2]

The homes of the early Jewish immigrants were not unlike those just described. The traditional pattern of Jewish family life of which the husband was the spiritual head was also retained. But it was not long before marked changes began to occur. The mezzuzah was no longer seen on most Jewish homes in Minneapolis. One may examine the outer doorposts and find the mezzuzah in no more than 10 percent of the Jewish homes. Though the houses of the early immigrants still bear the symbol, the children and grandchildren neglect this traditional practice.

"The mezzuzah may have had some meaning for my grandfather and my father, but it doesn't take such an outward symbol to remind me that I am Jewish. I live my life as a self-respecting Jew ought to live. There are too many symbols in Jewish life as it is. This is one I can do without."

The sons and daughters of these immigrants are less inclined to carry on the tradition of charity boxes in the home. It is "unscientific."

"It was a highly expensive collection method and seemed so 'personal' as against the more acceptable Community Fund idea which was finding ever-increasing acceptance."

In the late twenties, except for the homes of the grandmothers, one could hardly find charity boxes in Minneapolis. The businessmen of the community were still visited by the agents of the European eleemosynary institutions and collections were still rather substantial.

Only after 1917, the year of the Balfour Declaration, was it considered "proper" to retain a blue-colored Jewish National Fund box in the home, for the purpose of helping to purchase land in Palestine in the name of the Jewish people.

Since the organization of the Minneapolis Federation for Jewish Service which, among its other purposes, serves as the central community agency for the collection and distribution of all charities, local, national, and international in scope, the charity box has largely disappeared. The Jewish National Fund Box has gained in importance and prestige because the local chapter of Hadassah serves as the collection agency.

About the only collections of Hebrew books in the community are to be found in the several libraries of the Minneapolis Talmud Torah, in the Orthodox and Conservative synagogues, and in the personal libraries of the rabbis or the very few older Jews who are Hebrew scholars. Even among the latter, there are very few complete sets of the Talmud. Rather one finds Hebrew Bibles, prayer books for the various holy days as well as for daily prayers, and an occasional copy of the Shulchan Aruch. The Teitsch-Chumosh has disappeared.

Aside from a candelabrum in which candles are lighted on the Sabbath eve, there are few objects of specific Jewish character in the homes of most of the Jews of Minneapolis. Pictures and art objects of Jewish interest are few indeed. Books of Jewish interest are seldom found except in the homes of first-generation Jews. After a concerted campaign in 1940 by the Jewish Publication Society of America for memberships which would entitle the subscriber to a minimum of three Jewish books annually, about sixty subscriptions were secured. By 1945 the number had dwindled to thirty-eight subscribers in the entire city.[3] However, three of the synagogues — Temple Israel, Adath Jeshurun, and Beth El — hold library memberships in the organization.

The synagogues have recently undertaken to make their memberships aware of the wealth of Jewish materials, books, and art objects that are available to them by the establishment of book and gift shops. Displays of these items have increased their sale within the community.

The traditional type of art work has largely disappeared from Minneapolis homes. It has given way to copies of Van Goghs and Renoirs and the usual standard, highly impersonal "art" of the department store. In some homes one finds the works of contemporary Palestinian artists, or work by the students of the

Palestinian Bezalel Art School, in silver, copper, or brass. All Jewish homes still possess candlesticks, of either brass or silver. The emphasis upon Palestinian art objects is largely due to the renewed interest in Palestine.

The status of the Jewish woman in Minneapolis has changed markedly from the European pattern. Among the early German-Jewish families the wife was basically the homemaker. She did not enter into the business of her husband or assist in the matter of earning a livelihood for the family.

"Although my wife had nothing to do about earning a living for the family, I used to talk over many of my business problems with her. But I didn't depend upon her advice too much. It was just that I did want her to know how things were coming along in the business. We both regarded it as her duty to see to it that our home was as nice as possible, that the children were given every attention. She had much more to say about the children than I did because she was with them practically all the time. She used to entertain a great deal. We were always having company over to the house and she used to do a lot of baking in preparation for those evenings. Of course she belonged to some ladies' clubs but I didn't pay much attention to them because they met in the afternoons."

The wife of the East European managed the household and cared for the children. Especially if her husband was on the road as a peddler, it was up to her to care for the needs of her children. She acted as both father and mother until the return of the father to the city, usually over the Sabbath. She did share her troubles and problems with her husband and frequently left the matter of enforcing discipline upon the children to her husband. Though the husband would discuss his business affairs with his wife, it was likely to be only in terms of whether he had made or lost any money on his peddler's route.

If the husband had a small grocery or some other business in the city involving the maintenance of a store, the wife usually shared in the management. She acted as a clerk and knew the business as well as her husband. These women seldom belonged

193

to any societies or clubs. They found their pleasure within their own households, visiting friends and neighbors, attending the synagogue on the Sabbath and other holy days, and participating in its social affairs whenever possible.

As the economic status of the family improved, the wife had less to say and do about the husband's business. She had much more leisure time and could use this time in any way she saw fit. Her household duties decreased too because, with the improved economic status, the family was able to afford "help." Many of the functions which were originally associated with the family were gradually taken over, wholly or in part, by agencies outside the family. The introduction of electricity with its many time-saving household appliances, the introduction of canned foods, factory-baked bread, better homes, so constructed as to provide greater household efficiency, the introduction of the automobile — all these helped to provide the housewife with more leisure time.

Nor must we forget that during this transitional period the size of the Jewish family was also decreasing. Records of naturalization found in the files of the Minneapolis Talmud Torah indicate that around 1910 there were many Jewish families with five to ten children.[4] There were few childless marriages. Though we have no way of ascertaining with any degree of accuracy the median size of the Jewish family in Minneapolis in 1910, the testimony of old-timers supports the belief that families were considerably larger than they are today. In a sampling study of the Minneapolis Jewish community made in 1945, the median size of the Jewish family was found to be 3.82.[5] Families with two children, or even only one, are common.

The present size of the Jewish family varies with the economic status of the particular family. For example, the 1945 survey indicated that the average size of the families of children attending classes in the main building of the Talmud Torah, who come from homes covering the entire North Side (lower and middle class), was 4.7. The average size of families at Beth El Congregation (Conservative, North Side, middle and upper class) was 4.3. At Adath Jeshurun (Conservative, West Side, middle and upper class) the average family size was 4.1. At Temple Israel (Reform, West Side, middle and upper class) the family size was 4.0.

In general, the same factors that have made for a reduced birth rate in the general population are at work within the Jewish family as well. Birth control is generally practiced. No religious or social sanctions have been evoked against it.

Though most Jewish marriages are blessed with offspring, there are cases of childless marriages. Many requests for adoption come to the Jewish Family Welfare Association, but the number that can be filled are few. In most cases children are adopted from outside communities.[6]

Because the responsibility for the economic welfare of the family depended to a greater degree upon the husband, he had even less time than formerly to devote to his family. As a consequence the woman assumed a more important role in the rearing and training of the children. It was the wife who helped to make the important decisions with reference to the children's schooling, the question of whether Jonathan would take Hebrew lessons at the age of six or wait until he was nine, whether Shirley would take dancing, art, or music lessons, or all three. And it was the wife who played a dominant role in the decision as to which synagogue to join and which social clubs had to have the benefit of the family's membership.

"My wife had more to do with getting me to join a synagogue and a social club than I like to believe. To put it frankly, it wasn't very important to me one way or another which synagogue we should join, but my wife said that her friends belonged in Synagogue X, and besides she pointed out that if we wanted our children to meet the right people, they ought to be going to that synagogue's Sunday school. We simply had to join the golf club though I had never held a golf club in my hands before. It was important for our prestige, I guess. At any rate, we joined where my wife said we should."

The middle-class Jewish woman dresses very well. She knows styles and keeps up with the latest fashions. The better stores in Minneapolis acknowledge that Jewish women are among their best customers. It is generally believed that in proportion to the family income the Jewish woman spends more on her own clothes and her children's clothes than any other group of women in Minneapolis except the very wealthiest.

In the middle-class group the majority of the women have their own checking accounts in the city's banks. A goodly number of women drive their own cars, or if there is only one car in the family, they drive their husbands to the office in the morning, use the car throughout the day, and call for their husbands after work. A great number of Jewish women smoke, though there are still many who frown upon the practice. Practically all of the third generation smoke, as do most of the daughters of the early immigrants. The Jewish woman is not averse to drinking, but she drinks in moderation. Practically all the wives of the two hundred members of the Jewish Oak Ridge Country Club play golf and many are to be seen on the golf course almost daily during the summer months.

Perhaps because she is so devoted to club and organizational life, the Jewish woman has a healthy interest in world and Jewish affairs, which she expresses primarily through the study groups within such organizations as the Council of Jewish Women, Hadassah, the synagogue women's leagues and sisterhoods, the ladies' auxiliary of B'nai B'rith, Pioneer Women's Organization (Zionist), the ladies' auxiliary of the Talmud Torah, the Emanuel Cohen Center, the Jewish Family Welfare Association, the Minneapolis Federation for Jewish Service, the Community Fund (where she assists with fund-raising activities), the Red Cross, the Foreign Policy Association, the Parent-Teachers Association, the League of Women Voters, the College Women's Club, and so forth. There are, in fact, few organizations and causes of either a civic or national character, general or Jewish, in which Jewish women do not participate.

THE FAMILY AND THE HOME

"I honestly believe that the very best Jewish organizations in the city are the women's organizations. If it weren't for them, many of the projects which we have carried out in the city would never have been undertaken. Take the case of the Council Camp, organized by the Council of Jewish Women. This camp takes a goodly number of the children who are recommended by the Jewish Family Service Association and gives them a fine summer vacation in northern Minnesota. In addition, they were the first to provide camp facilities for the children of middle class Jewish families.

"The women seem to make a success of everything they do. They goad the men to take action. I think that's what happened with the B'nai B'rith ladies when they decided it was time to establish and furnish a house for Jewish students on the campus of the University of Minnesota, under the direction of the Hillel Foundation. Hadassah was keeping interest alive in Palestine and doing good work for the hospitals there before the men were actively interested in Zionism, as they are today. I think any rabbi will tell you that the women's league or sisterhood of his congregation is *the* basic organization in the synagogue. In fact the strength of the Minneapolis Jewish community is due, I believe, to the wonderful spirit of cooperation and healthy interest in all phases of the community life which was first expressed by the Jewish women of the community."

As the direct result of her interest and work, the woman now receives a greater degree of equality within the Jewish community. She is to be found on the boards of directors of practically all Jewish organizations, including the synagogues. She serves on the board of the Talmud Torah. Indeed, few important decisions with respect to the religious, cultural, or philanthropic work in the Jewish community are made without her advice and assistance.

She is, in the main, responsible for the successful study courses and lecture courses sponsored by synagogal and other organizations. She likes meetings that feature book reviews or reviews of plays, and attends them in greater numbers than any other type of cultural affair.

"If it weren't for our wives, I believe that most of us men

would stay away from these things which my wife calls 'cultural.' When I get home from the office, I don't like to go gallivanting around, but my wife keeps on insisting, so we go. I suppose that's why I go to the concerts of the Minneapolis symphony orchestra with her every other week during the season, and I've even had to go to the ballet with her. Whenever some show from New York comes to the Lyceum Theater, I'm sure to have her remind me to get tickets."

Husbands and wives will be found any night in the week eating out at the hotel dining rooms. They are among the well-known patrons of the better restaurants in the city. Wherever the food is good, the music pleasant, and the setting dignified, Jewish couples will be found in attendance. The family-night dinners at the Standard Club and the Oak Ridge Country Club, intended only for members and their friends, are well attended.

Jewish women like to give luncheon parties in great profusion.

"I came back to Minneapolis to visit my family and friends after an absence of a year. I was almost immediately engulfed by a flood of invitations to luncheons in my honor. I think that I attended a luncheon practically every weekday. They were all quite elaborate. In some cases, after the luncheon we played bridge or gin rummy. Usually the same crowd travels together, so I was meeting the same women each day. It didn't seem to me that these women were capable of any serious thoughts until I discovered that these same girls were all members of important societies in the community and were among the really active leaders."

There is a great effort on the part of the Jewish woman (and her husband must of course share the responsibility) to keep up with the Joneses. If one wishes to travel in the same crowd with one's friends, it is expected that the same standards will be observed.

"Each new home that goes up is bigger and better than the last. Everyone seems to be trying to make his home the last word. Sometimes it seems to me that most of these middle-class Jews are spending more on themselves and their homes and their children than they can actually afford. I know a good number of the men who have such homes and who are to be seen at this club and that party and I know from them that they are living up to almost everything they earn. How long it can keep up I don't know."

Whether or not this indictment is true, it appears that in proportion to income the Jewish family lives in far better surroundings and spends money much more freely on personal pleasure than does the non-Jewish family. It must, however, be pointed out that proportionally the Jewish community is known to contribute far more liberally to charitable causes, both civic and Jewish, than the non-Jewish community.

Despite the round of activities carried on by the parents, the children are usually close to the parents. Parents lavish fine clothes and elaborate gifts upon their children, as well as a great deal of love and affection. Parents, especially the mothers, devote much time to their children and their problems.

"I think that parents and children get along far better today than they did in the early days. Children were actually afraid of their fathers in those early days. He had to be listened to with respect, and you couldn't argue with him. Today children treat their parents as real friends. They talk over their problems with them. They bring their friends to their home to sleep overnight or to have dinner, and mothers take it very naturally. I think that in most cases children are a bit closer to their mothers than they are to their fathers but it is a truly wonderful relationship.

"Children feel that they have something to say about family affairs and I have actually seen Jewish families where the children are invited to give their opinions on matters affecting the whole family. Parents make their children feel that it's their home and I think that's why the children and the parents have retained such a fine family feeling toward each other."

Few Jewish girls continue their employment after they are married. Except during the war years, it was expected that the young man would be able to support his wife so that she need not work after marriage. Though the number of working wives is increasing, there is still something of a stigma attached. Mothers of such girls and, in some cases, the mothers of the grooms, half-apologetically explain the matter.

"My daughter went to school where she learned a profession. She's a social worker. She feels that she should not give up her work when there is a need for it. Besides when they get ready to have a family, she says it will be time enough to give up her work."

"What's wrong with her working? My son loves her even if he hasn't got a million dollars. So they say they'll both work and lay aside as much money as they can, and then after a few years they'll be able to buy the things they want. Then they will settle down and be happy."

The patriarchal family that is traditionally associated with Jewish life has largely given way to the "equalitarian" family, which Mowrer has described as a family "where there is a minimum of superordination or subordination in the relationship between husband and wife." [7] The interests of parents and children still center on the home. The family appears to be at least as strong a unifying force in the Jewish community today as it was in the Old World.

Though the traditional attitude of the sanctity of marriage appears to prevail, the divorce rate among Jewish families in Minneapolis is definitely increasing. As will be observed from Table IX, the changing attitude toward divorce is marked after the year 1920. Though the rate has not yet increased to the level of the general population in Hennepin County, it appears likely that the rates will be similar within another decade.

Jewish law has always countenanced divorce, even though it has frowned upon it. Family ties through the ages have always been so strong that divorce proceedings were rare indeed. According to traditional Jewish practice, a Get (Jewish bill of divorcement), prepared in the presence of witnesses by a rabbi, must accompany any civil divorce; otherwise the parties are still regarded as married.

Even though the divorce rate has increased among the Jews

THE FAMILY AND THE HOME

TABLE IX. MARRIAGES AND DIVORCES OF THE JEWISH POPULATION COMPARED
TO THE GENERAL POPULATION OF HENNEPIN COUNTY

Year	Number of Marriages	Number of Divorces	Number of Jewish Marriages	Number of Jewish Divorces	Ratio of Marriages to One Divorce for General Population	Ratio of Marriages to One Divorce for Jewish Population
1890	1765	125	13	1	14.1	13.
1900	2160	230	24	0	9.4	24.
1910	3447	401	74	5	8.6	14.8
1920	6381	652	182	10	9.8	18.2
1930	4562	1045	131	19	4.4	6.8
1940	5375	1166	112	16	4.6	7.1
1945	6785	2040	114	23	3.3	4.9

of Minneapolis, the number who seek a Jewish divorce in addition to the civil decree is rather limited. Except for those who call themselves Orthodox, few persons bother to acquire a Jewish divorce unless they expect to be remarried by an Orthodox or Conservative rabbi, who will require that a Jewish bill of divorcement be procured. The Reform rabbi makes no such request.

Judaism has always stressed the importance of right living. Violations of the moral code, either in private or public, were regarded as sinful. The biblical emphasis upon purity and the universally recognized high standard of fidelity in marriage have affected the outlook and point of view of Jews, even to the present generation. Religious and parental teachings have, through the centuries, had a wholesome effect upon the Jew. Any offenses against morality, both religious and civil, are regarded as casting a stigma upon the entire people, and as a consequence the indignation of the group tends to curtail such tendencies and often makes the offender a social outcast.

For religious and moral reasons adultery is regarded as a serious offense. The number of men who are unfaithful to their wives is believed to be exceedingly small. Prostitution by Jewish women is not known to exist in the community. The pressure of public opinion being what it is, no prostitute could hope to live for any length of time in the Jewish community without finding herself an outcast. The Jewish community is, by and large, a moral community.

Shortly after the great influx of East European immigration to Minneapolis in the early 1900's, the problem of delinquency among Jewish children was regarded as serious. A careful check has been made of the Hennepin County Juvenile Court records for 1905, the first year in which exact records were kept. Of a total of 219 juvenile delinquents, 14 Jewish boys were arrested, for the following offenses:

Driving over a cross walk faster than a walk.
Malicious destruction of property. Threw stones and broke a window.
Charged with breaking into a box car and stealing watermelons.
Pitching pennies.
Gambling with dice.
Stole a razor.
Assault and battery.
Got into a fight on the street while selling papers.
Stole two newspapers.
Arrested for burglary.
Trespassed on the railroad and stole wheat.
Stays out nights. Swears and fights members of his family.
Choked boy in argument over five cents and took two newspapers.

When we consider that these children seem to have gotten themselves into difficulties because, in most instances, they were on their own, earning money by selling newspapers and fighting for the privilege of remaining in business, and because they were, in many cases, unable to gain the understanding of their foreign-born parents, we may appreciate the apprehension of the Jewish community.

The report of the probation officer of Hennepin County for the year 1912 indicates that of 645 delinquents, 56 were Jewish. Little wonder that the problem weighed heavily on the Jewish community.

However, the amount of delinquency began to decrease after 1912. In 1913 and again in 1914 there were only 34 cases. Truancy brought about the arrest of 6 Jewish boys and girls in 1913. Of the cases in 1914, 15 involved petit larceny and 3 girls arrested for incorrigibility. By 1916 the secretary of the Associated Jewish Charities was able to make the following report:

Jewish juvenile delinquency is decreasing in Hennepin County, according to reliable figures computed on the number of cases brought into the Juvenile Court, as compared with the general increase in population.[8]

The report pointed out that the number of cases had been reduced after play facilities were provided for Jewish children on the North Side.

In 1940, 23 Jewish young people were brought before the juvenile court in Hennepin County (see Table X). That juvenile delinquency has ceased to be a real problem among Jews of Min-

TABLE X. JEWISH YOUTH IN JUVENILE COURT,
HENNEPIN COUNTY, 1940

Offenses	Number of Offenders
Traffic violations	13
Truancy	1
Sought ride from road	3
Disorderly conduct	1
Reporting falsely to police	1
Petit larceny	1
Grand larceny	3
Total	23

neapolis is further attested by the statement of Edward F. Waite, judge of the juvenile court in Hennepin County from 1911 to 1921 and again from 1931 to 1941: "It was a matter of comment that we had very few Jewish boys and girls in the Court, in proportion to the general population."

Judge Waite has placed the credit for this achievement upon

the watchfulness of the Jewish community itself as well as upon the program of the Talmud Torah. It is reasonable to suppose that the adjustment of the Jewish parents to their American environment, their better understanding of the American way of life, together with improved economic status, made for better relationship between parents and children and, as a consequence, reduced the tendency toward delinquency.

Though juvenile delinquency in Minneapolis showed an increase in 1945 of more than 13 percent over the previous year,[9] the number of Jewish delinquents did not increase, according to the Jewish Family Service Association. After careful study of the danger of increased delinquency, it reported that "there was no real problem of juvenile delinquency within the Jewish community and that what little there was had not increased as the result of the war."

Jews have been known for their temperance. Drunkenness is not now and never was a "Jewish vice." There is no record of any Jew ever having been arrested for drunkenness in Minneapolis until 1944, when a single adult, on his way home from a family party, was arrested for drunken driving.

Jews traditionally never drank wine or strong drink unless they had first recited the proper benediction. Under those circumstances it is clear why Jews are not habitual drinkers. Of course Jews, both men and women, take an occasional cocktail. However, Jews do not frequent bars in large numbers, and when they drink they do so in moderation: "We have been taught temperance, not abstinence."

Killing and crimes of passion are almost nonexistent among Jews of Minneapolis. In the past thirty years only one Jew was convicted of murder, and though he was a resident of Minneapolis for several years he was generally not regarded as a part of the Jewish community.

During the days of that "noble experiment," prohibition, some Jews, along with members of the larger community, were bootleggers. The Jewish community looked upon their activities with disgust and a sense of shame.

"What could we really do about these people and even about some who are gamblers? We have no real control over these people. The synagogue couldn't excommunicate them. They just were ignored as much as possible. We tried to keep out of their company."

Some Jews like to play cards, though most persons play for small stakes in the privacy of their own homes.

"Yes, there are a good number of us who play cards and for large stakes, but I'm sure the number isn't larger proportionately than is true of the public at large. We are interested in sports and some of us like to bet on the outcome of games. But the number of such persons is really very small. It's always the same group that does that sort of thing. As long as we don't hurt anyone by it and have a good time doing it, I can't say that it is very serious. You don't hear of Jews absconding with money or embezzling or doing a lot of other things like that. And very few Jews 'run around.' Yes, I know that there are such Jews but the majority are clean decent people."

The Jewish community of Minneapolis has never kept any records of mixed marriages. Nor is there such a record in the office of the clerk of the district court of Hennepin County. All information about intermarriage must come from the rabbis of the community, who would be expected to officiate at such marriages, or from a careful study of the membership rolls of the various synagogues and other Jewish organizations. The degree of social acceptance of the intermarried would thus be ascertainable. Allowance must be made for those persons who leave the community in order to marry where they are not known. There are too those who marry and take up residence outside the community.

Intermarriage is said to take place when a Jewish person, male or female, marries a person who is not born of Jewish parents, or who has accepted another faith and has voluntarily read himself out of the Jewish faith. Traditionally intermarriage was regarded as calamitous. When it occurred among the children of Orthodox Jews, parents "sat Shiva" — they observed the traditional seven-day period of mourning as if the child had died. Parents were distraught and ashamed to face their friends.

When intermarriage occurred, an effort was usually made by some member of the family to secure the formal conversion of the non-Jew to Judaism. Such conversion could take place if the non-Jew voluntarily desired it and if he engaged in a period of study of the Jewish way of life, its ideals, theology, and ritual. If the non-Jew were a male, the rite of circumcision was also required. In the case of either male or female, a formal conversion ceremony followed the period of study. The ritual bath, or cleansing, was required.

In the early days there was very little intermarriage in the East European community. Occasionally, it occurred in the German-Jewish group.

"Although we didn't speak much about it, my children knew that it would kill me if one of them married outside his own religion. Whenever we heard about intermarriage taking place, and we really didn't hear about it very much, we would all feel sick about it. But we were always afraid of it because it meant that we would be losing a child. I don't care what ceremonies people go through. Once you marry a non-Jew you aren't going to be as Jewish as you were before. That's why I always insisted that our children should receive as good a Jewish training in the Hebrew school and at home as possible."

Intermarriages take place in ever-increasing numbers within the Jewish community. They may be frowned upon, spoken against, and thoroughly disliked, but they take place nevertheless. Moreover there is a growing tendency to accept such persons without prejudice in the synagogues and other Jewish organizations (see Table XI).

In nearly all cases it is the Jewish youth who marries a non-Jewish girl:

"I have noticed that very few Jewish girls marry non-Jews.

THE FAMILY AND THE HOME

I guess there is pretty much of a stigma attached to it. But there are a fair number of Jewish boys who marry Christian girls. These girls are usually converted formally to Judaism by the rabbi. Still, I think the odds are all against intermarriage working out successfully."

Practically all those Jews who intermarry are native Americans. In most instances the Jewish youth is financially better off than the girl he marries.

TABLE XI. INTERMARRIAGE AS INDICATED BY SYNAGOGUE AND
SOCIAL CLUB MEMBERSHIP ROLLS, 1945

Synagogues and Clubs	Membership	Number of Members Intermarried	Intermarriages in the Families of Members
Adath Jeshurun (Conservative).....	403	14	9
Beth El (Conservative)............	387	8	4
Temple Israel (Reform)............	450	20	4
B'nai B'rith (Lodge 271)...........	527	12	2
Oak Ridge Country Club...........	200	13	3

Information on the number of marriages taking place within the Orthodox synagogues is not available. Because the Orthodox rabbis will not usually officiate at such marriages, the sons and daughters of Orthodox Jews usually go to either the Reform or Conservative rabbis. If they refuse to officiate, these young people are married by a civil authority. Practically all those who intermarry remain within the Jewish fold. They join synagogues and temples, the golf club, and other organizations. They usually go to the Reform or Conservative synagogues, feeling, correctly, that their wives will be more readily accepted than at Orthodox ones. Even when the wife has not been formally converted to Judaism, she is permitted to join the women's organization of several of the synagogues and occasionally even plays a role of some prominence in its affairs.

"What should we do? Drive these people out from us entirely? Isn't it better that we should do what we can to make them feel that they are Jews and get them to live like Jews? What good will it do us if we wash our hands of them? Besides many of these boys have married very fine girls. They want to be part of the Jewish community. If they do, give them the chance. If they don't, it is something we don't have to worry about."

Do intermarriages succeed in the Minneapolis community? It must be said that the number of divorces between intermarried couples does not appear to be high. There is, however, another measure of success or failure in marriage which should be considered. The number of intermarried couples who "do not get along" appears to this observer to be rather high.

"I have noticed that when intermarried couples do not get along, the wife usually drops her Jewish associations very quickly and seems to return to her original church group and she takes the children along with her. There are others who, despite promises made and even active participation in the Jewish community organizations, bring up their children as Christians rather than Jews. They send them to church Sunday schools or insist upon observing Christian holidays, such as Christmas, in their homes, even though the husband is upset and disturbed about it. These persons argue amongst themselves but they somehow remain married to each other."

Jewish family life is still strong in Minneapolis. Children are given every attention and consideration. Parents often provide comforts and cultural opportunities for their children at great personal sacrifice. Though the number of divorces among Jewish couples is on the increase, the husband-wife relationships appear to be good. The home is still the Jew's castle. Social activities and family life center around the home. There is every reason to feel that the strength and beauty of Jewish family life constitute assurance for the continuity of the Jewish way of life.

Part III   THESE ARE
           THE GENERATIONS

Introduction

A PHOTOGRAPHER often "works around" his subject. He may focus his camera from many different angles in order that all that can be known of the features, spirit, and personality of the subject may be graphically presented.

In this sense, this study attempts to photograph the Minneapolis Jewish community. Every effort has been made to present a complete picture of the individuals who comprise this community. The ethnic group itself has been "photographed" from many different angles.

Part I has presented the basic facts about the Jewish community. Every effort has been made to point out the important factors in the development and growth of the Jewish community. The relationship of the Jewish community to its non-Jewish neighbors has been discussed in Chapter 3. The questions and problems that confront the Jews of Minneapolis with respect to these ofttimes unsatisfactory relations have been discussed. The possible solutions for these problems, as the Jewish community understands them, have been suggested.

In Part II we have examined the changes that have taken place in every phase of the life of the Jewish community. Contact of cultures has brought about certain marked changes in both the personal and communal life of the Jewish people, religiously, culturally, socially, and economically. These changes have been recorded in detail.

Still another part of the picture remains to be presented. Cultural changes may be seen from the viewpoint of representative Jewish families who have lived in Minneapolis for many years. They become more marked when observed through the personal histories of members of succeeding generations. They help thereby to give added meaning to the facts that have been presented in the other sections of this study.

Here, then, we present the stories of these generations as told to the author by members of the present Jewish community. They have been changed only in detail in order to avoid identification of the narrators. Their stories, it is believed, are representative of the Jewish community as a whole.

Chapter 11 The Scholar Becomes a Merchant

An East European whose early years were spent in study of Hebraic literature and lore, of Orthodox tradition, comes to Minneapolis. He discovers a new way of life, retaining nevertheless his deep love for the traditional ideas and practices. He finds taxing the problem of rearing his children as Jews. His daughter, typical of the other children in the family, works out certain compromises in the religious pattern of her life. The grandson feels a greater sense of security in his Jewishness than his parents did. The tradition of family love and loyalty is retained through the three generations.

MORDECAI, SON OF JONAH

I was born in the town of Vidukla in the province of Kovno, Lithuania, in the year 1869. My father was the owner of a tailoring shop. I recall that he employed about fifteen people in his shop. It was pretty large as a business for those days. I still remember the excitement of all of the townspeople on the day he brought a Singer sewing machine into the town. My father was about thirty-five years old when I was born.

There were about two hundred families in this town. I think that it was an all-Jewish community. The Gentiles lived on the outskirts of the town. Now it may be that the reason I think that it was an all-Jewish city is because we all lived in Jewish neighborhoods, the Jews lived all together, and I do not recall ever seeing Gentile neighbors. In our town Jews and Gentiles did not mix socially, although on occasion business was done with them.

The synagogue was in the very center of the town. All the weddings of the community took place in the courtyard of the synagogue. There were about two or three hundred seats in that synagogue. We also had a bes hamidrash (house of study). There were always at least a dozen people about in this bes hamidrash learning the Gemarah (part of the Talmud). There was also a public bathhouse in the middle of the town. We had no such thing as a bath in our own homes.

My father possessed what for those days could be regarded as average Jewish learning. He could "learn" a chapter of Mishnayos (a portion of the Talmud) very well. Each Sabbath he studied the portion of the week that was to be read in the synagogue very carefully. He was regarded as a fine Jew.

My mother was a very pious Orthodox Jewish woman. She came from a little town near Tavrig in Lithuania. In her manner of conducting herself, she was certainly no different from all the other Jewish women of that time. She wore a sheitel (wig) in accordance with Orthodox Jewish law. Of course, all the other Jewish women of our town wore sheitels too. She knew how to recite her prayers by heart. The women of the community learned their prayers especially well from a man of the synagogue who would recite aloud the prayers for all the women in the women's gallery of the synagogue. As they listened they learned the prayers, and inasmuch as they all attended the synagogue, they learned them especially well. My mother never had any special lessons in Hebrew, but that was no different from most of the other Jewish women. It simply was not expected of them. My mother could speak Polish and Lithuanian, but not Russian. There were not many Russians in our territory.

The people in our town, whom I still remember, were engaged in various businesses. They were carpenters, butchers, bakers, innkeepers, purchasers of wood, wheat, dry goods, and a few were millers.

I had but one brother and no sisters. I did have another brother who was two years older than I am, but he died as a result of an accident. One day he swallowed a plum pit and it stuck in his throat. There was no doctor in town, so he could not be saved.

My older brother was a real Hebrew scholar. I did not see much of him because he left our town as a youth and studied at the university at Vilna. He also attended the yeshivoh (academy of higher Jewish learning) in Vilna. He acquired a certificate as a teacher. In those days that was regarded as a very great honor. Few Jewish boys were able to qualify. I did not really get to see or know my brother until I was about thirteen years old because he was away so much of the time. I was the only child at home.

I started my Hebrew education at the age of five when I went to a cheder. My teacher was Shmuel the Melamed (Samuel the Teacher). I recall that he lived about ten blocks away from our home. I studied with him until I was seven years old. This school had sessions which lasted from eight o'clock in the morning until five o'clock in the afternoon. I would then come home for supper. Then I would go back to school at night for a couple of hours. I always took my lantern with me at night to light the way. I used to have bread and syrup for lunch. My mother would give me a penny to buy some syrup, and I took the bread from home. When I was seven I already knew the five books of Moses together with the main commentary on the Bible by Rashi, and I had just begun to study the Talmud. When I reached that point I was regarded as an advanced student, and so I went to another cheder where I studied for two more years. I was then nine years old and I returned to my old teacher, Shmuel the Melamed, because my parents and I regarded him as such a good teacher. We used to study together at five o'clock in the morning. I used to sleep in his room in order to be there on time for these lessons. I studied with him until I was ten years old. Then I learned to write Yiddish. Most of the time I spent in studying by myself in the synagogue with other boys of our community.

When I was about eleven and a half years old, I had a talk
with one of my boy friends about our studies. We decided that
we weren't learning enough under those conditions, so we decided to leave Vidukla and go to the town of Rishane, where we
were sure we would receive better instruction. I didn't even tell
my parents about my decision. We told the driver who took us
to Rishane to tell our parents where we had gone and that we
intended to study in the Chasid's Klose (the Study of the Pious
One). When we came to the town, we met the rabbi and paid a
tuition fee of twelve dollars for the season. This meant that we
could study from September through March, or from the high
holy days up to the Passover festival. I remember that I used
to sleep on a bench in the synagogue. I bought a gunny sack
and filled it with straw which I picked up around the town.
This was my bed. I lived this way until I was thirteen years
old.

I was Bar Mitzvah (confirmed) at thirteen like all other
Jewish boys. They didn't make a fuss over Bar Mitzvah in those
days like they do today. I prepared my own Talmudic discourse
for the occasion. My parents' friends were invited to my home
after services, and it was a happy day for us all. After my Bar
Mitzvah I went back to Rishane and remained there until I
was fourteen and a half. I decided that there was still a better
yeshivoh in Kovno, and I decided to go to this large city. I came
to the city of Kovno on a Friday afternoon.

I know that I did not ask for or receive advice from either
my father or my mother as to whether or not I should go to
study in Kovno. I figured that I knew what I had to do if I
was to advance in my learning. The other boys and I received
our meals at the homes of the various Jewish townspeople free
of charge. I ate in a different home each day. I remember that
on the Friday afternoon when my friend and I arrived in Kovno,
we came to the synagogue and there Rabbi Isaac Elchanan, the
great rabbi of that city, whose name came to be known all
over the world because of his piety and learning, came over to

us and asked us if we had any place to stay over the Sabbath. When we replied in the negative, he took the other boy to his home and arranged for someone to take me to his home. There were, I think, about five yeshivos in the town.

I studied with Rabbi Zalman Charif, that is, Zalman "the sharp" or highly learned person. Rabbi Zalman Charif gave me an admission test, and after listening to me he received me into his class. During the first few weeks we slept in the old bes hamidrash (house of study). I gave the shamos (beadle) five rubles, and he arranged for us to eat at various homes for all days of the week but one. On that day we sat in the public soup kitchen. I studied in Kovno until I was seventeen years of age. After that I studied by myself. Shortly after I was seventeen I went on to the great city of Vilna. Most of the yeshivos were very crowded, and so we studied in a suburb of the city under Rabbi Joseph. Our meals here too were arranged for by the shamos. I went home to Vidukla to see my parents at the time of the high holy days. Of course, during all this time I used to write to my parents, and they would send me money with which to buy the few things that I needed.

About that time there was a government order that all the boys in the yeshivos had to have passports. I didn't have one. When the government inspectors came, I would hide somewhere until they had gone. That, however, did not disturb me very much because I wanted so to study in Vilna. I also had the chance to hear the greatest cantors in the world in the synagogues there. After a time, however, I became worried about the matter of the passport, so I decided to go back to my home town to find out what I could do about getting one. The army might at any time have picked me up and forced me to serve. So I became very much afraid to be seen out in public in those days.

My older brother, whom I had hardly known and seldom seen, had come to America, to the city of Minneapolis. A member of my family had come to America sometime before and had sent a ticket for my brother to come here. My brother was an up-to-date person. He just could not stand life in the small European towns. At that time just about everybody I knew was going to America. So I decided to write to my brother, and after a time he sent me a ticket to come to America. He purchased the ticket on credit and told me that I was to pay him back for it. That I did after I earned my first few dollars here. My parents and I talked the matter over carefully, and they finally agreed to let me go to America. I paid ten rubles as a bribe to someone to get me over the border without a passport. The Prussian border was about ten miles from my home town. I was then free. I went to Memel, then to Hamburg, and on to Berlin and Havre. From there I sailed to New York, and I arrived here in 1888.

One of my relatives came to America with me. I remember that in the few days that we were in New York, we were on a wagon together and someone threw rotten tomatoes at us because we were foreigners.

We were both anxious to go to Minneapolis. We got on a train and rode as far as Buffalo. From Buffalo we took the boat to Duluth, and we were on the Great Lakes for three and one-half weeks. My brother, who was in Minneapolis, could not imagine what had happened to us.

About three weeks before the Jewish New Year, Rosh Hashonah, in 1888, I arrived here. I recall that it was on a Thursday of that week, and we all sat down to decide what was to be done with us, how we were to earn a living, and where we were to stay. Some of my relatives who had provided the ticket for my brother's transportation to Minneapolis permitted me to stay with them, although their home consisted of only two rooms.

There were about two hundred Jews at that time who lived on the North Side. Of course, there was the South Side Jewish community, which was older, and the German Jewish community, which I did not know at all.

THE SCHOLAR BECOMES A MERCHANT

On my first Sabbath I went to the synagogue which was located on Sixth Avenue North and Second Street. It was upstairs over a grocery store and was called the Ohel Jacob Synagogue (Tent of Jacob). This synagogue was Orthodox in every respect and was very much like the synagogues I knew in Europe. The pulpit was in the center of the room, and there were wooden benches around it. There was a table in the rear of the room where we used to learn and learn the Talmud. I remember how happy I was to be called up to the Torah on my first Sabbath there. There were about twenty people present at this service.

On Monday of the next week, my friend and I went to look for work on Washington Avenue and Fourth Avenue North. I saw a crowd of people standing around, and I could tell they were trying to get jobs. I got into the crowd, and I too got a job using a shovel, working for the railroad lowering some tracks. I got a dollar and a half a day.

You can well imagine how hard it was for me to work with that shovel. I hardly knew what one was. I certainly had never had one in my hands before. I worked at that job for about three weeks. I was proud because I had made, what was to me, a lot of money. I then bought shoes, a suit, and a hat, all on credit. I remember paying ten dollars down for these things.

When I came here, I didn't have to change my ways very much from what they were in the old country. The Ohel Jacob Synagogue had its minyan (public service) for Rosh Hashonah at the Turner Hall, on Fifth and Washington Avenue. All the peddlers in town came to this service. We had a chazan (one who chants the liturgy). Services were very much the same as I knew them as a boy.

I got other jobs, after my railroad experience. I worked in a lumber yard at night. I worked there for a month, lowering lumber on trucks.

The peddling business attracted me. One of the Jewish men in town had a peddler's supply house. He gave my relative and me about seventy-five dollars' worth of goods with a canvas bag

219

and a box which we were to tie onto our chests, for notions. The whole thing must have weighed nearly seventy-five pounds. We were taken out to the Shakopee road and left there. Thus we began our peddling career. I didn't know any English. I talked as best I could, and I walked and walked.

I remember the first Shabbas (Sabbath) I was out in the country. I knew a Jewish family lived there. I tried to get them to take me in over Shabbas, but they laughed at me. He said he couldn't afford to do it. I went along the road two miles and came to another house. There I found another Jewish man, who was nice to me and took me in over Shabbas.

But after that, when I couldn't get a place to stay over Shabbas, I began to peddle on Shabbas. I peddled on foot until January first of 1889. I made about a hundred and fifty dollars' profit. I then went to the ticket agent and paid for my ticket, which my brother had secured for me. I also got tickets for my parents as well as for my brother's wife and his children. I ran up a debt of about four hundred dollars. My brother was also peddling, but we did not travel together very much. I kept up the peddling business for about five years. During all that time I davened (prayed) regularly. I wore my tefillin (phylacteries). I never ate any meat because I didn't want to violate the dietary laws.

I guess the reason for my observance of so many of our customs was because I was so alone. I didn't want to be alone. I wanted to be part of something. I didn't want to lose my identity.

I remember that a great number of the other Jewish peddlers did eat meat away from home. That always surprised me.

When I was in the country peddling, of course, I could do no studying, but when I was back in Minneapolis, I would go to shule (synagogue) on Shabbas.

In 1893 I decided to remain in town, so I began to peddle apples. My parents had come here in 1890. I bought some furniture from one of the Jewish merchants and set up a home on

THE SCHOLAR BECOMES A MERCHANT

Fifth Avenue and Washington North. I supported my parents. I also had to support my brother and his family because my brother just didn't make much. My brother became ill too, and that made matters worse. He was too refined for that kind of life, I guess. He couldn't stand it. He was a scholar. He became ill, and he died a short time later.

After I made a few dollars, I decided to open a grocery store. It was very small, but I was able to get along fairly well. Many people from the South Side would place their orders with me, and I established a fairly decent business.

In 1896 I married my wife. She had lived in Minneapolis for some time. She came of good Orthodox stock. We were married on Rosh Hodesh Tammuz (the first day of the Hebrew month Tammuz), in the bride's home. Rabbi Jaffe of the Ohel Jacob Synagogue officiated. A chazan was also there. His name was Golling. It was a strictly Orthodox wedding. We fasted before the chupa (wedding canopy) on the day of the wedding. We were married on a Friday.

We lived upstairs of the grocery store which I operated on Washington Avenue North. At first we had two rooms in back of the grocery; then we rented five rooms upstairs. I had saved up three hundred dollars when I got married. We kept no budget. But we had enough to eat and for clothes.

Seven children were born there. My wife never went to a hospital when any of the children were about to be born. The same doctor was there for all those children.

During those years my grocery store was always closed on Shabbas. But I went to the market to purchase goods for the store on Shabbas. My wife did a lot of the work in the grocery store. We had a horse and wagon for delivery of our merchandise. We lived there above the grocery until 1906.

My boys went to cheder. It was a private cheder in a man's home. They were taught how to read Hebrew, also how to translate the five books of Moses. It was an old-fashioned cheder, like in the old country. I didn't send the girls. They studied privately.

My boys used to go to shule with me, even to the Selichos services at five o'clock in the morning. The girls didn't go to cheder because it wasn't the style to send girls. Girls didn't study Hebrew in those days.

I think I was a good father. My children minded me. They had to mind me, that's all. I gave them everything they wanted in good and bad times. Even when times were very hard, they got everything.

In 1906 I started buying damaged or unclaimed freight from the railroads. My brother-in-law and I decided to come together as partners. We opened a store at Sixth and Hennepin. We worked the business up very nicely. Then we went into the wholesale end of the business. Things were very good.

Of course we kept the dietary laws at this time. But our place of business was open on Shabbas, although I used to go to the synagogue every Shabbas and come down to the business after the service was over.

Before I started in the grocery business, I used to study Gemarah after 6 P.M. in the shule with several other people. I always liked it. I wore a little beard, a goatee, in those days. I shaved it off on my first trip to New York, where I went on business. I did so because people used to laugh at me. They just weren't wearing any kind of beard.

I never studied English at any kind of school. I had just enough time to earn as much as I could for my family. I had many debts to pay. Besides in those early days they didn't have any Americanization classes for me. I had applied for my citizenship papers about the second year after I arrived here. I became a citizen as soon as possible. I was proud that I served on the jury many times.

We finally moved to another house. I had purchased two houses. I rented out one and we lived in the other. Three more children were born there. The business prospered. We had a cottage at one of the lakes not far from Minneapolis, and in the summer time the whole family went out there, that is, my wife and the girls. The boys were either going to school or working during the summers. Of course, all the children went to public school and then to high school. Three of the children went on to the university. Two of my daughters became school teachers. Another daughter became a social worker. Three sons went to the university. One graduated from law school; another became a doctor. The other boys were interested in my business.

Although I studied Talmud at the Ohel Jacob Shule, I was never what you might call a member there. I joined the Fourth Street Shule to which Rabbi Silber came later. That synagogue became the Kenesseth Israel Synagogue later. I kept on my studies of Gemarah whenever the time permitted until I started doing such a large business in 1928 that I just couldn't spare the time any more.

My oldest son was Bar Mitzvah at the Kenesseth Israel Synagogue. He knew Chumosh with Rashi (the five books of Moses with commentary). He never went to the Talmud Torah (the modern Hebrew school). He studied with a private teacher. He recited the haftorah (the prophetic portion of the week) and delivered a speech before the congregation, and then I invited the whole congregation to come home with me for kiddush (sanctification of the wine) and refreshments. I remember that I was angry because my mother-in-law took it on herself to invite her friends to that Bar Mitzvah. They took too much authority. I was active in the Kenesseth Israel Synagogue. Later I became president of that synagogue and was in office for thirteen years.

I think that I gave liberally to all causes, certainly to all the visiting rabbis from overseas. They all used to come to see me after they came to town.

When my other sons became Bar Mitzvah, I didn't make quite as much of a celebration over it as I did for my first son. We made a b'rocho (blessing over the wine) in shule and that was all.

For a time we had a room fixed up in the newer house into which we had moved, for study. It was the children's study room. I engaged a private teacher, and he taught the boys as well as the girls Hebrew. Later my younger sons went to the Talmud Torah.

One of my sons was quite a businessman in his own right when he was only ten years old. After school he got a job selling candy in a theater. He would come home very late. He received many lickings for doing that, but he just went on. Nothing could stop him.

My home was always strictly Jewish even though I didn't keep Shabbas because of the business. At home Friday night, the beginning of Shabbas, was always special. There was special food. Everyone dressed up for Shabbas. It was fine. Friday night was always family night at our home. Even through all these years, all the children gather with us for Shabbas dinner and to hear kiddush.

Some people may think that I have changed over the years because I do not do things the same as I used to. I didn't really change. I was always doing the things that were done by everybody else in my neighborhood or the people I knew. I followed the majority, that's all. When I was president of the shule, I went with the crowd. I didn't even in those days believe everything the older folks did. Of course, I have always observed the dietary laws. That's simply because I'm used to it. Let my children do what they want. If you stop to question everything, it's just no good.

In the early days no one asked the reason for every religious question they followed or were supposed to follow. People used to say, "You mustn't ask," so we didn't ask. We just had faith — that was enough. You can't learn faith. Today people want to know the reason for everything. That's why it's no good.

People growing up in this country are living more American lives. The old folks are dying off. This generation isn't any worse from the point of view of the way it lives than the earlier generation. Today they go to schools and universities and they just know more. Children do what they think is right when their parents die.

I think that the old type of synagogue, the Orthodox synagogue as I knew it, just isn't good for young people. They need the newer type of modern synagogue. Otherwise they just won't come at all. Not so many years ago we wouldn't think of kindling the lights in our home on Shabbas because it was against Jewish law. We used to have a Gentile turn off the lights for us. Today the whole world has changed and everybody, I think, thinks nothing of turning on lights on Shabbas.

Another thing that has changed is the establishment of Talmud Torahs. Maybe it's better that there are such modern institutions. Time will tell if our young people are better Jews because of them. I think that it's a good thing that there are Sunday schools for our children today. The synagogue should be what I tried to make the Kenesseth Israel Synagogue, the second home for the people.

There are ever so many changes in the lives of this generation from the way it was in the past. Formerly everybody spoke Yiddish. Today our children certainly don't speak it as a regular thing. They have almost forgotten it. In the early days in this community, many women wore sheitels (wigs) in accordance with the practice of shaving off the bride's hair before marriage. Today no one wears such a thing. Formerly everyone prayed every day, or at least most people did when I first came here. Today they just don't. I remember that when one of my sons was attending university, I found out that he hadn't been praying in the mornings, and I slapped him because of it. We used to call our children by their Hebrew and Yiddish names. That stopped when the teachers in the public schools actually gave our children American names. In early days here we used to make the motzi (grace before meals) at every meal. My children don't practice that. Another change I can think of is that when there was a circumcision ceremony, we would have the mohel (a Jewish person skilled in the rite of circumcision) perform the ceremony. Today I think that most people have regular doctors. People used to come to shule in early days to give their daughters and sons names in the presence of the congregation. I think that few people do these things today.

I can think of other changes too. In our early days here funeral services were conducted for practically all but the very finest, pious people in their homes. A eulogy was never delivered except for the very righteous. Today everyone gets a eulogy and some very unworthy people are even brought into synagogues for their funeral services. Maybe, though, it's better this way.

Yahrtzeiten (observances of the anniversary of death of members of one's family) were always observed. Everyone observed it. Today ever so many people either forget it or have someone else say kaddish for them. There used to be no embalming. Today practically all bodies are embalmed, even though it's against Jewish law. And they bring flowers to funerals today, another custom that was forbidden. Today every young Jew seems to like sports. In the early days that certainly wasn't true. In fact we got rid of a rabbi here because he used to like to ice skate and ride horseback. People weren't used to those things in their rabbis, although there was really nothing wrong. We used to have study groups in the synagogues of 50 or 60 people right here in Minneapolis. Tell me where they are today?

Not so many years ago children listened to their parents. There was real discipline. Today parents are relegated to an inferior position by their children. In the early days people entertained by visiting with their friends or playing a friendly game of cards. Today they spend so much for entertainment, and they don't enjoy the same kind of entertainment we did. I don't think that many people keep kashrus (the dietary laws) today the way we used to in the early days.

Of course there were freethinkers in those early days as well as today. They were the people who came over from Europe trying to rid themselves of their Jewishness as quickly as possible. But they were only a small group.

THE SCHOLAR BECOMES A MERCHANT

I think that most of the differences of which I am talking are due to the influence of American schools. The children would go to school, listen to the teacher, and then wonder why the home wasn't like the teacher said. First they would wonder, then they would try to make it that way.

Despite all these changes, I do not think that Judaism is dying in America. I think that Orthodoxy is losing ground very quickly, but I think that the Conservative movement is helping to keep Jewish life up very nicely.

Of course, my children are all grown. Practically all of them are married and have their own families and homes. They do things differently from the way my wife and I did them. But I think that they're not such bad Jews, everything considered. They're also good Americans.

HANNAH, DAUGHTER OF MORDECAI

I am one of a large family of children. I was born in the home of my parents, which was located above a grocery store owned by my parents. I guess that it was still not considered safe to bear children in a hospital. The fears of the older generation with respect to the danger of dying, if brought into a public institution like a hospital, were still very great. Certainly my mother never thought of bearing children in a hospital and would have refused to do so had her physician suggested it. I was born just before the turn of the century.

As I have indicated, my father owned a small grocery store. The store was located in the heart of the Jewish neighborhood, on Washington Avenue North just off Fifth Street. My father would see to the buying and would take care of the deliveries. His customers were located in various sections of the city and practically all of them were Jewish. My mother was a very important member of the firm. She spent a great deal of her time in the store, waiting on the trade and taking care of the books and, I suppose, making small talk, which was a very important matter. Storekeepers in those days knew all about the personal lives of their customers and were just as apt to advise on all personal matters as they were to take the grocery orders.

Despite the fact that my mother spent so much of her time in the store, we were certainly not neglected. The older children cared for the younger ones. Then too there was my grandmother, who lived with us. She was a real matriarch. She was my father's mother. We all loved her very dearly and she looked out for us almost as much as my mother did. I think that during those early years of my childhood, I remember my father more vividly than I do my mother. Mother always was so busy, between the store and the house. All our clothes had to be cared for and everything had to be left in shape for us children and my grandmother to take over. My mother went into the store after we children got off to school each day. I remember my father more clearly because he was always bringing us little presents, sometimes clothes, and my sisters and I, to whom he was partial, enjoyed the many gifts he gave to us. I remember Dad taking us to the Bijou where we would enjoy the plays and the vaudeville. Just as Dad favored the girls, so mother favored the boys. Nothing was too good for us. Our home was far from elaborate. You may well imagine that a grocer trying to earn enough to meet the household expenses for a large family of growing boys and girls would hardly be in a position to have any kind of luxuries around the house. The older children passed on their clothes to the younger ones. It was seldom indeed that the younger members of the family ever got new clothes.

Dad was very strict with his sons. He watched over them and really dictated to them. He saw to it that they studied their Hebrew lessons and that they did all the assignments given them by the Hebrew teacher who used to come to our home to teach us. He was always watchful about the hours they kept. He was concerned about when they went out and with whom and when they returned home.

Yiddish was the language used most frequently by my parents. They spoke Yiddish between themselves, though they used

English in speaking to us. We, of course, always spoke English, though we understood Yiddish very well.

Though we knew many other children and liked other people, we always seemed to be happiest among ourselves. The children always got along together exceedingly well. The girls usually associated with the girls and the boys with the boys. As we grew older we became even better friends. We really were a family in the best sense of the word.

We were so close together in age that four of us actually started public school together. After all, our parents were not as strict about public school in those days because the schools themselves weren't really too strict. There had been some illness which delayed several of us from getting started in school at an earlier age. But it didn't take long after we started going to school for us to find our proper levels. We all got along well in school. My parents had a very healthy respect for education. My mother had attended public school classes, that is, she attended elementary school. She never got as far as high school. She never lost her foreign accent, despite her school experience. But that must be laid to the fact that her associations were always with persons who were themselves of foreign origin.

During our early public school days, business improved and the family increased in size. So we moved to a nicer and much larger home, which my father rented at first and then later purchased.

You may well imagine how much my parents thought about education, when I report that one room of the house was fitted out as a classroom. We used this room in which to do our homework. We also used it for our Hebrew lessons. The Hebrew teacher used to come to our home to teach us. We did not yet attend any organized Hebrew school. My father still believed in the direct method of teaching which he had himself used when he was a student in Europe. There were desks in the room. We never studied Yiddish, though we did study Hebrew. We learned to read our Hebrew prayers and we learned simple translations as well as simple portions from the Bible. Of course, it was the Hebrew text of the Bible from which we studied.

To get back to the matter of the Yiddish language, Mother always spoke to us in a Yiddish that was mixed with English words. My grandmother always spoke Yiddish to my parents and to us. Father did not speak Yiddish to us though he did use that language in talking to mother. But Dad always used to read the Yiddish newspaper. That was his only way of keeping up with the events which were of concern to him as a Jew. Of course, he used to read the English newspapers too. But he was more completely at home with the Yiddish press which was published in New York City and which could be purchased in Minneapolis. I remember that I did so well in my Hebrew lessons that they used to speak of me as *Die Frume,* that is, the "religious one."

Each of the children had friends outside the family, boys and girls of our own age. But basically, our family relationships were so fine that we just took it for granted that we were closest to our own brothers and sisters.

About that time the business had expanded. Dad had gone into another business, an expansion of the grocery business. And before we knew it, Dad was doing quite a big business. This business necessitated his traveling a good deal. At that point mother came back into the home on a full-time basis. She was out of the business and she then began to devote her full time to the care of the home and her large family. My grandmother was still there, helping us all.

Mother never did the laundry at home. It was always sent out. I guess there were just too many of us to have it done at home. Mother had the help of a colored woman who came in from time to time, especially on Fridays, in order to help prepare for the Sabbath. The Sabbath was something extra special at our home. Mother always prepared her special delicacies. There was always fish and chicken and kugel (pudding) and all the other dishes we liked so well, all the traditional dishes, prepared with extra special care. The house was always immaculate. The Sabbath candles were lighted. The kiddush was always chanted by my Dad over the wine. And we all loved it. About the only time mother went out from the house was on the Sabbath, when she went to the synagogue, or on the other holy days when she would go out to visit or just take a walk.

I shall never forget the Saturday night baths which we children took. We used to line up for the baths. Mother used to wash the girls' hair. It was an exciting night around the house.

The house we lived in at that time was really a great big house. It had to be to take care of us children. It was very modern for those days. We used gas. We heated the house with a coal furnace. We had hot water and inside plumbing. The big family dining room was the center of the house for us. Mother knew the special foods each of her children liked and she always saw to it that the children had exactly what they liked. Our clothes were always made by a dressmaker, that is, for the older ones. Then, when the clothes became too small, they were passed on to the next in line.

None of us children was ever given an allowance for spending money such as I give my own children. Money was provided when we needed it but only as we needed it.

Mother used to attend the parent-teacher meetings. She was very good in arithmetic and used to help us with our homework.

There was very little quarreling in our home. As I look back at those years, I think I understand now why we got along so well together. It was because of my mother's philosophy, which was *Alles mit Guttens,* that is, "do everything in a kindly spirit." We used to hear her use the phrase regularly. And it may be that the phrase and its implications sank in.

Of course, that did not prevent my Dad from exercising his disciplinary measures. He never lifted a finger against the girls. But he did, on occasion, spank the boys. He really made them toe the mark. It was always interesting to see the boys march off to the synagogue with Dad on a Sabbath or on the holy days.

He watched over them very carefully. Whether or not this method was better than mother's, I do not know. Mother was strict in her own way. She knew when to be strict. She exerted a great influence upon us all. She exerted a great influence upon my Dad, though I suppose he would hardly have wanted anyone to believe that he listened too closely to what she said. He believed that this was really a man's world. Even when he went into his new and larger business, mother still knew what was happening and would offer her advice, even though he didn't always listen as carefully.

Mother lived for her husband and her children. She put herself into second place. She would never think of getting new things or doing something special for herself if she felt that any child of hers wanted anything, or if her husband was in need of advice or counsel. But she never imposed herself or her views upon him or upon us.

Dad's horizon broadened when he went into the new business. He was traveling a good deal. He met some of the big businessmen in the country. He visited many new and interesting communities and he liked that kind of life. Whenever he returned from one of these trips, he would always bring us, the girls especially, extra nice gifts.

The social life of my parents was centered in the synagogue. My father had become a very important member. He had even assumed office in the synagogue, and later he became the president of one of the largest Orthodox synagogues in Minneapolis. Dad was always bringing people over to the house for dinner. Many of the synagogue meetings took place in our home. Important Jewish people from other cities or other lands would be our guests. Mother enjoyed being the hostess. We enjoyed the excitement.

When we were young, Dad arranged for us to spend the summers at a lake resort about twenty miles from the city. Mother did her own cooking and baking out there. She was very exact about the observance of the dietary laws. The girls would spend all summer with Mother. The younger boys would be with us too. When the boys grew old enough to help in the business, they would stay in town with Dad and drive out, first with a horse and buggy and later with an automobile. Those summers were really glorious. Our cousins and our friends would visit with us out at the lake. I think that Mother used to spend all or most of her time just looking out for us, cooking, working. But she loved it. I never heard her complain.

Yes, mother was a homebody. She lived for her family and her home. Perhaps that is why she never quite lost her foreign accent, though she used to speak English very well. The people who knew her, our Jewish neighbors and the few non-Jews with whom she came in contact, all liked her very much. Of that, I am very certain. She was always so friendly. There was always a very pleasant smile on her lips. She carried herself erect and she was a very handsome woman with clean-cut features.

We children always had our special jobs around the house. We were all assigned to special duties. There were rooms to clean, beds to make, stairs to wash, woodwork to look out for, and so on. The older girls supervised the younger ones. Even the boys were expected to take care of their own rooms.

All the boys had newspaper routes. They always wanted to earn extra money and they followed the general practice of selling newspapers by delivering them on their particular routes. My father not only did not object, he thought this was a good idea. As I look back, I believe that he was right. Since their public school days, each of the boys earned his own spending money. Of course, they attended school. All of us went through high school. Several of the boys and girls graduated from the university and two took graduate work in preparation for professional careers. Two of the girls became school teachers. I was one of the teachers. In addition, we all studied Hebrew. For a considerable amount of time we studied Hebrew under private tutors at home. Then, when the Hebrew school system became

well established, several of the boys attended and were graduated from the city Hebrew school.

Dad, despite his strictness, was really a lovely person. We
not only respected him, we truly loved him. He was always sweet,
soft-spoken, mild-mannered, and really genteel. He had many
of the characteristics that were associated with the Old World.
I suppose he acquired his notion about strictness and discipline
from the Old World. But through it all, he was very close to
his sons and daughters. I would not say that he was always
up to date. He had little mannerisms that were definitely not
modern. For example, he believed that he ought to go to the
synagogue with the boys. He never took the girls to the Sabbath
services. We girls, even on the high holy days, would just run
into the synagogue for a moment and run right out again. We
would run up to the women's gallery in the synagogue, where
our mother and grandmothers prayed, let them see that we were
there, and then we would run out again. Dad used to sit with
his sons in the very first row of the synagogue. That was regarded as an important position in the synagogue.

I remember that in my early childhood, Dad used to have
a little Vandyke beard. But over a period of time that beard
kept getting smaller and smaller, until one day it disappeared
completely. Dad always retained his mustache, though.

Despite the fact that our home was kosher and all the ritual
and ceremonial was observed in the home, all of us children
gradually began to eat nonkosher foods. I do not think it was
ever done in the spirit of rebellion. Rather, it became the natural
thing for us to do when we were at school, or when we began
to work. Even during our school days we never stayed home
from school except on the most important holy days such as the
New Year and the Day of Atonement. I suppose both mother
and dad knew what was happening but nothing was really ever
said to us about it. We just followed all the rules and regulations within the home. Now that we are married, three of us
have kept our homes kosher, using meat that is prepared in

accordance with Jewish ritual and not mixing milk and meat dishes at the same meal. With one exception, even those who now keep kosher homes, eat out and do not observe the dietary laws outside their homes.

None of us children ever attended Sunday school classes, except for one of my sisters. I think the reason for that is because the Orthodox synagogue did not have such classes. The only Sunday school my father finally sent my young sister to was the Reform temple. There was a Sunday school in a Conservative synagogue. But my Dad, at that time, did not like the Conservative synagogue because it was a kind of modern Orthodox institution and with him it was "either all or nothing."

We girls, however, used to attend the classes conducted by the ladies of the Reform temple in what was called a settlement house. We learned how to sew. And we also took music lessons. Several of the children learned to play the piano and the violin. All in all we were really very busy youngsters.

Throughout our school days we got along very well with the other pupils, both Jewish and non-Jewish, and our teachers, who were all Christians, seemed to like us very much.

There were very definite social classes in our younger days. There were the educated Jews, who constituted the aristocracy of the North Side community, and the unlearned. Of course, the learned were those who knew Hebrew, the Bible, and the Talmud. The others were looked down upon. Because of my father's background and because my mother's parents, who also lived in Minneapolis, were regarded as among the learned, our family was regarded as "select."

I didn't start dating until I was a senior in high school. Dad never believed that it was right for us to go out. And if and when we did, we had to be in early. I remember that once a boy invited me to go to the movies. But I had to be home by nine o'clock. I had no Jewish boy friends at high school. My friends were non-Jewish. In fact, most of the children had a great number of non-Jewish friends. But with few exceptions, we didn't invite them to our home. I suppose this was due less to a dislike or fear of the non-Jew than to the fact that most of these friendships were so casual. We really were so self-contained within the family group. As we grew older, I know that my brothers invited their non-Jewish friends to the house and were really very close to them.

During our summer vacations, after we grew up, we began to work, doing a variety of jobs. But they were the usual kind of things boys and girls do, just to earn spending money.

I still remember the time when I first ate nonkosher food. I was out on a party. One of my brothers was with me. We all went to a Chinese restaurant. Everybody was ordering chow mein, so I ordered it too. I was upset when it was placed before me because I had never eaten nonkosher meat before. But because all the others did, I ate it too. I still don't eat pork, bacon, or ham. When my children were born, I gave them bacon because the doctor ordered it.

In the early days of my marriage, I tried to keep a kosher home. I used to serve the bacon for the children in a special pan. But gradually I started to change things because my husband really didn't care about such things. In fact, he had been reared in a small town and hardly knew about such things as kosher and nonkosher. However, when another child was born to me, I did not serve him bacon. He was managed quite well without it.

When I began to work, during summers, I also worked on the Sabbath. The folks said nothing about it.

When I was in my teens, I used to go to a great number of dances, parties, and on occasion, went to picture shows. I went to these parties with Jewish boys and girls. I do not think that I attended any affair where the gathering was exclusively non-Jewish. We always had a very good time. The relationship between the other members of the family and myself is extremely good and I always think of the family most pleasantly. The many affairs that the Gymal Doled Club used to hold, that is the club which was made up of young men in business and in the professions, used to be attended by these young men and their girl friends. My older brothers used to take me to some of these affairs, and I would, of course, go with many of my other boy friends.

I met the man whom I married at a party. It happened that it was on a blind date. My husband had come from a small town in the Midwest. His family had been Orthodox originally; however, they had moved to this small community and had had very little Jewish background, although he was Bar Mitzvah. I am sure, however, that he had little opportunity to gain very much from the point of view of Jewish information or knowledge.

When the children began to grow up, that is, when they were in their late teens, my husband's family moved to a larger city because the various members of the family had begun to associate with non-Jews and their parents were afraid that they might marry non-Jews. The relationship between these children and their non-Jewish friends had always been most cordial, as had been the relationship between the parents in the community as a whole. I am sure that there was nothing in the entire relationship which would reflect in any way upon the ability of the parents to associate with or to get along with their non-Jewish neighbors. However, there was always the fear that intermarriage might take place, and as a consequence the family moved to the city of Minneapolis.

At no time, however, did the family have a kosher home, at least, so my husband told me. When they came into the larger community of Minneapolis, they proceeded at once to join the Reform temple and attended on occasion. I am sure, however, that basically it was a matter of attending on the high holy days more than on any other particular occasion.

My husband told me that in his early days, in the small town in which he lived, the family had kept a kosher home, but that there had been a mix-up in the matter of keeping the meat and milk dishes separate. As a consequence, the matter of kashrus was soon forgotten. Then too there was the matter of trying to bring kosher meat into the smaller communities. It was a terrific problem because kosher meat was only slaughtered and prepared in the larger communities. The meat would often come in spoiled and would therefore be worthless. All these factors tended to make it impossible for the family to continue to keep a kosher home very long.

To get back to my own immediate family now, we are not what might be called a particularly observant family from point of view of ritual, and yet I think that we do basically maintain a religious attitude. We never used to recite the kiddush at a Friday evening service at home before the Sabbath meal. However, since my sons have attended the Talmud Torah, at least one of them is able at any time to chant the kiddush and that helps us to feel the presence of the Sabbath. I have always lighted the Sabbath candles whenever I was home on a Friday evening. However, it has been the practice with us, over many years, to spend the Friday evening with our parents, when all members of the family assemble, and it makes it a special holiday for all of us.

As for the Sabbath day itself, it was not very much different from any other day, inasmuch as my husband worked. My children, when they began to grow up, also attended school on Saturday or would work. I think that my boys have always enjoyed the Friday evening with the family and the Sabbath spirit to a very great degree. I am sure that my older son, who was in the navy, missed the Friday evening at home to a very great extent. Since he has returned home, he has been especially close to the family. My daughter, however, doesn't seem to enjoy it to the same degree as the boys.

I sent my sons as well as my daughter to the Talmud Torah. I did so for several reasons. First of all, I felt that it was really important that the children learn Hebrew, particularly because I wanted them to understand how to be able to translate the prayers which they recited in the synagogue. And I felt too that because Minneapolis had a Talmud Torah of such excellent reputation it would be too bad if they did not take advantage of this great opportunity. I also sent my children to the Talmud Torah because I knew that my parents, particularly my father, would feel slighted or hurt if I did not do so. As far as my daughter is concerned, she went to Talmud Torah for only a few years. Because she was the only girl in the class, she gave it up after just two years. I do feel that there is a great value in knowing Hebrew, and I know that whatever Hebrew I have acquired has been of extreme importance and value to me through all these years.

I believe that customs and ceremonies ought to be followed, not particularly in so far as the Orthodox manner of conducting them is concerned, but rather in a more modern manner. I like to see to it that children know the value and meaning of such holidays as Chanukah, which comes around Christmas time. I have always tried to have them feel that we would make the occasion one of at least as great significance and beauty in meaning as the Christmas festival. And so, in so far as practically all our holidays are concerned, I think that I have always tried to see to it that our home was especially arranged for the occasion and that in every way there was something beautiful and significant about the holidays.

As far as my family and I are concerned, I think we not only know that we are Jewish, but I think that we feel Jewish. It isn't that we have a particular isolationist point of view with reference to other people, but rather that we have a sense of dignity and I think a sense of self-respect with regard to our Jewishness. I like to observe certain of the customs and traditions of our people. I like to see to it that many of the dishes which we serve at our home are what you might call Jewish dishes, because I feel that all these little values help somehow or other for us to retain our identity as Jews. I feel too that there is something of beauty and value in them in their own right.

My children have never had any feeling of resentment because of the fact that they are Jewish, or because they are members of a minority people. They do, however, feel this dignity of which I speak, and I think that they have accepted their Jewishness in as dignified and fine a fashion as I should like.

I do not feel the need for maintaining the dietary laws in my home. Nor do I feel any need for maintaining them outside my home. I eat in restaurants. I will eat any kind of food excepting those pork products which I have referred to before. I do so because I feel that the whole question of sanitation today is entirely different from what it was in the Bible days. I feel that meats are cured and cared for, and that hygienic arrangements are such that it is no longer required that meat be slaughtered and kept for a particular short period. I feel that the fact that blood is regarded as uneatable in so far as Jewish law is concerned is actually contrary to the fact. I believe that blood retained within the meat is essential both for human life and for its improvement. That is why I like meat rare and do not resent or feel upset because I see traces of blood in the food. I believe that the modern method of butchering cattle is such that I can accept the idea of eating any kind of meat without fear, and certainly I do not feel that by so doing I am any less Jewish than I was before.

I like the observance of the Sabbath, particularly the Friday night meal in association with the family. I think that here is one custom or tradition which surely ought to be maintained as long as I possibly can do so. I think, however, that the Sabbath day ought to be a day of fun, a day of recreation rather than a gloomy day in any respect, and I have always insisted that my family make of the Sabbath a day in which they can really have lots and lots of fun.

You may say that the kind of kashrus which I keep is really no kashrus at all. Yet for me it has some significance. I buy meat from a kosher butcher most of the time. Yet I do not hesitate, on occasion, to buy meat from a nonkosher butcher. I do, nevertheless, prepare steaks or pheasant or other foods which my husband brings home, without any particular compunction. Of course, my parents would not regard this as keeping kosher in any degree, and yet it does not upset me nor has my family ever considered it in any way an infringement upon our particular interpretation of Jewish life.

I think that there is one major problem that does confront us these days, and that is anti-Semitism. To me it is a very serious problem. I know that my children feel it in some degree, although they are quite satisfied with their Jewishness and have never felt a sense of inferiority because of it. They do, nevertheless, run up against the problem every once in a while, and I think that in this community, there are many indications that anti-Semitism is a rather serious problem.

Our social life, however, is entirely free from the problem of anti-Semitism, because we do not really associate in any major degree with non-Jews. That is, we do not have non-Jews call on us, nor do we call on them. This does not mean that we do not have extremely friendly relations with our non-Jewish neighbors, and all around us there are non-Jewish neighbors, as there have been for many years. It does mean, however, that somehow our associations are carried on rather exclusively among ourselves. It means too that in a business way my husband and I find our Christian friends very delightful. When my husband is away from home and I travel with him, we find the relationship with our non-Jewish friends extremely pleasant. Yet somehow it is neither expected nor does it seem desirable that there should be too much association between us in the residential section in which we live. I have always felt that intermarriage was wrong. I feel that it is likely to produce not only the disruption of family ties, but the weakening of basic loyalties to one's people and to one's faith, and I have always opposed it. I am, of course, hopeful that intermarriage will not occur in my own family. As to what would my reaction be, or the reaction of my husband, should intermarriage occur, I cannot at this

moment say. I am sure that I would try to make the best of
the situation, but I think that I would certainly not be very
happy about it. However, my attitude would undoubtedly be far
different from that of my mother, for I know that she would
have felt that she had lost a son or a daughter by intermarriage.
I think that I would try to adjust to the situation. This despite
the fact that I know that I should feel unhappy about it.

I do not know whether anti-Semitism is worse today than it
ever was. Perhaps because of all that has happened since the
advent of Hitler, the situation seems far worse today than I can
recall it during my early youth. I am sure that in my father's
day in the old country the situation may have been at least as
aggravated and as serious as it appears to be today. But as far
as I am concerned, I know that I feel it very much. I am very
much distressed and upset because of the large degree of anti-
Semitism that I see. To me it is a serious challenge and a dangerous sign. What tomorrow will bring in this respect, I do not
know. Except that despite anti-Semitism and despite the many
forms of hatred and prejudice I see about me, I feel that there
is nothing about my Jewishness which ought to make me feel
that I want to put it by the boards. I do not wish in any degree
to give up my identity, even if I could, with my Jewish people. I
shall always have a very great love and a very great respect for
my people.

I want, however, to state that not infrequently I find individuals among our people who do things in public or who say
things that cause me to feel a sense of shame and a sense of
hurt. I somehow or other feel that any Jew who violates an
ethical or moral standard, or who may do anything which in
any way reflects upon the good name of our people, is thereby
reflecting upon me as well, and as a consequence I am very
much disconcerted by these things. I know that when I read the
names of those who have been involved in any crimes, whether
minor or major, I always look for Jewish names. Perhaps this
will be regarded as a weakness on my part. Yet somehow I can-

not avoid the feeling that others, non-Jews, do very much the same sort of thing. Whether they do or not, I feel that Jewish people ought to do everything in their power, whatever that power may be, to exert an influence upon those who may be bringing shame upon our people to change their way of life. Some people, of course, say that no matter what one does, the finger of scorn or the finger of prejudice will be pointed at us, and that the good will inevitably suffer with the bad. That may be true. Yet I am simply expressing my feeling even though it may not be at all logical.

The life which I and my family live is far different, of course, from that which has characterized my parents. My relationship to my husband is a far different one. We are both in charge of our household. Our children look up to both of us, they turn to both of us for advice and counsel. Yet they do regard their father as the master of the home. They know, I think, that I too play a rather important role in the home, and they know that our relationship — and by "our" I mean the relationship between my husband and myself — is a fine one and an understanding one. Because of this fact, they too have a greater sense of security. I think that ours can be regarded as a happy home which, though not purely traditional in form, is at least a good Jewish home, one that has through these years maintained its identity with the Jewish people, which takes pride in the fact that our ancestors made some contribution to the enrichment of society, and which also has helped to enrich our lives. My generation may be less religious in a formal sense than the generation of my parents, but I am sure that it is as sound Jewishly and as loyal Jewishly as my parents' generation.

NATHANIEL, SON OF HANNAH

I'm sure that you will soon discover, as I tell you all about myself, that there is really nothing particularly distinctive about me or my life. I'm very much like any other American boy, I guess. The fact that I'm Jewish won't change the story very much from the story my non-Jewish friends would tell you about themselves.

I was born in 1925 — on the twenty-first of March, to be exact. My birth took place in a hospital. I'm told that we first lived in an apartment building which was owned by my grandfather. Later we moved to a duplex. We lived in that house for a good many years. I recall that my parents saw to it that my sister and I had the best of everything. I recall that we not only had lots of toys, but the very best that my parents and all the family, my aunts and uncles and grandparents, could buy for us. I have very pleasant memories of my childhood.

Ours was a really happy home. My parents were very happy together and things were always kind of easy around the house. I'm sure that no one would call my Dad rich, but he was certainly always able to live nicely and we all had the nice things we wanted.

My mother was never the one to discipline us children with harshness. She certainly never slapped or beat us. I do remember that if we did anything that displeased her, she would say, "Just wait until your father comes home." That meant that if we were to get a licking, it was Dad who would give it to us. And I do remember getting a number of good lickings from Dad. I don't think that I was ever really afraid of my Dad. He wasn't the kind of a person who would ever make us children afraid. But I certainly always had a very healthy respect for him. I mean, there just was no telling when he might get very angry and discipline me. I think though that on the whole I deserved the few really good lickings I got. For the most part both Mother and Dad would talk the matter through with me, and as a result our relationship was always on a very high plane.

You may have gotten the idea already that Dad was really the boss around the house. It wasn't because he was ever harsh or mean to any of us. On the contrary, we all loved him very much. We all, my Mother included, listened to him. We did what he liked. He got the kind of food he liked best. Mother always tried to please him and his word was final around the house. He was the one to make the decisions for the family. He was the boss — no question about it.

When I was a youngster, I went to John Burroughs Elementary School. I do not recall ever having any special problem around the school. I got along well with the teachers. My mother was especially active in the Parent-Teacher Association. I certainly never had any problem because I was Jewish and I never felt anti-Semitism as a problem in any degree.

To get back to my father. I want to be sure that you don't get any wrong impression about him or my relationship to him. When I was a youngster and, in fact, all through the years we always spent much time together. He was certainly a real pal to me. We used to play ball together. When I was old enough for scouting, my father became active in our scout troop too. He was a troop committeeman. My father always has loved nature. He could, if given the opportunity, spend all his time in the outdoors. He loves to fish. He loves all sports. He likes nothing better than sitting in a boat on some Minnesota lake, with his fishing line in the water, waiting for the "big one." And he can handle a gun too. In fact, when he was a child in this part of the country, I'm told that he used to do a lot of hunting and fishing. My father would always take me along on fishing trips when I cared to go. I'm afraid that I was really never the sportsman that he hoped I would be. When I was eleven years old, he took me on a trip to Yellowstone National Park. Once he took me on a three-week business trip out as far as Montana. We really got to be real friends and I know that I enjoyed hearing the comments of the other boys and their fathers when Dad would undertake to make all arrangements for our hikes and camping trips when I was in the scout troop.

Both my parents were born in this country. They are midwesterners by birth. Though their backgrounds are not the same, they certainly cannot be mistaken for anything other than Americans.

I was not conscious of being Jewish until I was five years old. Then I was introduced to Sunday school. I guess I never thought about any differences between my friends and myself from point of view of religion. I suppose that one of the reasons for this was the fact that we really were not very observant of Jewish customs and ceremonies during my younger years. My Dad never recited the kiddush at the Friday evening meal. Except for the fact that my parents would go to my grandparents' home for the Sabbath meal on Friday night, where I used to love to go because there was a holiday spirit which I didn't quite understand, I was not aware of anything particularly Jewish in our lives. My Dad had always worked on Saturday. My mother shopped on Saturday. My father may have known some Hebrew, but very little, when he was a boy. I know that he was Bar Mitzvah on his thirteenth birthday just as other Jewish boys were, but I don't think it "took."

My mother's background was far more Jewish. She came from a home that was quite Orthodox. If she was really more religious than my Dad, I really never felt it. But mother has always had a way of not showing her real feelings about things and I suppose that she would not have wanted to impose her ideas on my Dad. Though she came from a kosher home, we never observed the dietary laws in our home. My parents did attend services in the synagogue on the high holy days. And I suppose they came into the synagogue on other occasions too, but I wasn't really very much aware of that sort of thing.

Yet when I was eight years old, my parents started me in the Talmud Torah, which met in the synagogue building after school hours. Classes were held five afternoons a week, or rather four afternoons, Monday through Thursday. On Sunday mornings I attended Sunday school. Because I was required to attend Sabbath morning services in the synagogue, as a part of my requirements for confirmation, I attended. I think I enjoyed it about as much as other boys. I really never complained about attending. I just took it all for granted.

THE SCHOLAR BECOMES A MERCHANT

We really had a happy home. The relationship between us all, my brothers and sister and my parents, was very fine. We always felt close to each other. I think we were really a family, not just a bunch of individuals living in the same house. I always felt close to the synagogue, too, and to the Hebrew school. I never felt like a foreigner because I attended.

Now that I have grown up, I think I appreciate the Talmud Torah more than I did when I was attending. If I ever have any children, I would certainly want them to learn Hebrew. I think that it did me a lot of good. It made me feel closer to the Jewish people and to my religion and certainly never made me think of myself as someone apart or different from other people. Just as other people have their own particular churches and schools, so I think we ought to have ours.

Not until I went to Talmud Torah did I pal around with Jewish boys. We had never lived in what might be called exclusively Jewish neighborhoods. I think that it was a good thing that I did go to Hebrew school. I am still closest to those boys with whom I attended the Talmud Torah classes. I have found a definite advantage in being able to read Hebrew even if I don't understand everything in Hebrew. It has helped me to enjoy the synagogue service and I use the word "enjoy" advisedly. I like to attend synagogue services. In fact I think I attended rather frequently until I joined the navy where for three years I served during World War II as an officer.

I attended high school and got along very well with all the other boys and girls. Once again I want to make it clear that I never found any conflict resulting from the fact that I was Jewish. I did see occasional instances of that sort of thing but they were never situations which bothered me personally. When I was graduated from high school, I went on to the University of Minnesota. I attended that school until I decided to join the navy. Since my naval experience, which lasted for three years, I have gone back to school and I shall soon be graduated. I hope to get into business of some kind. It may be that I will go into my Dad's business or I may go into something else. I don't quite know yet just what I shall do. I suppose that Dad expects me to go in with him, but I intend to make my own decision when the time comes for me to do so.

I have a great number of boy friends. I never have gone out very much with girls. I just have enjoyed the companionship of the kids with whom I grew up, I guess. All my friends were in the service at the time I was in the navy. What will happen now that we're back about our relationship I don't know. We do see a good deal of each other still, but some of the boys have already married. One of these days I suppose I'll be meeting the right girl, and I'll get married too. But when I do, it will be a Jewish girl I'll marry. I don't believe in intermarriage. It isn't because I feel superior or regard other religions as inferior. It's rather that the family is really very important to me and I know that our family would never be quite the same should I intermarry. I just can't see intermarriage at all.

I suppose you are surprised that I say this because you know that I really haven't been a very observant Jew. That is, I certainly don't observe the dietary laws. I eat milk and meat together. I eat nonkosher meats except pork and ham. I guess the reason I follow this way is because I was brought up that way. There is no other explanation for it. It is just a matter of upbringing, not a matter of religious principle. I *do* eat bacon. The reason is that I was given bacon as a very small child because the doctor recommended it. So I have eaten it all these years. It's just what you get used to, I guess.

Despite what I have said, I think that I am a religious Jew. I sort of feel that people take religion more lightly these days. They just don't seem to have as much time for it as they did in my grandfather's day. I think that the reason is to be found in the fact that our present-day civilization is based upon technology and science rather than upon spiritual values.

When I was in the navy and all over the Pacific and into the Orient, I didn't find that my Jewishness was affected very much.

THE SCHOLAR BECOMES A MERCHANT

All my fellow officers knew I was Jewish but that seemed to make no basic difference in their attitude toward me. I believe, though, that seeing as much as I did of the suffering of Jews, a sudden awareness of what it means to be a refugee made me more conscious of my Jewishness. I think that all the suffering of Jews which I have not only seen but read about has helped to make me more conscious of being a Jew. I don't think that I am aggressively Jewish or anything like that, but I am Jewish and I feel that the suffering of Jews must be of direct concern to me. In fact I think that if those persons who believe that Jews ought to disappear from the face of the earth had any real sense, they would cease their attacks upon Jews. If there were no animosity toward us I doubt if the Jews would be so strongly united.

But I never feel a sense of responsibility for the acts, good or bad, of my fellow Jews. I am not one to read the papers looking for Jewish names in the news and, seeing one, to feel that I have been directly involved just because some Jew may on occasion get into trouble. I don't think that being a Jew is a handicap. Being Jewish is a handicap only as far as one permits oneself to be handicapped by it. I have always set my mind against such an attitude. If I were turned down by some club because I was Jewish I think my answer would be "so what?" I just don't think those things matter. If someone doesn't want to have anything to do with me because I am Jewish, I doubt that it would bother me very much.

Of course, I may be talking this way because I have really never been confronted by the problem of discrimination against me because of my Jewishness. I say that after reflecting over my school days as well as my experience in the navy.

That does not mean that I have not seen discrimination against other Jews. I have certainly seen a lot of it around the university, not by the faculty or the university authorities, but rather by the students themselves. I have seen it in the attitudes of fraternities and sororities and even in veterans' organizations.

249

JEWS IN TRANSITION

Since my war experiences I have become a Zionist. For many years I did not feel strongly about the subject of a Jewish state. That was because I just didn't feel that Jewish aims with respect to Palestine were possible of fulfillment. I never really opposed the idea but it just didn't mean anything to me, one way or the other. I have always felt perfectly secure in America. I am about as American as anyone else in this country. But I am beginning to see signs of anti-Jewish prejudice here in this country as I have seen it through the refugees with whom I came in contact. Today I believe that it "can happen here." For these reasons I feel rather strongly about the need for a Jewish state and that state ought to be in Palestine.

I regard myself as a good American. I also believe that I am a good Jew. I certainly would never want to discard my Jewishness, even if I had the opportunity. My last name is quite Jewish. They tell me that I don't look Jewish. In fact people often think that I am Scandinavian because of my light complexion. But I would not want to change my name or alter it in any way. If people don't like my name, they don't have to.

Since I began going to synagogue and Talmud Torah, many of the traditional Jewish customs were re-introduced into our home. I like them too. I enjoy hearing the kiddush recited on Friday night. Either I or my brother recite the prayer because we really know more Hebrew than my Dad, due to no fault of his. If I had a family, I would certainly introduce these customs associated with the Sabbath into my home. The lighting of the Sabbath candles and these other customs please me.

I think that my Mother's parents have played a very important role in my life. They have helped me to see the nice part of Jewish custom and ritual. And certain other members of my family have influenced me. They had an effect upon my whole life which is hard for me to describe, but I know that it is what I am grateful for. If my parents had lived far away from the other members of my family, I doubt very much if I would have had the kind of Jewish training I received.

THE SCHOLAR BECOMES A MERCHANT

Despite what I have just said, I see a very marked difference between the Jewishness of my grandparents and their children. Of course, I'm only a grandson but it seems to me that the religious feeling that was true of my grandparents just isn't to be found in their own children.

I have always been close to my grandparents. I'll go one step farther. I'll say that I enjoy my grandparents very much. I feel completely at home with them. We visit them at least once a week. But their influence is with us all the time. I don't know whether this tie between the generations is something characteristic of the Jews but I know that I like it. I like family life. I feel close to my family and I feel close to the Jewish people. I guess I'm proof of the fact that one can be both a good Jew and a good American at the same time. I don't think that requires proof, but I just don't see that there is anything to the idea that the two are incompatible.

Chapter 12   Father, Son, and Grandson

THIS is the story of a Rumanian-Jewish artisan, his life in Minneapolis, tensions arising out of the relationship between the son and the father. The son feels a great sense of personal insecurity, which manifests itself in various ways. Though maintaining extremely close ties with his father, the grandson is remote from and unsympathetic to the religious viewpoint of the grandparent.

NATHAN, SON OF FISCHEL

I was born in Rumania, in the town of Botosani, in the year 1861. I lived in Botosani until I was twenty-five, when I left the old country and came to Minneapolis, in 1886. I was married in Europe, and my wife comes from the same town in which I lived. As I recall the town in which I lived in Rumania had a population of about 25,000, which is a pretty good-sized place.

My father had a kind of general store in the town. He sold all kinds of merchandise. He did his business with Jews practically entirely. The Jews, who constituted the largest part of the townspeople, lived in the center of the town. The Gentiles lived on the outskirts of Botosani.

My wife's father was a harness-maker by trade. But her own father had died and she had a stepfather who earned a living grinding salt by hand. We were married when I was twenty-four years old. My wife was eighteen.

As a youth I went to shule (synagogue) every day, morning and evening, as was the general custom. I think that practically 99 percent of the Jews kept kosher in those days. The 1 percent who didn't were some of the very wealthy people, the owners of the big farms. Everybody observed the Sabbath by keeping their businesses closed. I do not remember anyone who kept his business open on Sabbath. It was an all-Jewish town. There were always plenty of minyanim (ten males required for public worship) in those days. A Jew who would work on the Sabbath was regarded as a "goy" (a Gentile).

There were four children in my family. In my wife's family there were thirteen children, but only three grew to adulthood.

Although I said that my father had a store, it was really my mother who was the "businessman." She ran the business. My father just assisted. He used to spend most of his time davening (praying) at the synagogue. My mother ran the family too. But whenever any of the children did anything wrong, it was my father who punished us. It seems to me that all of us children were pretty well under control. There was very little disobedience. My father used to take me to shule with him from the time I was five years old. I even went with him at night to say T'hillim (psalms). I used to go with my father until I was about twelve years old.

I went to cheder (Hebrew school) along with the other boys. I was religious. I wore tzitzis (fringes on the inner garment) and I had payos (earlocks). I don't remember how old I was when I cut my payos, but I did it without my father's permission. I remember that I had to hide from my father when I cut them, I was so afraid of what he might say and do.

My wife, as a girl, had a melamed (Hebrew teacher). He taught her in her home. She also learned how to write and read Rumanian and German. Of course she knew Yiddish. Everyone did. She didn't go to the regular town school because there were classes on Sabbath. She learned how to sew and cook from her mother, as well as from the neighbors. She was one of the people whose family could afford to give her some kind of education.

I learned the tinsmith trade in Europe. Before my son was born, my wife and I decided to come to America. We wanted to earn a better living, and we didn't want our son ever to be a soldier in the Rumanian army. I went to Austria and got a passport, and I came on alone to the United States. We decided to come to Minneapolis because my wife had two brothers who were already living in this city.

I was in Minneapolis about one year before my wife and our six-month-old baby son came over here. I lived on Nicollet Island with one of my wife's brothers. I remember that he gave me three days' lodging, free of charge. Then I found work in a tin factory. I was lucky because I had a trade. Of course I spoke only Yiddish and it was very hard for me to understand, but I got along after a while. I had to quit my first job, though, after three days because I couldn't understand what they wanted me to do and they didn't understand me.

I recall that I did not work on my first Sabbath here in Minneapolis. But the following Sabbath things really happened. I was on the street when a friend of the family whom I had known in my home town came up before me on Shabbas riding on his wagon. "Come," he said. "Go see the town." Here it was Sabbath, and he was asking me to get on the wagon and ride. Well, I didn't know what to do, but I went. I figured that this man, who was much older than I, was riding on Sabbath and that I ought to.

After my first experience as a tinsmith, I decided to go out in the neighborhood to fix tinware. I earned about seventy-five cents to a dollar a day.

My wife's brother used to peddle in the country. They decided that if I was to earn a living, I would have to peddle too, so they took me over to Aaron Goldberg's store where he outfitted me for peddling. He knew all the peddlers. They used to come to him for advice and help. He had a big business. I remember that I first peddled out near Forest Lake. It was then that I first began to peddle on the Sabbath. I forgot about kashrus (the dietary laws). I wore my tzitzis yet for just a short while after that.

We lived on the South Side when my wife and baby came to this city. I peddled for a year after that time.

On the Yomim Noroim (high holy days) I went to shule on

the North Side of the city, because there was still no synagogue on the South Side. They did have a little place upstairs in one of the homes on the South Side, but I wanted something better.

Now there was a man from my home town who was really a fine, pious Jew. He knew how to do most everything connected with a synagogue service. He tried to get a post with the congregation on the North Side, but he didn't get the job because the people who conducted that synagogue were Lithuanians, and they didn't want a Rumanian to get in. People used to say "Litvakes (Lithuanians) are too smart."

There were quite a few Jews already on the South Side, but very few people went to minyan (daily prayer service) during the week. They only went on the Sabbath. Services were first established in a hall on the South Side at which this man Schreiber, of whom I spoke, officiated on the holy days. The Rumanian synagogue was first established in this way. After the hall, they bought a small building and built another one in 1892. In addition to the synagogue, I belonged to the Woodmen of the World and to the Order Sons of Abraham, both fraternal orders. Most of us men belonged.

I peddled in the country altogether about two years. I walked most of the time. Then I graduated. I bought myself a horse and wagon and began to sell fruits and vegetables. We had two children by that time.

We got our kosher meat from the North Side. There was no kosher butcher shop on the South Side in the early days. We also got our milk and butter from the North Side.

I never earned very much, just enough to get by. It was a hard life for all of us, but we managed.

As I said, I never went to any school to learn English. I was working. But my wife heard that all people had to learn English and learn how to read and write, so we got one of the schoolteachers in Adams School to come to the house. She gave my wife lessons.

My oldest boy was growing up. We started him in public

school. I think that I was a good father. I tried to take care of my children. Of course I insisted on discipline. If the children didn't behave, I punished them. My wife says that I was pretty strict. The children used to go to their mother for protection when I got angry with them.

Our home has always been a good Jewish home. We tried to bring up our children to be as good as possible. I tried to help my children when they needed help. We got along on very little money. My wife used to ask me for money whenever she needed it for the family, and she says that she never bought anything unless there was money to pay for it.

Up to the time I had to stop working because of my age, I peddled fruits and vegetables. Later I had a fruit store. The children, even though they went to school, elementary and high school, used to work as newsboys and shining shoes. We always spoke Yiddish in our home. My wife and I are now supported by our children in our old age.

As I look at the Jewish community, I think that their Yiddishkeit (Jewishness) is much worse today than it was years ago here. They give more charity today than they ever did before, but their Jewishness is not as strong.

JONATHAN, SON OF NATHAN

When I was a child, I do not recall that there was ever any religious feeling in my home. Yes, the candles were lighted and they kept kashrus (the dietary laws), but there was never any burning feeling about such things. My parents never said to me, when I started going downtown to shine shoes or to sell papers, "Be sure to eat kosher." It never bothered me very much one way or the other.

My parents both spoke mostly Yiddish around the house. We always talked Yiddish to my grandmother. But aside from that I can't say that there was anything particularly noteworthy in their Jewishness.

We had no books, no newspapers in our home. It's true that

FATHER, SON, AND GRANDSON

I was taught by a melamed (Hebrew teacher) in my home. But I don't think I was impressed with it all.

I went to public school and then on to high school. Most of the kids who had any ambition at all went on through high school. But I never finished high school. So I decided to go to business college and learn to be a bookkeeper. My father gave me ten dollars a month to pay for the course of study. I then got a job in the office of a very large concern. Later when I had earned my degree at the university and had to decide whether or not to give up my job as an office clerk for which I was paid ten dollars a week, my father advised against it.

My father was a strict disciplinarian. I had to turn to my mother all the time. She was our protector. Otherwise we might have gotten more lickings than we did.

I used to go to the synagogue with my father on the holy days. I didn't daven (pray) at home or in the synagogue. I was given tefillin (phylacteries) at the time of my Bar Mitzvah, but I didn't use them.

I was a newsboy, selling papers on the downtown streets of the city from the time I was twelve until I was sixteen. I also used to shine shoes. Sometimes I have nightmares these days, imagining that I am still carrying a big shoeblacking box on my back. Apparently I was ashamed of this way of earning some money. I was fifteen when I shined shoes.

After the job I had as bookkeeper, I got another job with another large concern and earned quite a bit of money. I had expected to be advanced. But when the opportunity came, I was passed by and someone else who had a high school diploma got the job.

At about the same time, a Gentile girl whom I knew played an important role in my life. This disappointment over the job and her urging finally convinced me to try to study engineering at night school. It is of interest that my parents made no objection to my friendship with this girl. She was a frequent guest in our home. My father thought I was stupid for wanting to give up a job where I was making a fair amount of money. This was a point of controversy between us for many years. But I did quit my job, and I went on to night school at the university. I could not graduate from night school until I completed my high school requirements, which I did. So I received my degree and started to practice my profession.

I was married when I was a little over twenty-six years old. I haven't given my children very much of this thing you call "Jewishness" in a formal sense. My children do not fast on the Day of Atonement (although I always do). My children neither speak nor know Yiddish. I haven't provided my children with a Jewish background because I had other things I wanted them to do which I considered more important.

I saw, and I still see, no importance in studying the Hebrew language. They certainly do not observe the dietary laws, nor do they see various Sabbath ceremonials in our home, and they do not practice it in their homes.

Of course, I believe that there is something of value about the Hebraic culture. It kept Jews together. They all felt they belonged to something. However, it kept them from becoming thoroughly Americanized.

It takes a big man to be able to live in two cultures. Most people can't do it. We haven't enough leisure for that sort of thing. We must make a choice. So I feel that we ought to learn just enough of Jewish history, philosophy of our religion, something about the Old Testament, to make us feel that we are the heirs of a certain culture and know its value. I think that this is all that we can expect from the modern Jewish child.

I think that it would be nice if we had observed more Jewish ceremonials in our home. I think I miss that. I miss such ceremonies as the lighting of Sabbath candles. I would like to have my children enjoy them. I think that it is a mistake to drop everything. Yet I believe that the reason I dropped so many things is because it wasn't made meaningful to me when I was a child.

I believe that children should receive a liberal education, that they should understand above all else the meaning of democracy. We need something to be tied to. In Judaism it is Jewish history, not Hebrew, which provided that tie. In American life it is democracy.

My wife and I have a happy home. Externally I'm supposed to be the head of the house. But she certainly has as much influence as I. She isn't as strict a disciplinarian as I am. I used to punish my first child on occasion, but I have never given the others a licking.

Since we were married, my wife has had her own checking account at the bank.

I belong to many different organizations in this city. I belong to a synagogue. I have sent my children to Sunday school. I belong to other organizations in which there is opportunity for me to express my philanthropic interests as well as my interest in young people. I do not belong to any local service clubs because no Jews are invited to join. I belong to certain professional groups and believe that Jews should, as much as possible, participate in the affairs of their community, helping to make it a better community in every way and to make the meaning of democracy of increasing value.

I think that there is need for greater democracy in the Jewish community. I am opposed to seeing the same people run things year after year. It remains to be proved that others are not equally as capable of managing the affairs of our community.

I never experienced any real anti-Semitism in my younger days that can be signified by that term. There was name-calling in my day, but it wasn't particularly harmful. I do not think that the problem of anti-Semitism is to be dealt with by saying that we need more Jewishness. Rather, I believe that we need to teach men how to understand and appreciate *all* peoples more than we do at present. I have always believed that.

I had many non-Jewish friends as a youth, both girls and boys. I think there ought to be as much of that kind of relationship as possible.

I think that I am regarded as a successful man. In many ways I am. My wife participates in organizational life in the Jewish community in a minor sort of way. We have people, many different kinds of people, over to the house regularly. All in all, we are enjoying the good things of life and in my own way I am trying to serve the best interests of America and the Jewish people.

BENEDICT, SON OF JONATHAN

I was born thirty-one years ago in Minneapolis. My parents are well known and, I believe, highly respected Jewish members of this community. Our home was definitely one of the "better" homes in so far as opportunities for us children were concerned, and it may certainly be so regarded in so far as its general standards of culture are concerned. Aside from personal reputations for integrity and honor, my parents have always attempted to give me and the other members of the family every advantage, culturally and materially.

My mother was born in the city of Cleveland and when she was about six or seven years of age, her family moved to northern Minnesota. There are some fine, but smaller towns located in that area. I do not know how much Jewish training my mother received, but in those days, surely, there were few opportunities to acquire a very extensive Jewish background. As for my father, his story has already been told. I happen to know that my father met the girl whom he later married and who is my mother when she came to Minneapolis on a visit. They were married when my mother was quite young.

Through all the years I recall that my mother was really closer to us children than was my father. It is not that he wasn't close to us, but I think that in most instances we turned to my mother. My father wasn't too much of a disciplinarian. He did not punish us physically very much, but he certainly attempted to influence us with his ideas. And as a matter of fact I know that I happened always to accept his ideas and to guide my life by them to a very great degree. My mother, however, was easier to talk to. That may be due to the nature of my father rather than to any particular failing on his part. I followed my father's judgment in most things because what he said usually seemed right to me.

Our home was always a nice place. We had many advantages that money could purchase for us. I think that when I was a youngster I did not bring my friends into the home the way the younger members of the family are doing it today. But that was due to me, not to anything that my parents neglected or failed to do.

I received the usual public elementary and high school training, and then I went to the University of Minnesota for my academic training. I then went on to the Yale Law School and received my law degree after three years. I was graduated some years ago.

My father is a professional man. But I cannot say that he influenced me unduly to study law. I really wanted to study law. His influence undoubtedly helped me to make up my mind on this score, but if I were to do it over again, I believe that I would take exactly the same course.

Our home was never what might be called a religious home. I'm not sure just how religious my father really is. But I know that my mother is definitely less religious and gives the subject less thought than my father. We did not observe the dietary laws in our home. We would see the candles lighted on Friday night on occasion, but I do not think that my mother ever recited the traditional blessing when she lighted the candles. And I am sure that when they were lighted, it was for the beauty of the candle glow rather than for religious reasons. We would light the Chanukah candles at the Feast of Lights some years. Other years we would forget all about it. I was never Bar Mitzvah, but I was confirmed at the religious school. I did have private Hebrew instruction for about three or four months, but today I can't read any Hebrew. I do not think that even when any of the ceremonials were observed there was any particular sincerity involved in so doing.

I went to the Sunday school as I have indicated, but it had no special significance, and I believe that I went just because they wanted me to go. Whether my parents wanted me to go is something about which I am uncertain.

Our family life and relationship was, I think, normal and healthy in all respects. Our relationship to our parents wasn't as close as some I've seen, but it was surely normal. There was never too much of a display of affection. This is in the case of both my father and my mother. My mother was always accustomed to going out to luncheons, meetings, and shopping during the day. She was away from home a good deal because she always had plenty of help around the house. She used to attend meetings of various organizations, go shopping, attend study classes, meet with her friends. Although I have said that she belonged to various local clubs and organizations, she was never, as far as I can recall, an active participant in any of them. She never had a very great interest in social issues. My father, on the other hand, was always interested in various issues of the day.

I never had very many Jewish contacts while I was at school here or away at Yale. True, I did have Jewish friends, but I never thought about the matter of having friends on the basis of whether or not they were Jewish. My Jewishness never bothered me very much. I don't think that I was ever concerned about it particularly. I think that I regard myself as a rather well-integrated person. I have, since my return to the city, been fairly active in Jewish organizations. I don't feel deeply about many causes, however. I work with those who feel they can use my assistance. I work with and for Zionists and Zionism because I think that it's good for our people. I think Zionism and Palestine are needed for our people. I also belong to B'nai B'rith and work along there as best I can. I think that its work is important. But I am interested in it primarily because of the fellowship it affords me. My interest in B'nai B'rith results in a measure from the increase in anti-Semitism that I see round about, and I have a desire to do what I can to combat it.

It seems to me, though, that most of the things that we are doing in attempting to fight anti-Semitism are negative in character. We ought to do something positive, like having the organized Jewish community assist the public authorities in stamping out and driving out any and all Jews who may be involved in wrongdoing.

I think, too, that as a whole the Jewish community has false notions about what is important and what values are worthwhile in life. Far too many think about things material, about clothes, wealth, and so on. They set their standards accordingly. There is a great deal of that type of thinking and acting in this community. I like to judge people on the basis of what they are, their intelligence and sincerity, not on the basis of what money they may or may not have. I'm not interested in making friends on that basis at all, and I don't think I've ever been. Of course there are times when I have to compromise my position, or at least feel that I ought to, when I may stand to lose a client or offend someone in business because of my attitude.

I was married shortly after I graduated from law school. I had known my wife for four years before marrying her. My wife had absolutely no Jewish background. She was reared as a Humanist, I believe. Her training was received in their Sunday school. Our home has nothing of Jewish ceremonialism or anything like that.

I joined the temple (Reform) several years ago. It was the same place I received my Sunday school training. I belong, not for religious reasons at all, but because my friends belong and because it is the thing to do. I suppose my father might have expected it of me. I never attend services except on the high holy days. I would be subjected to much pressure from my friends if I did not attend then. I believe that a very small percentage of the people who go attend because of sincere convictions. I think they and I are motivated by the desire to live up to the conventions of our society.

I have a good number of friends, and I like people. My wife has her friends and sometimes our ideas about people do not agree. She won't ever associate with them if they aren't what she thinks they ought to be. I find it necessary, though agreeing with her on principle, to meet and associate with those who aren't my ideals in any respect.

My father has influenced me a great deal. I have tried to please him, but it hasn't been any sacrifice on my part because I have usually seen his point and agreed with him.

We never used Yiddish in our home. I do not speak it, read it, or write it. My association with my grandparents is very limited. I really do not see very much of them. I cannot read Hebrew at all these days. I have forgotten what I learned, and frankly I really find no real need for the language.

I do not think that there is enough contact between the Jewish and non-Jewish communities. I think we ought to try to find more and more means for participation in the affairs of the community. I would try to break into the work. I am really not very much interested or concerned because there are clubs, service clubs and others, that do not accept Jewish members.

If I had a child I think that I would try to see to it that he got more out of his Jewish training in Sunday school than I did. I would try to have it done right. But the training, on the whole, would not be much different from my own.

I think that the most important thing that my parents have taught me is a sense of honesty, a desire to live honorably and a righteous life. My mother may have emphasized social values and social life to a greater extent than I deem necessary, but she surely participated in teaching me these ideals.

Chapter 13   Intermarriage Is a Problem

A FATHER, of Russian-Jewish background, an artisan, Orthodox in religious thought and practice, is at a loss to understand
a son who, despite early Jewish training in home and school,
intermarries. The son feels himself to be a Jew, wishes to maintain contact with Jewish communal life, is devoted to his father,
and sees no problem in intermarriage.

ISAAC, SON OF SHOLOM

I was born eighty-five years ago, in August 1860, in a little
town in Lithuania. The town, situated not far from Telz, in the
province of Kovno, was small in size. I recall that it consisted of
about five hundred Jewish people with about an equal number
of non-Jews. I lived there until I was twenty-six years of age.
In my town there was a big synagogue, probably one hundred
years old at that time. There was a bes hamidrash (study room),
also a klose (little synagogue). The people of the town earned
their living as tailors, shoemakers, blacksmiths, buyers of grain,
flax, and cattle. These goods would be shipped to Memel for ex-
port. There was no railroad in the town. All goods were carried by
wagons.

There were four children in the family, two boys and two
girls. I was the oldest of the lot. Of course, there were other
children, but they died before I was born.

My father made his living as a merchant, buying and selling.
His name was Sholom Block. I recall that the whole family was
named "Block." I cannot recall any change in the family name
at any time. My father made an honest living. Twice a week in
our town we held a market and farmers would come in with their
supplies. Father would buy from them and then either sell his
goods to bigger dealers in the same town or haul the goods, what-

ever it was, on to a larger town. Father was an honorable Jew. He did his best for his family. He was never a melamed (teacher of Hebrew). He was always a merchant. He went to synagogue three times daily, but who didn't in those days? He was a true believer. Whenever he failed to earn enough to take care of his family, he would say "God will give it to us tomorrow." I don't think that he knew any Talmud. You see, he was an orphan and had no chance to learn. Father was neither very tall or very stout. He was just a good-natured, friendly person. Of course, everybody knew everybody else in that town. He had been born in the town of Kroz and later moved to our town.

I had a real mother. She had been a midwife in Europe. As a girl she had lived in Kelem, just two miles from Kroz, the town from which my father came. My mother was about nine years younger than my father. My mother spoke Yiddish as did all the people. She understood Russian, Polish, and Lithuanian as did my father. She could daven (pray) and could use the Teitsch-Chumosh (the Bible translated into Yiddish with its folklore). People spoke of her as "learned." I don't know just who taught her these things. She was also a very charitable woman. When she had a dollar or two, she would put it in the pushke (the charity box) and purchase some clothing for some poor woman. My mother came to Minneapolis and lived here for about five or six years before she died. She was seventy-five years old when she died here in 1909. My father also ended his days here in Minneapolis at the age of eighty-seven. He died in 1915.

My childhood home consisted of two rooms. In these rooms the six of us, my brother, sisters, parents, and I lived. I remember starting to go to cheder (Hebrew school) when I was six years old. My rebbi (teacher) didn't know Talmud or other higher learnings. He taught me how to read and how to recite Tehillim (psalms). In the winter we would go to cheder at six or seven o'clock in the morning and spend the whole day there, taking lunch along. We would come home when it was dark. When I had learned to daven I would daven at home before I went to cheder. I remember that the rebbi had ten children of his own. On Shabbas I would pray with him. I went to cheder until I was Bar Mitzvah.

The Bar Mitzvah wasn't very attractive in the old country. Nobody made any fuss about it. It certainly isn't like it is here in this country.

I was never able to go to any school but the cheder. I helped my father in his business until I was fifteen or sixteen years old, and then I started to learn a trade. My father's cousin used to build mills which were run by water or wind. I worked with him until I was twenty-one years old. I remember receiving twenty dollars a month and board for my work, which was a great deal in those days. I followed this trade and worked in different towns. And I also had a good time. There was plenty to eat, and I didn't work so hard. I got to know my job so well that I supervised other workers. Traveling around, of course, I got lonesome. Then I would go back to my home town to see my parents. Of course, I don't think that I was ever more than ten or twenty miles away from my home during these travels.

At twenty-one I was taken into the Russian army. I was in the army only nine months. How I got out is interesting. I said that I was sick and they put me in the hospital and kept me there for seven weeks. Then I managed to bribe one of the doctors at the hospital. So they let me go home for a year. After that year was over, I went back for another examination by the doctor and they gave me my discharge. I remember that during my army days, I still kept my tefillin (phylacteries) and wore them whenever I could.

It may appear strange to you that I did what I have told you about getting out of the Russian army. But none of us wanted to serve in that army. When my boy was in the army here (in the United States) I visited him. They treated him wonderfully. But it was different in Europe and especially in the Russian army. Then too I didn't and wouldn't eat trefoh (non-kosher) meat, and in the army they expected me to. I still remember the rations I got while I was in the Russian army — a loaf of hard bread, so hard you couldn't break it, a spoonful of cabbage, a piece of meat on a toothpick. That was what we were given to eat. Then I remember one day they made me slap some soldier. That I couldn't stand. Just think of it! Slapping another man because some officer wanted to punish him.

During my days in Russia I never saw a pogrom. I always got along well with the Christians. In fact I got along well with them in this country too.

I was twenty-two years old when I was honorably discharged. Then I began to think of getting married, and I started looking around for the right girl. I used to travel to the town of Telz and I met my wife there. One of my friends told me about her and about her nice family. I made it my business to see her before she could know anything about what my friend said. She had no father, only a mother. Now in my time boys had to ask their mother and father. But I didn't ask too much. I just saddled up the horse and rode over to her town to see her. I didn't even ask her mother for permission to marry her. But her mother did come over to my town to find out all about me. Apparently I wasn't too bad, for we got married.

Our marriage took place in a private home. Her uncle, who was a rabbi in Telz, officiated. The chupa (marriage canopy) was placed in the courtyard of the shule. I was married on a Sunday even though it was customary to be married on a Friday (for good luck).

Ours was not an elaborate wedding. After the ceremony, there was something to eat and drink. On Monday we all came together again and had a party.

After my marriage we stopped for a time with my parents. I think it was about two years. I was then about twenty-five or twenty-six years old.

Everybody used to say to me, "You're a pretty handy man. You'll make money if you go to America." I thought that I would take their advice, come to America, make a few dollars, and then go back to the old country. But it turned out otherwise. I saved about fifty dollars in order to make the trip to America. I already had a son before I left home. I went to Memel, took the train to Hamburg, and from there I took the boat to America.

First I came to New York. I didn't like it at all. Of course, I had left my wife and baby in the old country. I stayed in New York for one week. I had only a dollar left.

A funny thing happened when I got to New York. It was the Sabbath. An expressman came up to me and took my clothes and the dollar I had left. But even that didn't upset me as much as the fact that for the first time in my life I rode on Sabbath. I went to the home of an old friend from my town. He didn't ask me "Are you hungry? Are you thirsty?" He just made me feel unwelcome. So I looked around for another landsman. He was more friendly and took me over to his home. This friend, Gedaliah, was a real gentleman. When we came to his home, he said to his wife, Leah, "Let's have some food." He took care of me that night. We davened maariv (the evening prayers) and then I went with him to East Broadway where he introduced me to his father-in-law. His father-in-law wore a yarmelke (skull cap). My friend explained who I was and said he wanted to help me. The father-in-law took me into his fine home, where they even had a piano, and gave me room and board through Monday. I remember that Tuesday was Tishah B'Av (the ninth day of the Hebrew month, Av, commemorating the capture of Jerusalem), and I fasted on that day as was the custom.

A Minneapolis man came to New York at that time. He heard that I was there and came to see me. We were from the same town.

I was so poor then that I sold a watch that my wife had given me at our marriage. With the money I bought tinware to peddle in Connecticut. I went with a few other peddlers. We hustled and made out pretty well. Every two or three weeks we would come back to New York. During all that time I spoke only Yiddish, but I guess I was smart enough. I peddled for nearly two years. I saved money. I bought some clothes.

During all this time I still davened every day. I even put on tefillin. I never wore a yarmelke and I never had payos (earlocks), not even in the old country. I always ate kosher food and I never peddled on the Sabbath.

I was about thirty-two years old when I came to Minneapolis. It happened this way. I told a cousin of mine whom I had met in New York that I intended to go back to the old country because I had a few hundred dollars saved up. He advised me instead to come to Minneapolis because he had been there. So the two Weinberg boys who had peddled with me decided that all of us would come to Minneapolis.

When I came here, I tried to figure out what to do in order to earn a living. One of the cousins and I decided to buy some dry goods, get a team of horses and a wagon, and peddle. We bought about seven hundred dollars' worth of goods, but business was no good. Finally I decided to become a junk peddler, and I peddled in the country, stopping in hotels. I always got a private room so that I could daven in the mornings. I really suffered from hunger in those days.

The Gentiles used to treat me fine in the country. I remember one Sunday stopping at a farmhouse and getting the smell of turkey they were having for dinner. I hadn't eaten meat for a couple of months (because I was observing the dietary laws). The folks passed a plate of food to me. It was a great temptation. I remember that my partner ate. He and they urged me to eat, but I didn't eat.

I remember the first Friday my partner and I were out peddling. We came to a farm just before Sabbath eve and we begged the people to let us stay overnight. But they wouldn't, so we stayed in the field. Sabbath afternoon the farmer saw us in the field and drove us out. I remember walking fourteen miles behind the wagon so as not to ride on Sabbath. Yet that couldn't keep up forever. One of those Sabbaths I finally had to ride. I remember never lighting a light on Sabbath. This meant that I was very cold out in the country most of the time. I always wore a tallis koton (a small prayer shawl) under my shirt, since I was a little boy. I still do to this day.

After I was in Minneapolis for two or three years, I finally was able to bring my wife and son to Minneapolis. I brought my parents here about five years after my wife came here. My child was not given his English name by my wife or me. We called him by his Hebrew name. His teacher in public school really gave it to him.

My wife was a very pious woman and a good woman. When she and my son came I fixed up a home at Sixth Avenue North and Washington. It had four rooms. We furnished the house. I was then making a living. It wasn't good, and it wasn't bad. But people didn't need much to live on in those days.

In Minneapolis there were already quite a few Jews. They were nice people. Most had stores, or they were peddlers, teamsters, butchers. I do not recall any shules (synagogues) then. We rented a place above a grocery store on Sixth Avenue North and Second Street. We had a minyan every day including Shabbas. All the people were shomrei Shabbas (strict observers of the Sabbath). At first they had a hall on Washington Avenue around Sixth Avenue North for services on Rosh Hashonah and Yom Kippur. The crowds got pretty big in the place above the grocery store, so we rented a store on Ninth Avenue and Second Street. It was after that that we really started to build a shule.

I used to belong to the Kenesseth Israel Synagogue when it started. I started going there in order to say kaddish (the mourner's prayer) for my mother when she died in 1909. Later I went to the Shaarei Zedeck Synagogue.

I have three boys and three girls. All but one were born here. I tried to bring them up as Orthodox Jews. A lady we knew used to teach the girls. One of my boys went to the Talmud Torah. The older one had a rebbi. The younger one knew Hebrew so well he would even talk Hebrew on the telephone.

My children went to public school. The boys went on to North High School. I provided for them until they graduated. The girls did not graduate from high school.

My older boy used to sell papers while he was at the university. I gave him the money for two years so that he could finish high school. After that he started to make some money by giving lessons in English while he was going to school.

I never attended any Americanization classes. As for my children, when they grew up they went out to work. Of course, there were problems about my children. Things bothered me. My boy ate trefoh (violated the dietary laws). He worked on Shabbas too. We felt very badly about it, but what can you do?

All through the years until 1930, when I developed high blood pressure, I peddled. My wife died in 1929. I have always been a shomer Shabbas (strict observer of the Sabbath) and I have always observed kashrus (dietary laws).

I believe that Jewishness has changed greatly since my early days. America is a good country. Tzedokoh (charity, philanthropy) is the greatest virtue of American Jews. All the rest is lost. I think that for this loss we have to blame the Jewish mothers. Fathers have to work in order to make a living, but if the mothers don't work, why don't they set an example?

I do not see enough of the fulfillment of the Fifth Commandment, "Honor thy father and thy mother." My children have always been wonderful to me. You see my chair over there? It is mine. No one ever sits on it but me.

When my children were small, we spoke Yiddish in the house. All the children spoke Yiddish. They still can speak it and understand it.

In the early days in Minneapolis the Jews and Gentiles did not get along very well. They used to throw stones at us. They thought we were wild people I guess. Today it is much better.

INTERMARRIAGE IS A PROBLEM

People are more civilized today. That's because they go to school today.

My son left to work in another city. It was a place where there were few Jews. You know he intermarried. That fact may account for it.

ARTHUR, SON OF ISAAC

I was born in a little town in the province of Kovno, Lithuania. I was about five years old when my mother brought me to this country. My father had preceded us to Minneapolis by about two years. I had a younger sister who was brought here at the same time, in 1890.

Although I did not begin to go to the elementary public school until I was eight years old, my parents sent me to a cheder conducted by a private party when I was six years old. As a child, until I started public school, I spoke only Yiddish in my home. I studied in the same cheder until I was Bar Mitzvah at the age of thirteen. There were about twenty other children in the cheder also taking lessons. I studied Hebrew reading, translation of the Chumosh (five books of Moses), as well as the books of the Prophets and writings.

Ours was a thoroughly Orthodox home. My father would go to the synagogue with me every Sabbath. It never occurred to me to regard this as unusual because it wasn't really. Other boys did much the same thing, and I did what my father did as a perfectly natural thing. The discipline in our home was of the kind that none of us ever thought about it as discipline at all. My father was probably the boss at the house, but there was no disciplinary problem in the sense that we think of it ordinarily.

My parents never attended any classes for Americanization. I do not believe that there were any such classes in the city then. Yiddish was spoken to us, but English was gradually used as we started going to school. My parents usually used Yiddish when speaking to each other.

As for the discipline of which I spoke, I think it can best be explained in this way: When my father asked me not to play ball on the Sabbath, I just didn't play ball. When he asked me or the other children not to keep company with certain other people as we started to grow up, we just did as he said. We never questioned his judgment. It was perfectly natural for us to obey both his, as well as my mother's, wishes.

I was eight years old when I began to sell newspapers on downtown street corners. Most of the boys who were selling papers were very decent. Seldom did we have any trouble. I will say that the language used by those newsboys was better and more refined in those days than it is today on the part of many children. I think too that the language of the adult was better in those days than it is today. There seemed to be more gentility. Of course, every once in a while some newsboy would get out of hand, but by and large the boys were fine, and I always treasured memories of those days and those boys. They were a good lot of Jewish boys.

With the money that I earned as a newsboy, I bought the things I needed for myself, and I always gave my father the balance. It wasn't much, but it was good enough for a child in those days.

My parents just naturally assumed that I and the other children would get as good an education as possible. There was never any question about our going to school. I had four sisters and one brother by that time.

I attended Sumner School, Blaine School, where I graduated from the eighth grade, and then I went on to North High School. In my class there were sixteen graduates of whom two were Jews.

No fuss was made about my Bar Mitzvah. I had an aliyah (called up to the reading of the Torah in the synagogue) and that was all. I recited the b'rochos (blessings) and that was the whole Bar Mitzvah ceremony.

When I was thirteen I gave up peddling newspapers downtown, and I took a newspaper route. I continued with that work all the time I went to the University of Minnesota. At the start I earned seven dollars a month. Later I earned more. I was a

INTERMARRIAGE IS A PROBLEM

pretty good student at the university. During my undergraduate days I used to teach private persons mathematics as well as English. That supplemented my income and helped to put me through school. I remember that I earned sixty-five dollars a month doing these many jobs.

After I was graduated, I went to work for a large corporation in another city. Through my student days, I never ate nonkosher food. Even when I went out of town for the first time, I managed to live at the home of some Jewish people and I continued to observe the ritual laws.

Later, in 1907, I got a fine position in another city. After several years I was advanced to a position of some prominence. I never encountered any difficulty because I was Jewish. The people there knew that I was Jewish because I had so stated.

There never was a Jewish issue or problem for me in those days. My contacts were simple and my relationship to the people was always very wholesome. I never had a serious problem in those days that resulted from my Jewishness.

Of course, I was not as observant of things Jewish during those days as I had been earlier. Even while attending the university, I observed the Sabbath. I always stayed out of school on holidays, and on those holidays which were traditionally observed for two consecutive days I simply stayed out and that was all there was to it.

Sometime later I married a Christian woman. It may be surprising that I, the son of Orthodox Jewish parents, and myself quite observant of traditional Jewish ritual through all my days, should have done such a thing. I know, of course, that many people will not and have not understood me as a result of this intermarriage. I know how it has affected the members of my own family. My father has grieved over it, I am sure. Yet he does not speak about it to me. The story of my marriage may be interesting.

The lady I married, some eighteen years after I first met her, was a very well-educated person. We first met in the town where

I was working. She remained there for two years and then left for several other communities where she taught school over a period of years. But she returned to my town. We were both interested in each other. I think that the one thing that kept us from getting married all that while was the fact of my Jewishness and her acceptance of Christianity. I can assure you that it was not an easy decision to make. It meant a certain break with my family and friends. It meant some of these things for her as well. But after long hours, days, and weeks of debate and consideration, I decided to ask her to marry me and she accepted. We were married by a Christian minister. I was never married by a rabbi. During all these years, while I was in this small town, I was one of the minyan at high holy day services. I no longer had much of an opportunity to observe the dietary laws or the Sabbath in the way in which I had done as a youth, but I was not opposed in any way to any phase of my religious heritage. To this day I still do not eat pork nor do I eat lobster, both being forbidden according to Jewish ritual. I had put on tefillin (phylacteries) daily until the time I came to this small town. During my university days, I took courses in Hebrew grammar, the Prophets, and another course on the book of Deuteronomy. So you can see that I was not one to oppose Judaism or the Jewish way of living particularly. I had never intended to give up my faith as a Jew.

As I say, the question of whether or not to intermarry was not easy for me to decide. But I finally decided in favor of it. It was understood by each of us that neither was to give up any particular faith. There certainly was no question about my giving up my religion. My wife had been a Congregationalist and she continued to be one in a minor sort of way. The reason for my decision was simple enough. It just came down to this. It was my life. I had my own life to live. I wanted to marry this girl. We had much in common. I never once thought about giving up my way of looking at Judaism. So we were married.

I do not have very much feeling for ritualism in religion. Of course, years ago ritualism seemed very important to me, but all that has changed. I am not violently opposed to it. It just has no great meaning for me. Ritualism does not seem to me to stress the real values that are important to me. I do not believe in formal worship particularly. Of course I am not opposed to it. I do go to the synagogue services, especially on the high holy days. I do believe, however, that *all* religions stress form too much. We need to develop a sense of spirituality rather than ritual. I have thought about the matter considerably, and I have concluded that ritual does not have sufficient effect upon the individual in developing the kind of character or spirituality that is desirable. For that reason I just do not regard ritual as important any longer. I do not seek to impose my notions on this score upon others. I just feel that with my life I do as I please.

I still feel myself very much a part of the Jewish people. I am proud when Jews generally are proud of some achievement or accomplishment. I am hurt when my fellow Jews are hurt.

I believe that through the years Judaism has actually become stronger than it was in many respects. I see that strength in the more positive expression of real values on the part of Jews. There is less stress generally upon rules and ceremonies. There is an increase in national sentiment and feeling.

The increase in solidarity of Jews may have resulted — in fact, I am sure that it has resulted — from the effects of Hitlerism upon the people generally. The more people have to overcome, the stronger they seem to become, the greater appears to be the strength that is theirs to overcome the evil that threatens them.

I have always believed that Hebrew as a language should be retained as part of the synagogue form of worship, and I feel that Jewish children and adults ought to make every effort to know the language. I feel about Hebrew as the Swedes feel about Swedish. They ought to know the language of their people even while knowing the English language. I have never regretted studying Hebrew.

The problem of our relation to the non-Jewish community is

graver today than ever before. There is a serious threat to us, and it ought not to be overlooked. I see instances of it ever so often. Sometimes in my work I find that discrimination against Jews is being carried on even by those who have what are generally considered high educational standards. I see it manifested in discrimination in clubs. I am reasonably sure that even today Jewish people would have a hard time getting placement in businesses operated by men of high intellectual attainment. Jews have all the necessary qualifications, but unless there were dire need I do not think that they would be accepted very readily.

Chapter 14   German-American Family

Born in America, of German-Jewish parentage, the grandfather believes himself to be different in some way from East European Jews. He still speaks of the early immigrants as "refugees." Though regarding himself as a Jew and associated with the life of the early Jewish community, he has ceased to practice many of the customs and ceremonies that he knew in his parents' home. His son, with little Jewish education, is troubled by a sense of insecurity. He moves farther away from Jewish group life and devotes himself, with increasing fervor, to those movements that will help to label him as a "good American." The granddaughter, who has received no Jewish training, feels the need for closer ties with Jewish people and resents the emphasis upon country of origin of her fellow Jews which still seems to be important to her parents.

SAMUEL, SON OF ISRAEL

I was born in the city of Albany, New York, in 1862. The family from which I come is of German origin. The home from which I came was quite religious. My mother had an absolutely kosher kitchen. We observed the Sabbath too. There was no cooking done in my parents' home on the Sabbath. The observance of the dietary laws included the use of two sets of dishes for meat and milk products. I attended the public schools in Albany and was admitted to the bar to practice law in that city. However, I was one of those who wished to follow Horace Greeley's advice, and I decided to go west immediately after passing the bar examination.

I had originally intended to go to Mandan, North Dakota, where I had a friend who had come from Albany. I thought later that I would go on to Bismarck because I had a cousin in

279

that town. I got as far as St. Paul, where I met an uncle of mine who was interested in land settlement in this area. He influenced me to stay in this section. He said that because I was an attorney he could give me some business and get me acquainted with people who might help me get started. So I decided to practice law here in Minneapolis. I was the third Jewish attorney in this town.

I came here alone. That is, the members of my immediate family did not come with me.

As I recall the scene in 1883, when I came here, there were not really so very many Jews. There were three divisions of the community. The most prominent Jews, who came here in the early seventies, a group of about twenty-five or thirty families, were mostly of German origin. They were engaged in various businesses. As I recall it, they were clothing merchants (some had very fine businesses in the center of town), dry goods merchants, jewelers and pawnshop owners, owners of liquor stores, cigar merchants and makers, and one lithographer. There was one very fine attorney with an excellent reputation. You will recognize the names of some of these families because many of them are regarded as the old-timers of Minneapolis. They were such families as the Reeses, Rothschilds, Weiskopfs, Segelbaums, Nussbaums, Weils, Sam Jacobs, Harpman and Gronauer, Abrahams, Max Wolff, Pflaum, Mikolas, Kayser, Ed Bernstein, Isaac Buxbaum, Henry Deutch, Joe Jonas, Sam Alexander, Weisman. With but few exceptions, this group was all of German-Jewish origin, though most of them did not come here directly from Germany. They had lived in other sections of the United States before they came here. There were, among these families, a few Jews of Polish origin. But their number was not very great proportionately. There was another Jewish attorney in town but his reputation was not good.

The outstanding Jewish person in the city in those days was Mr. Segelbaum. He was truly a fine man. There was, excepting for the temple, no Jewish organization in those days, except one voluntary body to help the refugees (the immigrants from Russia).

We had a social club in those days which we called the Apollo Club. It was a private club, limited in membership to the group I have just mentioned. It had its own club rooms on one of the upstairs floors on the corner of Second Street and Nicollet Avenue. It had about forty or fifty members. I would call it a club for card-playing mostly.

The temple had already been organized. It met in a frame building on Fifth Street, between Marquette and Second.

In those days there were no pavements in Minneapolis. There were wooden sidewalks. The town had about 50,000 people. There was one car line. The University of Minnesota had only one building.

There was quite a colony of Rumanian Jews. For the most part they lived on the South Side of town around Franklin Avenue and Fifteenth. They had some nice people among them, notably, Joe Schanfeld and the Harris family.

None of us Jews ever engaged in the banking business, nor were we in the milling or lumber businesses. We never got anywhere near the really big businesses of this area. We did not belong to civic organizations. The Jewish people never stood very high with the non-Jews even in those days. As an attorney I had non-Jewish clients and friends, but on the whole, excepting for business relations, we never saw very much of our non-Jewish neighbors.

In those early days the temple had a Sunday school. It was started when the temple moved to Fifth Avenue and Tenth Street. My sister, who came here with my mother after I was successfully located and with whom I made my home, taught in the Sunday school. I do not recall that any of the families with whom I was acquainted had kosher homes. I never observed it except in my own home. We certainly had no mezzuzahs on the doorposts of our home. I do not recall many of these homes where the kiddush was recited on Friday evening at the beginning of the Sabbath. We had no study groups for adults. Nor do I know any of this group who put on tefillin (phylacteries).

Most of the people to whom I refer were not affluent. Only one family owned a horse and buggy. People lived in rather large houses of seven to nine rooms. But their rent was very small. Most marriages took place in the homes. There were no inter-marriages in those days, except for one case, that I can think of.

The people certainly did not speak German to each other. They all spoke English. Our children received typical Ameri-can names though many of the original group had truly biblical names, such as Simon, Isaac, Samuel, Joseph, Abraham. Our children attended public schools and received their Jewish edu-cation in the Sunday school. Boys were Bar Mitzvah at the tem-ple. Boys left school earlier than the girls in those days because it was expected that they would learn some business.

We used to do a lot of visiting among ourselves in those days. We had card games on Sunday nights. There was ladies' night once a week at the club and there was dancing. On Rosh Hashonah most Jews held open house. All places of business were closed on both Rosh Hashonah and Yom Kippur.

The anniversaries of death (yahrtzeiten) were strictly observed. We did not embalm the remains in those days. We used plain coffins and there was never any music at funeral services. We always had a minyan (ten males for public worship) when one of the group passed away.

The rabbis of our congregation played no important role in the community, and I think I can say in all truth that the Jews paid little attention to them. They were "offish." We really hardly knew them. I think that the function of the rabbi has changed and improved wonderfully since those days, in so far as his relationship to both the Jewish and non-Jewish communi-ties is concerned.

I was married here in Minneapolis in 1892.

An example of the degree of our religiosity in those days may be gathered from the way in which we observed the Passover. Although we all bought matsos, we didn't all observe the Passover strictly. I think, however, that most people did not eat out during the week of Passover, but went home to eat.

The Jewish people in those days were largely isolated. They did not mingle to any great extent. I think that we always had as much anti-Semitism in those days as we do today. The anti-Semitic situation became worse for us here after the refugees began coming to Minneapolis. People used to throw rocks at them and call them sheenies. Some never shaved and some dressed different, and that was the cause of it.

I was an attorney with a fine practice, and I had, as I have said, many non-Jewish friends. Later I was elected to the state legislature of Minnesota. But in all fairness I must say that I found that Jews seldom got a fair verdict from a jury here.

Although I had studied Hebrew five days a week up to the time of my Bar Mitzvah in Albany, I never thought much of Hebrew, and I didn't teach my children any Hebrew. They went to Sunday school. I think Hebrew is a dead language. We are living in an age when there are too many important things to bother about it. There isn't such a great amount of religious feeling in any of us, I guess. But I have always believed in God. My faith in Him is still strong.

I believe that our synagogues and temples are functioning far better today than they did. I believe that there is greater respect for the Jew in certain quarters of our community today than there was in those early days.

HENRY, SON OF SAMUEL

I was born in Minneapolis in 1893 in a house on Linden Avenue, which is located just a short distance from the Catholic church. I recall that it was a corner home. It was a very large house consisting of some twelve rooms. It must have been one of the fancy homes in the city before that time. It was still a very beautiful and impressive home when I was a child. We used gaslight and we heated the house with coal. There was also inside plumbing. I recall that the front walk of the house was cement, but on the side of the house the walk was made of wooden planks. Of course, most of the sidewalks in the town consisted of wooden planks in those days.

Although my parents were certainly not religious Jews, they tell me they had quite a celebration at the house at the time of my circumcision ceremony. My parents often spoke of the large gathering of Jewish people who came to the house on that occasion. My father was considered pretty much of a good fellow. People liked him very much. In his day he was regarded as a very successful lawyer. He was also active in politics. He was a staunch Republican. My sister was born seven years after my birth. The neighborhood in which we lived was non-Jewish.

I do not recall that we ever had any Jewish neighbors. However, we never really had any serious trouble because of the fact that we were Jewish. Occasionally there were anti-Semitic manifestations in the neighborhood. The word "sheeny" was always used, but somehow none of us worried very much about it. I remember that I did have a fight as a youngster while I was at public school because somebody called me a dirty Jew, but on the whole I have rather pleasant memories of the neighborhood and of the people who lived there.

I never had any Jewish children to play with and I never missed them. I went to Sunday school at the temple when it was located at Fifth Avenue and Tenth Street. The family and I used to go to the temple on New Year and the Day of Atonement. We never attended services on Sabbath. I never received any Hebrew education, and I cannot read or understand Hebrew at all. My parents never prepared me for my Bar Mitzvah. My sister, however, was confirmed at the temple. We never observed any Jewish rituals in our home. My father certainly never recited the kiddush on Friday evening, and we never observed the dietary laws or other rituals. We never had a mezzuzah on the doorpost of our home. As a matter of fact, I think that my parents looked upon all Jewish customs as obsolete.

GERMAN-AMERICAN FAMILY

Of course, we used to discuss the other Jewish persons in the community. Our friends were all members of the temple. In those days the North Side was getting a lot of the East European Jews, and I remember that we felt that these people were bringing disrepute upon us all, that they were putting us in a bad light here in the community. Some of these people, with their long beards and long black coats and funny black hats, looked so strange that we could not "take" them very well. I remember that other Jews, the older settlers, used to call them "kikes."

I think the reason we children got to know about these strange newcomers was because Dad was a lawyer, and as a professional man he often gave them advice. Even though he handled their business he didn't like them very much.

My family associated exclusively with Jewish families. Their real friends were among them. My father belonged to a social club with other Jewish men and used to have a good time playing cards with them. Of course, there were families among the German-Jewish element whom we didn't like either. We felt that those Jews who were engaged in the liquor business were also bringing our people into disrepute. I will say, however, that there was never any indication that these people were at all dishonorable in their practices.

When I was a youngster I attended home parties given in various other Jewish homes. Games and ice cream and cake always constituted the afternoon's entertainment. There was a group of Jewish children who attended a dancing school conducted by Mrs. Noble on Hennepin Avenue. My parents sent me to dancing school too. This class met once a week and consisted of boys and girls from the age of about eight or nine up.

My mother was always a rather quiet woman. She didn't belong to many of the activities that were taking place in town. She confined her social activities to entertaining other Jewish families in our home.

I had a perfectly normal youth. I graduated from public school and then in 1910 went on to high school. There were not very many Jews in my class. Most of my friends' children, however, went to high school. In fact, some of the girls were actually given private school education here in Minneapolis. I didn't stay in high school after my first two years there. We lost our house around 1911, and we moved to another neighborhood on the South Side of the city. Although it wasn't a Jewish neighborhood, there were several Jewish families who lived rather close by. I decided that I wanted to go to work, and my father didn't object when I took a job as an errand boy for Butler Brothers. I think that there was so much talk in our house about the financial straits we were in that I made up my mind that I would try to be independent and earn my own income. I think that this attitude has colored all of my thinking since that time.

I seldom dated a Jewish girl when I started going out when I was about sixteen or seventeen. There were never any serious objections from my family on this account. I remember that my folks expressed the hope that I would take a Jewish girl out, but there wasn't any real serious concern about the issue of intermarriage. In my day there were quite a few intermarriages in the Jewish community. Yet I guess that my parents had no real fear that I would intermarry.

Our home life was then quite different from what it is today. I think, however, that the differences are characteristic of the times in which we lived. It was generally true, for example, that women were regarded in a very much different light from what they are today. When I was a child I looked upon a woman as a very strong creature. I certainly never saw a woman smoke or drink. My parents taught me that women should be respected, protected, waited upon, and cared for. Certainly the whole attitude toward women has changed. Women have far more freedom today and are regarded as equals.

My father played a most important role in my life. I always looked upon him as my chief advisor and later as my partner. I always consulted him about everything I did, and even though he was quite stern, certainly more so than I am with my daughter today, I always respected him, and I think admired him.

My first job brought me a weekly salary of five dollars. I held onto this job for a short while and then I became a bank messenger with the Security National Bank, which later merged with the First National. I held this job for about four years and earned twenty-five dollars a month. I then became a teller in the bank and earned around sixty dollars a month. About that time my father had joined with several other men and had purchased a building. This was about the year 1915. I was given the job of taking care of the building and collecting rents. I held onto this job until the United States entered World War I.

When war came I enlisted. I wanted to become a flier. However, my dreams did not come true, and I found myself a second lieutenant in the infantry. I was not sent overseas. When the war ended, I was furloughed from active duty, and I came back to Minneapolis and started looking for a job. There were several jobs which I held, none of them very important. Finally, through one of my friends, I started a business in a small store in Duluth, and I did very well.

I have never, throughout these many years, participated in Jewish affairs, nor have I had very many Jewish friends. Most of my friends were Gentiles. I simply was never interested in Jewish life or Jewish organizations. As for Jewish customs, I do not see any sense to them. I certainly never went to the temple on Sabbath morning, and the whole thing never meant anything to me. My folks were not religious, and I was even less concerned than they. My father had always been associated with the temple, but when I began to earn my own money I never wanted to affiliate.

During the years when I was coming up financially, I had no Jewish friends and I have very few of them today.

I married in 1925. The girl I married is, I believe, more religiously inclined than I, but certainly not very much more. I have a daughter who attended public school and high school in Minneapolis and also went to a private girls' school outside the city. She never joined a Jewish sorority, perhaps because the school to which she went did not have other Jewish girls.

I never sent my daughter to any Sunday school. She knows absolutely nothing about Hebrew or Jewish history, although she has in recent years expressed a desire to know about these things and has indicated that she has felt cheated in this respect by me. If my daughter were to marry out of her faith, I do not think that I would seriously object just so long as she was in love. I don't think that I would particularly like the idea, but I certainly wouldn't raise any question about it. I would simply feel that if this is what my daughter wanted, then it is the best thing.

To get back to my reasons for not becoming a member of the temple: First, I never really felt any need for it. Second, I had lost a lot of money at one time and I didn't want to assume other debts. Third, I felt that I could not carry any other obligations than those pertaining directly to my business. I always objected to the manner in which the dues one paid at the temple were decided. I remember that some Jewish lady was seen wearing a sable coat. The next day her husband was visited and told that his dues were being raised.

I do have many social contacts, and they are some very fine people. I do not play cards, and I do not play golf. I do not now belong to the Oak Ridge Country Club, although in 1923 I did. One of the reasons why I have not rejoined the club is because the club has taken on a lot of members who are not, in my opinion, the kind of people I care particularly to associate with. I have not joined B'nai B'rith. I had no special interest in that organization, and I have always tried to keep away from it as much as possible. Although I contribute to the Minneapolis Federation for Jewish Service in its annual campaigns, I have never taken an active role in the campaign.

I think that the Jewish community today is much better than it was in the early days. In these days the Jewish men are certainly more prosperous, and because of that they have better homes and their children are much better educated and they are much finer people. I do not see such bad living conditions today as I used to. Of course, there are some persons of the lower straits who are still getting into trouble of one sort or another, but on the whole things are much better. The Jewish people are really much more Americanized and much finer.

Despite that, anti-Semitism has grown in this community and I am very much concerned about it. I think things are really getting very much worse. When I was a young man growing up there was no Henry Ford with his *Dearborn Independent*, no Hitler, no Silver Shirts organizations and other anti-Semitic groups. Of course things happened in those days that were not pleasant, but the anti-Semites were not as well organized then and they did not do things as openly as they do today.

Around the year 1925 I had an experience here in Minneapolis that upset me. I met an old friend of mine when I had come back to Minneapolis after a stay on the West coast. This non-Jewish friend asked me to join the Minneapolis Athletic Club, so I gave him my application. After some time he said "I want to talk this thing over with you. Frankly, I have found out that they don't want any Jews in the club. I don't know why. Your family is a good one and you are an honorable person. You served with distinction in the war. Still they don't want you." Well, the same thing happened with the Automobile Club, and I see it happening all the time. Naturally I am very much upset about it.

I became interested in the American Legion and have been active in it since 1933. I believe that there is room for such an organization, but I heartily disapprove of such an organization as Jewish War Veterans, and I have never become a member of that organization. I don't believe that there ought to be Jewish War Veterans or Catholic or Swedish war veterans. I just don't believe in it.

When German refugees started coming into this country before World War II, I was in sympathy with the movement. Anything we could do to help others should be done. I feel that Palestine is important as a place of refuge, as a home or country, but as a religious state, never. Of course some of my friends tell me that there is no intention of setting up a religious state in Palestine, but that is how I have felt about it.

When I was in California around 1925, I was at a low ebb financially. This made me very nervous and I think I was a pretty sick man. Upon the advice of friends I joined the Christian Science church, and I followed its program for about six or seven months, but I threw it overboard because it didn't do me any good. I just joined because I wanted it to help me. I didn't care too much about their doctrine one way or the other.

I think that the worst thing that the Jews can do is to set themselves apart. They make themselves conspicuous. I do not think that Jews ought to keep the Sabbath because we ought to keep the Sabbath of the majority. I do not think that there ought to be Jewish clubs. Members of a minority group must give up their differences and conform to the majority in all respects when they come in contact with the majority.

I think that we have changed considerably from the days of my parents. Certainly my sister and I were disciplined by our parents. We were never allowed to talk back. Children were to be seen but not heard. The word of the parents was law. We were not supposed to argue with our parents. Today all of that is changed, and I think for the better. There is much more give and take between parents and children, a much healthier relationship.

When I was a child I remember that my father doled out money to my mother weekly in order to meet the household expenses, but today my wife has her own checking account, and my daughter too has her own bank account. Generally I think that there is a much healthier relationship between parents and children. We discuss, we talk things through, but the whole idea of discipline as it was practiced when I was a child has certainly disappeared. My father certainly never went hunting or fishing in his early youth, as I have done and do. I enjoy these sports and prize fights and other outdoor activities. My wife was active in the Red Cross during the war. She goes out on Jewish Federation drives and does things like that. We have our small group of friends, and we live pretty much by ourselves. We do not feel that we need the Jewish community particularly, and we think that we are being pretty good Americans, as well as pretty good Jews, by the way in which we live.

BERNADINE, DAUGHTER OF HENRY

As an only child, I have had about every advantage that parents can provide. I am twenty-one years old. Minneapolis is my home town. I was born in Swedish hospital.

When I was five and a half years old, I was introduced to my first schooling. I became a kindergarten pupil at Kenwood School. Just about the time I was to enter the first grade, my parents moved to Los Angeles. I went to the public schools there until I was in the sixth grade. For reasons best known to my parents, they moved back to Minneapolis and into the very same neighborhood in which we had lived before. I went to Kenwood School once again. From there I attended Jefferson Junior High School until 1941 and I then went on to West High School, where I was a student until my junior year. I wasn't doing too well in my classwork and for reasons that seemed right, I was advised to attend a private girls' school. So, I was sent to a prep school for girls out of the city.

There is a quota system there for Jewish girls. The entire student population is about two hundred. I really don't know why it was this school to which I went, more than any other. I am sure too that my parents knew about the fact that this school had a quota for Jewish students. But it really didn't make too much difference. I never felt as if I were a person on the outside just because I was Jewish. My friends, both before I went there and while at the school, were Christian. I was required to attend chapel services daily at this school. On Sundays I was required to attend some church in the town just as all the other girls were. There was no temple there. I went with my friends to their services. I went to mass on some Sundays. I went to the Christian Science church. I also attended the Episcopalian church. The school itself was Presbyterian. I think that this experience broadened me considerably. I think that I understood religion better because of it.

When I was graduated in 1943, I registered in the general college of the University of Minnesota. I enjoyed the school very much. I received the A.A. degree (Associate of Arts) very recently. Since then I have had a most interesting job as physical education instructor at the Sumner Field housing project playground. I have learned a great deal there.

I have always had friends among Jews and Christians. Until my days at the university I think that the majority of my friends were Christian. Lately I find that I am going with Jewish boys and girls in greater number than ever before. My real friends are, I think, in the Jewish group.

I have never attended Sunday school here at the temple. My folks were not members. I did attend Sunday school for two years at the Wilshire Temple in Los Angeles. That's all the Jewish training I ever had. I have never observed any of the Jewish laws or practice with respect to diet and other such things. Sabbath is no different than any other day for me. Sunday is the only day I know as a day of rest.

I belong to a nonacademic, philanthropic sorority. I have never belonged to any college campus sorority. We meet at the homes of the girls.

When I was at prep school, I had no awareness of my Jewishness. I lived in the dormitory. I had a number of friends. I never resented the fact that there was a quota system at the school. I just didn't think of it one way or another. About the only time I would go into the temple would be on Rosh Hashonah and Yom Kippur. My parents never went with me. I just went in myself. I never fasted on those days. My parents didn't either.

My parents give me an allowance on a yearly basis. This is supposed to cover all my needs for the year, such as tuition, books, clothes, and so forth. I do not pay anything for room and board. We live in a very nice home in a good neighborhood. I have about everything I want from point of view of comfort. If I run short of money, I am on my own and must earn it. This is particularly true now because I seem to have used up my whole year's allowance in less than six months.

I have often felt that I should have had more Sunday school training. In fact I've mentioned it many times to my parents. I think one should know one's own religion. I've missed something I should know. I'm sure that my parents have been surprised to hear me say that, but it's really the way I feel about it. The fact that they may not feel too keenly about it doesn't mean that I should have been kept from being confirmed along with other Jewish boys and girls. I have often felt left out because of this. I think that whether one is really religious or not there are certain conventions that ought to be followed. These are points on which my parents and I just don't agree.

I have never felt any need to pray. I think of God in a vague sort of way, as the Creator of the universe. He may or may not be a Person. He is, I believe, Somebody above us.

I think that my relations with my parents have been good. Of course, there are differences of opinion. But that isn't really too serious.

I see my grandfather, who is a real old-timer in this community, very often. I still do his errands for him or drive him around in the car. I have learned a lot about Minneapolis from him. He feels, of course, that it's a mistake for me to be making friends with so many of the boys and girls on the North Side. Once he said that he knew the grandfathers of these friends of mine and that they used to have long beards and look like foreigners. He thinks I ought to stick to my own set and for him that means I ought to stick with German Jews.

I run around with a lot of the boys and girls from the North Side. I think it is perfectly silly to be concerned about who were the grandfathers or grandmothers of these boys and girls, just so long as we have the same interests, the same likes and dislikes.

I never had any Hebrew training. I don't know how to read Hebrew. I never really felt any need for it.

I have never studied piano or any other instrument. I have always been interested in sports. I like tennis and swimming best. I guess that's why I took the civil service exam and became a playground instructor. As you know, this is the field used by the housing project people. There are Jews and Christians, Negroes and whites. Every once in a while I have some trouble over there. Little fights take place between the Negroes and whites. I think, though, that all this trouble is due to the parents rather than to the children. Mothers often come over to me and tell me they don't want their children playing with Negroes. Even when the children don't hear what their parents are saying, they know how they feel and before you know it they copy their attitudes.

My mother does not come from the same background as my father. She is really of Polish origin. She was born in America, in Los Angeles to be exact, but her father was Polish. Her father came to the United States through Canada. Mother's mother was born in San Francisco. Mother is no more interested in Jewish ceremonialism than is my father. We serve pork products in our home. In fact I've heard my mother say that there is really no major difference between us and our Christian neighbors. Their homes are run exactly the same as ours. We do not have any Jewish books in our home. We don't celebrate the Sabbath. We have no Jewish symbols around the house.

I don't know any Yiddish. I hear Yiddish expressions from my friends. I like to go with them to the Jewish delicatessen stores around town for kosher corned beef, but not for religious reasons, only because I like it.

I feel absolutely no insecurity because I am Jewish. If anyone ever asks me what I am, I always answer "I'm an American." It never occurs to me to say "I'm Jewish."

Of course, I am concerned about anti-Semitism. I think it's a shame that such things happen. As I said before, I think that these things continue to happen because of the way in which parents teach their children. I am upset when I see Jewish names involved in any crime. It makes things worse for all Jews. I don't know that there is anything that can be done about it, however.

I do not favor intermarriage. I would want to marry a Jewish boy. I think that both parties ought to belong to the same church. If intermarriage takes place, I think there ought to be no children because it is harder on children than it is on the intermarried couple themselves. I have never thought about intermarriage for myself because I have no desire to be outside the Jewish group and because too I am going around with Jewish boys and girls.

Around our home my Dad is the master of the house. He is really in charge. When I was younger I remember getting a licking. But it didn't happen very often.

We always had a maid in our home. When I was a child I wasn't dragged around everywhere the folks went. I have learned how to manage a home. I think that I am quite domesticated. I can cook, sew, make the beds, and be generally helpful around the house.

I think today that there is too much snobbery in the Minneapolis Jewish community, at least the part of it that I know. I cannot understand why there should be such discrimination between the Jews of the North Side and the South (west) Side of town. It just isn't right. When I go out with my friends, I choose them because I like them, not because of who their grandfathers were or reasons like that. But people, my own parents in fact, tell me that it "isn't the thing to do." I do it anyhow because I like their company. People seem to judge you for what you have and not for what you are. I think that's the worst fault with the Jewish community today. Of course I may be describing not the faults of an entire community but those people in my own immediate circle. At any rate, I don't like what I see and I am fighting it in the only way I know how, by going with those I like regardless of where they live or what they have or who their grandfathers were.

Part IV   LIVING IN
          TWO CULTURES

Chapter 15   Living in Two Cultures

ຂ❧ THE *future of Judaism in America is problematic. The conditions under which Judaism must maintain itself, if it is to survive in the modern American environment, are so different from those that have confronted the Jewish people in other times and places that Jews nationally ask themselves what sort of Judaism, if any, will emerge as a result of Jewish efforts at adaptation.*[1]

THE story of what has happened to the Jews in Minneapolis since the coming of the first Jew in 1866 is, in a sense, the story of America. For America is the sum total of the various ethnic groups that have taken leave of other lands and built their homes and lives here.

Germans, Irish, Russians, Italians, Greeks, Scandinavians — each group has written his story in American annals in terms basically similar to those that have been described for the Jews of Minneapolis. Each has found it necessary to accommodate itself to new conditions in a new land. Each was required to adjust the way of life it knew and loved to a new pattern that was characterized as American. It was not to be expected that the national and religious culture by which these ethnic groups had lived could be wiped from their memories or erased from their hearts upon setting foot on American soil. Nor is it clear that it was ever their intention to discard their cultural heritage. Indeed American history demonstrates, in a sense, that the facts were otherwise, because all ethnic groups continue to live in two cultures.

The early immigrants of all groups lived among their own kind whenever and wherever possible. They sought to perpetuate their folkways and mores, even retaining their native language and dress for a time. They usually resented and distrusted the American school system, which often weaned their children away from their cultural moorings and unwittingly created rifts between parents and their children. The immigrant groups formed their own societies and cultural organizations, hoping thereby to retain as much of their native heritage as possible. They created schools of their own that would help their children know the language and tradition of their people. In the main, however, their efforts did not succeed as well as they had hoped.

The process of acculturation was too strong for them. Foreign language and dress, ideas with respect to courtship, marriage, and parental disciplines, to mention but a few, were gradually changed. The cultural ideas and practices of the majority were adapted to their own uses. Native-born children of foreign-born parents were usually far removed in outlook and practice from their parents. Often they rebelled against what they considered to be the foreign customs and practices of their parents. They sought to associate themselves with the culture of the majority people, with the American way of life. All accommodated themselves in varying degree to the newer patterns.

The Jews, in this sense, have been no different from all other ethnic groups. They have experienced the same problems and have reacted similarly to them. As we have observed, the Jewish immigrants, particularly those of Eastern Europe, sought to retain not only their religious beliefs and practices but the ways that were associated with their national cultures as well. Their first synagogues were organized on the basis of national origin. The necessity of earning a livelihood under new conditions, aided by the reactions of their children who were attending American public schools, tended to produce certain marked changes in their ways of living. Though the practices within the home changed more slowly, the changes that resulted from direct contact with a new environment were marked. Foreign dress was rapidly discarded in favor of American styles. Beards were gradually trimmed and finally removed. The English language was acquired, although Yiddish was retained as the language of the home.

In the main, changes were slowest in the field of religious thought and practice. Only where such practice impinged upon the necessity for earning a living were changes made. Where the Sabbath had been a day of rest, many Jews found it necessary to keep their places of business open on the Sabbath. Even then Jews worshipped in the synagogue on the Sabbath and after the service went to their shops or offices. However, whether slow or fast, changes in the religious thought and practices of the Jews did take place.

What is the significance of "Jews in transition"? Has contact with American culture in a midwestern community assured the gradual decay of Jewish religious life? Will the process of cultural loss continue to the point where little if anything that is distinctively Jewish will be retained by the group? The author is neither a prophet nor the son of a prophet. Yet certain prognostications may be made, based on the facts that have been assembled in this study.

The Jews of Minneapolis have indeed suffered a marked culture loss. They have discarded, wholly or in part, many of the religious practices that were regarded as vital to the perpetuation of Judaism. There is a decreasing emphasis upon ritual and form in the religious life of the Jewish community. The dietary laws are gradually disappearing from the home, as they have almost totally disappeared in the Jew's practices outside the home. Separatism, as such, no longer has a marked appeal for the Jew. He does not feel that he requires quite as much ritual as his fathers did in order to make for his survival as a Jew.

Although he has reduced the number of ceremonials and ritual practices that characterized his people in the past, he has returned to or revitalized other practices that have meaning for him as a Jew. The Jewish housewife appears to be reviving the practice of kindling the Sabbath lights. The Bar Mitzvah and confirmation ceremonies for the Jewish child are far more elaborate and meaningful than the Bar Mitzvah ceremony of an earlier day. Many holidays like Passover, Chanukah, and Purim are infused with a new spirit. Parents and children celebrate these festivals with greater joy and understanding today.

There are fewer fundamentalist Jews in Minneapolis today than there were a generation ago. The number of Jews who take the Bible literally has decreased markedly. The same holds true for their attitude with respect to the God idea. The hold of religious experience on the individual Jew has weakened. But Christians too have been faced with the same problem during the past half century.

The Jews of Minneapolis believe in God. They think of Him as One. But they think of Him, in ever greater numbers, as an impersonal Force or Cause. There is a marked increase in the number of persons who are members of the synagogues and temples in the city.

The Jews of Minneapolis, as a body, have no desire to lose their identity with the Jewish people or the Jewish religion. They do not even give thought to the idea of accepting any other religion.

They contribute huge sums to philanthropic causes. Having acquired more of worldly goods in recent years, they contribute liberally, even sacrificially. What is more, inasmuch as their contributions to philanthropy serve to identify them with the Jewish group and help to give them status within the group, they look upon charity as a badge of honor.

Even though parents are less learned, they provide their children with a better Hebrew educational program than they received in their own youth. The "learned" Jews of two decades ago are no longer in their midst. Yet the children of these parents seem more likely to know the Hebrew language, as the language of the Bible, than do their parents, who have often been termed "the lost generation."

The Jewish home has changed in many respects. It is today an equalitarian home in greater degree than ever before. Husbands and wives share their joys and their problems. They are equally responsible for the family life that exists within the home. The family is still a potent influence in the Jewish community. The relationship of children to parents is excellent. There is no problem of juvenile delinquency in the Jewish community. Both divorce and intermarriage are on the increase.

Institutional life of the Jewish community is strong. The degree of Jewishness is often measured by the number of Jewish organizations to which one belongs. Status is acquired thereby.

The ideals of democracy and freedom appeal strongly to the Jewish community. Jews stand ready to make any sacrifice in order that these ideals may be realized. They fight off all efforts toward parochialism on the grounds that parochialism sabotages the democratic ideal.

In appearance the Jews of Minneapolis, except for a very few of the old-timers, are as American as their neighbors. They have assumed not only the dress and mannerisms of their neighbors, but their practices as well. They have become sportsmen, fishermen, and hunters. They often talk like advertisements for the local tourist bureau.

They are, in short, "good people." They are no better and no worse than their neighbors. They live moral and ethical lives. They seek to live as completely as possible in the larger community, while retaining their interest and concern for the welfare of the Jewish community. They believe that they have a responsibility toward their brothers overseas and make every effort to fulfill their obligations in this respect.

The Jews of Minneapolis fall generally into two classes, so well described by Mordecai M. Kaplan. These are the "affirmative Jews" and the "marginal Jews."

Affirmative Jews are those who, despite being troubled by the ill-will of neighbors and the difficulties created thereby, accept their fate without demur. Most of them are identified with the synagogue and all that it represents; it is their principal link with the Jewish people. If they are Orthodox, they adhere to the traditional belief that God manifested, through miracle and self-revelation, His special concern in their ancestors. If they are non-Orthodox, they regard the ethical and spiritual truths underlying the ancient traditions as inherently worth fostering.

There are affirmative Jews, also, among those who have become detached from the synagogue. They find creative possibilities of Jewish life sufficient reason for wishing to maintain it. On the basis of what Jews have been able to achieve as individuals in modern times in all fields of human endeavor — economic, social and cultural — they are convinced that, if Jews were permitted to live in peace, they would contribute to civilization more than their share as a people among peoples.

Marginal Jews regard Judaism as a liability and a misfortune. Since they cannot advocate its forceful suppression, they would like to devise for it some kind of euthanasia or death-kiss. . . . They are known as Jews, least by what they themselves are or do, more by the company they keep, and most by their antecedents. Some belong to temples; their membership, however, is motivated not by religious convictions but by loyalty to the memory of parents, or by the desire to conform to social expectation. As a rule, to which there are few exceptions, these Jews are abysmally ignorant of the Jewish past and of its cultural treasures. They may be highly literate otherwise, but as Jews they are not even embarrassed at being illiterate. Everything connected with Judaism is for them an exotic orientalism which is entirely out of place in, and out of step with, the occidental way of life.[2]

These two groups live side by side in Minneapolis. They even work together when the occasion demands. Despite the numerous and often radical departures from the ways of their fathers, the "affirmative Jews" are still in the majority in the community. By their practices they have demonstrated their unorthodoxy, yet they seem to regard the "ethical and spiritual truths underlying the ancient traditions as inherently worth fostering." They may be confused about the exact nature of these ethical and spiritual truths, yet they grope and search for the way that will help to give them greater security in their Jewishness than they now possess. And *that*, in the opinion of this writer, augurs well for the future.

Will the Jews of Minneapolis, in another generation or two,

give up those distinctive ways of thought and practice and blend into the larger community? Will they, of their own volition, assimilate into the total community? The answer to these questions depends upon two sets of conditions, external and internal.

If anti-Semitism ceases to be a problem and a source of worry for the Jew, if he finds that he is wholly and completely accepted by his Gentile neighbor, the forces that now draw him closer to his fellow Jew may disintegrate. Having attained status and full equality — politically, economically, and socially — he may discard whatever remains of his religious and cultural heritage and merge into the larger community. If he finds that both here and abroad there is complete acceptance of him as a human being, he may come to feel that the Messianic era has at last arrived.

Despite the valiant efforts of members of the larger community to bring this condition about, prospects for its attainment in the near future are dim indeed. If there were no prejudice, hatred, or even bigotry on the local level, Jews would be reminded that it still exists on the national and world levels. As long as there remains a single Jew or a lone Jewish community that is troubled by anti-Semitism, Jews in Minneapolis and, for that matter, everywhere will remain uneasy.

Memory, and history too, play their roles in making it improbable that Jews will give up their identity with the Jewish way of life. If they are prone to minimize the implications of the narrative that is read on Passover eve, concerning the fact that "Once we were slaves unto Pharoah in Egypt," they will not soon forget what Hitler did to the Jews of Germany in their own day. As a consequence it seems unlikely that the Jews of Minneapolis will either individually or as a community give up their identity with the Jewish people.

There are factors too operating within the local Jewish community, and within the Jewish people generally, that make complete assimilation unlikely. Though the forms of Jewish practice have changed, it has not yet been demonstrated that the vast majority of Jews in Minneapolis have other than a sense of security in their Jewishness. They may not be as observant as their fathers from a ritualistic point of view; they may be "modernists" in increasing numbers in their interpretation of the Bible — but they still think of themselves as Jews. They continue to support Hebrew schools, synagogues, and temples and the programs sponsored by these institutions. The synagogues and temples, the rabbinic and lay leadership, are expending greater effort and are certainly more ingenious in their approach to the problem of how to foster interest in the Jewish way of life than they were a generation ago.

If there has been a lessening of the ties of formal religion, there has also been a stronger tie with the Jewish people. Palestine and the modern Zionist movement have helped to bring this about.

Ever since the Viennese Jew Theodore Herzl in 1896 inaugurated the modern Zionist movement, Jews throughout the world have envisaged the possibility of creating a Jewish state.[3] Though Eastern Jews, impelled by a great idea, took up residence in that ancient land, worked its soil, and brought hints of the land's potentialities to the Western world, for many years the Jews of the West contributed little of their means or skills toward the development of the country.

The Balfour Declaration helped to bring about a change in the thinking of many Jews who had been lukewarm to the idea of Zionism. In greater numbers they contributed to the upbuilding of the land. They watched the early Palestinian pioneers as they transformed barren desert land into veritable garden spots. They were impressed with the heroism of these chalutzim or pioneers who founded colonies, villages, and cities in Palestine. They could not help noticing that the contemptuous statements that Jews generally were incapable of toiling with their hands and a thousand other canards were, in Palestine, demonstrated to be unfounded and untrue. In Palestine they saw the men and women who had come from the ghettos of Europe build a new land, even as they heard these pioneers sing a new song, *Am Yisroel Chai*, "Israel lives."

The Jews of all the world saw a miracle being performed in their own lifetime. They saw — and they believed. They believed in their fellow Jews and they came once again to believe in themselves and their own potentialities. Where they had once listened and believed what the anti-Semites had to say about them, Jews throughout the world, in ever-increasing numbers, began to see themselves as a people reborn. Fascinated by the numerous physical and manual achievements of Palestinian Jewry, they were witnesses to a cultural rebirth as well. They saw the revival of the Hebrew language as a spoken tongue. They witnessed the development of the arts, literature, painting, drama, and music, the experiments in communal living, even the creation of new religious forms and holidays. The Jewish people was indeed a living people once again.

Now that Israel has established its own government and appears likely to be officially represented among the United Nations, the sense of insecurity and often of frustration, as the result of being a homeless people, seems in the process of being reduced. Where, until yesterday, the Jew qua Jew could see nothing but sorrow and prejudice and inequality round about him, his mood is now, more frequently, one of hope.

The Jews of Minneapolis, in ever-increasing numbers, have worked for the upbuilding of Palestine. They see in the state of Israel something more than a land of refuge for the displaced Jews of Europe. To them it is the land from which flows the spiritual and cultural riches of an old-new people. As they have, during the years, sung and danced to the music that has emanated from The Land, as they witnessed the ancient land being rehabilitated, and saw the Palestinians being rebuilt spiritually thereby, they were themselves inspired and spiritually refreshed. Hence they ask, rhetorically, "If ancient patterns have given way to newer patterns conceived in modern Palestine, what does it matter, so long as these new modes help to give meaning to our lives as Jews?"

There is yet another effect that the land of Israel and its people has had upon the Jews of Minneapolis. Though they paid lip-service to the idea that they, along with all minority groups, had the "right to be different," Jews were, in many cases, not too sure about it. True, the American way of life, in theory at least, supported this contention, but from point of view of practice, differences have rather been frowned upon. Many Jews have, as a consequence, "played down" differences and even argued that it was "un-American" to be different in any respect. It is this observer's belief that the reawakened interest in the land of Israel and its people will tend to cause more Jews to point with pride to the cultural and spiritual values they receive from Israel.

The Jews of Minneapolis will not be less American because of their return to their people. On the contrary, the creation of the state of Israel provides each Jew with a choice of citizenship he has never before possessed. Today he may, if he so chooses, renounce his American citizenship and all that the American way of life means, and accept citizenship in the state of Israel. The fact that the Jew does not do so makes it doubly clear that his loyalty to America and its culture is unequivocal. He, like other ethnic groups, has made his choice free from duress and pressure. Like Americans of Irish or German or Polish origin, he will look with pride or sadness upon the achievements or failings of his cultural homeland. But it will be, for him, the land from which springs his Hebraic culture. And he will realize, in ever-increasing degree, that he may make his greatest contribution to America by helping to infuse the prophetic ideals of justice, morality, and ethics into the warp and woof of American life and culture. All these positive forces at work in the Minneapolis Jewish community seem, to this observer, to outweigh the negative forces which have been pointed out in detail throughout this study.

LIVING IN TWO CULTURES

Though the Jews of Minneapolis seem to be departing from the minutia of traditional observance, there still remains a regard for ritual per se. Whatever ritual practices will be observed in the future, it is clear that the choice will be made on the basis of whether or not these practices will help the Jews to survive as a people rather than on the basis of divinely ordained Law. Peril besets such a course, to be sure. But there remains at present no other way for the Jew to follow. His desire to accommodate his religious and cultural life to the culture of the majority while avoiding complete assimilation — that is, loss of identity — will make his task difficult indeed. But the goal is worthy of his effort.

Reference Matter

Notes

Preface

[1] *American Journal of Sociology*, 46:331–43 (1940).

Chapter 1. The Setting

[1] A Minneapolitan as described by Lincoln Steffens in "The Shame of Minneapolis," *McClure's Magazine*, vol. 20, no. 3, p. 228 (January 1903).

[2] Collegiate enrollment exclusive of summer session, according to T. E. Pettengill, recorder of the University of Minnesota, is the following:

1900–1	2627
1910–11	3822
1920–21	8657
1930–31	13,864
1940–41	17,383
1945–46	22,703
1946–47	32,448
1947–48	31,946

[3] Sophia M. Robison, *Jewish Population Studies* (New York, 1943), 154.

[4] Franz Boas, *Race, Language and Culture* (New York, 1940), 60–75.

[5] This information was obtained from a "Self-survey of the Minneapolis Jewish Community" made in 1945. The survey was directed by E. Picheny, staff member of the National Jewish Welfare Board.

[6] F. Stuart Chapin, "The Effects of Slum Clearance and Rehousing on Family and Community Relationships in Minneapolis," *American Journal of Sociology*, 43:745 (March 1938).

[7] *Ibid.*

[8] Reported by the "Self-survey of the Minneapolis Jewish Community."

[9] *Ibid.*

[10] John Hope II, *Industrial Minorities in the Minneapolis Labor Market* (mimeographed, Minneapolis, 1948), 37.

[11] Sophia M. Robison, *Jewish Population Studies*, 155.

[12] These figures were submitted by Charles I. Cooper, executive secretary of the Minneapolis Federation for Jewish Service.

[13] *The Minneapolis Jewish Communal Survey* (3 vols., 1936) reports ninety-two organizations. Since it was published, two organizations have been created: the Jewish Hospital Association and the Home for Jewish Convalescents.

[14] This figure is based on an estimate given in *The Minneapolis Jewish Communal Survey*, 3:2.

Chapter 2. Community in the Making

[1] Mordecai M. Kaplan, *The Future of the American Jew* (New York, 1948), 325. Reprinted by permission of the author and the publisher, the Macmillan Company.

JEWS IN TRANSITION

[2] See the article by Ruby Danenbaum, "A History of the Jews of Minneapolis" published in the *Reform Advocate* in Chicago on November 16, 1907. This article provides much information about the early German-Jewish community.

[3] Though Messrs. Altman and Lauchheim were the first Jews known to have located in Minneapolis, Mr. Ralph Rees, who arrived in 1869, is known to have had the longest continuous residence in the city. Also in 1869 the brothers Plechner arrived in Minneapolis, to remain only a short time before moving to St. Paul. Messrs. Henry Behrens, Theodore Rees, and Samuel Alexander were known to have located in Minneapolis late in 1869. Each of these persons operated a clothing and dry goods store.

In 1870 Joseph Robitshek came to Minneapolis to serve as a clerk in the business establishment of Ralph Rees, and Simon Gittleson was employed by Jacob Cohen for a short time. In 1871 Cyrus Rothschild came from Philadelphia and acquired the business established by Samuel Lauchheim; also the third of the Rees brothers, Gustave, came to Minneapolis. The Chicago fire of 1871 was responsible for the addition of several Jewish individuals and families to the city of Minneapolis. Messrs. Jacob Cohen, Jacob Skoll, and A. Krutzkoff established clothing businesses in the city in 1871.

Beginning in 1873 we find a further increase in the Jewish population. The Jacob Deutch family, Emanuel Kayser and his bride from Philadelphia, Gustave Pflaum, Isadore Monasch, a Mrs. Dittenhoefer, and the parents and sisters of Ralph Rees, who were brought from Germany to make their home here, as well as Max Benson, are among those known to have established themselves in the community.

In 1874, Max Segelbaum opened a dry goods store on Washington Avenue and in the following year his brother Sander and family came to the city. Together the brothers opened the largest dry goods business in the city on Nicollet Avenue near Third Street. Jews known to have moved to Minneapolis in 1875 include Max Wolff, who had been making frequent business trips from the east up to that time, Lewis Brin and family, K. Brin, Leopold Ehrlich, and Louis Metzger and family. The name of Sol Sulzberger is recorded for 1876. In 1878 Edward Bernstein, Louis Werth, Morris and Herman Wilk, Isaac Faller, George Jacoby, and the Harris Brothers, and in some instances their families, helped to increase the size of the Jewish community. All these men established themselves in dry goods and clothing businesses along Washington, Hennepin, or Nicollet avenues. The first Jewish lawyer, Albert Levi, arrived in 1878, together with his brother, Gerson. Gerson Levi engaged in the wholesale clothing business on Washington Avenue North.

A yellow fever epidemic in the Southern states caused many Jewish families from that area to move to the germ-killing zone of Minnesota. Among them were the David Lowenstein family of Memphis, Tennessee, Josephine Yancy, Miss Ella Milius, Sarah Rau, Mr. and Mrs. Jacob Harpman, and the Jacob Gronaur family. The early eighties brought a considerable number of western European Jews to Minneapolis. Known to have arrived in the city during the first half of that decade are the Mikolas family, Samuel Jacobs, Isaac Weil, the Weiskopf families, Mayer Levi, Emanuel E. Abrahams, Joseph Kantrowitz, Louis Michaels, and Louis Shilt, and their families.

Although the first Russian Jew, Jacob Cohen, came to Minneapolis in 1871 after a brief stay in Cincinnati, he cannot properly be regarded as typical of the East European Jews. He found himself among German Jews and became

314

NOTES

an important member of their community. Of him, however, it is recorded: "he was recognized as the best Talmudic student in the community and was interested in all things relating to Judaism and its elevation."

[4] Danenbaum, "A History of the Jews of Minneapolis," *Reform Advocate,* November 16, 1907, p. 8.

[5] The leader of the Minneapolis Council of Jewish Women and one of Minneapolis' most representative Jewesses was Nina Morais Cohen. Mrs. Cohen was the wife of Emanuel Cohen, a prominent attorney, and the daughter of Rabbi Sabbato Morais of Philadelphia. She was a woman of great personal charm and scholarly attainments.

[6] *American Israelite* (Cincinnati), vol. 44, no. 16, p. 7 (1897).

[7] Calvin F. Schmid, *Social Saga of Two Cities* (Minneapolis, 1937), 77–79. This material was abstracted from a special term paper written for the course in Population Problems by Lyle Patterson, under the direction of Calvin F. Schmid.

[8] *American Israelite,* June 9, 1882 (vol. 28, no. 50, p. 394).

Chapter 3. The Jew and His Neighbor

[1] Milton Steinberg, "The Jew Faces Anti-Semitism" in *Jewish Reconstructionist Papers* (New York, 1936), 17.

[2] Letter from Mr. David Liggett, former secretary of the Minneapolis Council of Social Agencies and director of the Community Fund campaigns, to the president of the Minneapolis Federation for Jewish Service, on file in the office of the federation.

[3] Based on the records of the Minneapolis police department.

[4] Carey McWilliams, "Minneapolis: The Curious Twin," *Common Ground,* Autumn, 1946 (vol. 7, no. 1, p. 61). Reprinted by permission of *Common Ground.*

[5] *Nation,* May 29, 1943. Italics added.

[6] Selden Menefee, *Assignment: U.S.A.* (New York, 1943), 101–2. The book was published by Reynal and Hitchcock; the quotation is reprinted by permission.

[7] Maurice Lefkovits, *American Jewish World,* September 1922.

[8] *The Minneapolis Jewish Communal Survey,* 2:3.

[9] The results of the study were originally printed in *Jewish Social Studies,* vol. 5, no. 1, pp. 27–42 (1943).

Chapter 4. Beliefs and Practices

[1] Milton Steinberg, *A Partisan Guide to the Jewish Problem* (Indianapolis, 1945), 183–84.

[2] Israel Cohen, *Jewish Life in Modern Times* (London, 1914), 279.

[3] *Ibid.,* 281.

[4] For a fuller discussion of Orthodox Judaism see Cohen, *Jewish Life in Modern Times.* See also Milton Steinberg, *Basic Judaism* (New York, 1947), for a discussion of Orthodox, Reform, and Conservative viewpoints.

[5] For a discussion of Reform Judaism see David Philipson, *The Reform Movement in Judaism* (New York, 1931).

[6] For a discussion of Conservative Judaism see Robert Gordis, *Conservative Judaism* (New York, 1945).

[7] Micah 6:8.

JEWS IN TRANSITION

Chapter 5. The Dietary Laws

[1] Morris Joseph, *Judaism as Creed and Life* (London, 1920), 178–79.
[2] Cohen, *Jewish Life in Modern Times*, 51.

Chapter 6. Feast and Fast Days

[1] Israel H. Levinthal, *Judaism, An Analysis and An Interpretation* (New York, 1935), 107.
[2] For a description of the Sabbath see Morris Joseph, *Judaism as Creed and Life*, 200–11; see also Cohen, *Jewish Life in Modern Times*, 60–66.
[3] From the traditional High Holy Day Prayer Book.
[4] See Exodus 34:23.
[5] Exodus 12:1–20; also Leviticus 23:4–8.
[6] Exodus 34:22; also Leviticus 23:9–21.
[7] Leviticus 23:33–36, 39–43.
[8] Maccabees I.

Chapter 7. From the Cradle to the Grave

[1] Mordecai M. Kaplan, *Judaism in Transition* (New York, 1941), 43.
[2] This figure was obtained by checking the number of deaths listed in the *American Jewish World* for three successive years (1943–45).

Chapter 8. The Changing Synagogue

[1] Joseph, *Judaism as Creed and Life*, 288.
[2] George Foote Moore, *Judaism* (Cambridge, 1927), vol. 1, chap. 5.
[3] Danenbaum, "A History of the Jews of Minneapolis," *Reform Advocate*, November 16, 1907.
[4] *American Israelite*, May 31, 1882 (vol. 28, p. 394).
[5] *Ibid.*, June 4, 1896 (vol. 42, no. 49, p. 2).
[6] *The Minneapolis Jewish Communal Survey*, 3:2.
[7] *American Jewish World*, November 23, 1945, p. 20.
[8] From the minute book of the Kenesseth Israel Congregation.

Chapter 9. The Educational Process

[1] David Aronson, *The Jewish Way of Life* (New York, 1946), 44.
[2] The facts regarding the fraternal orders were provided by members of these organizations.
[3] Samuel N. Deinard, "Minneapolis," *Jewish Encyclopedia*, 8:599.
[4] *American Jewish World*, October 29, 1915.
[5] Fourteenth United States Census.

Chapter 10. The Family and the Home

[1] Joseph H. Hertz, *A Book of Jewish Thoughts* (New York, 1926), 11.
[2] Cohen, *Jewish Life in Modern Times*; Eugene Kohn, *The Future of Judaism in America* (New York, 1934), 19–46.
[3] This information was provided May 28, 1946, by Mr. Maurice Jacobs, vice-president of the Jewish Publication Society of America, Philadelphia.

NOTES

[4] The records are incomplete and are therefore not useful for statistical purposes. They serve only as a basis for an estimate on the size of families.

[5] "Self-survey of the Minneapolis Jewish Community."

[6] The Jewish Family Welfare Association has a long list of applicants for child adoption.

[7] Ernest R. Mowrer, *Family Disorganization* (Chicago, 1927), 111.

[8] Julia Felsenthal in the *American Jewish World,* January 21, 1916.

[9] Reported by Paul Segner, research analyst for the Minneapolis Council of Social Agencies, March 2, 1946.

Chapter 15. Living in Two Cultures

[1] Eugene Kohn, *The Future of Judaism in America* (New York, 1934), 9.

[2] Mordecai M. Kaplan, *The Future of the American Jew* (New York, 1948), 3-4. Reprinted by permission of the author and the publisher, the Macmillan Company.

[3] See A. Bein, *Theodore Herzl* (Philadelphia, 1940); also Robert Nathan, *Palestine Problem and Promise* (Washington, 1946); H. Infield, *Cooperative Living in Palestine* (New York, 1944); M. Samuel, *Harvest in the Desert* (Philadelphia, 1944); A. Revusky, *Jews in Palestine* (New York, 1935).

Appendix. Name Changes among Jews in Minneapolis (1901-1945)

FROM	TO	FROM	TO
Aberman	Tamires	Cohen	Sherman
Abrams	Haskvitz	Cohen	Snyder
Abromovitz	Abern	Copelovitz	Copel
Abromovitz	Bromowitz	Coplinsky	Coplin
Altrowitz	Alter		
Andovitz	Avid	Daskoske	Dash
		Danzeker	Gross
Bernstein	Brandon	Deitch	Bohn
Beugenstein	Beugen	Duzansky	Duzan
Blumenberg	Kelly	Dworsky	Dewor
Blumenfield	Brenner		
Borosky	Barr	Epstein	Evans
Breslowsky	Briss		
Browne	Brandon	Finkelstein	Fenn
Brownstein	Brandon	Fischman	Fisher
Burnstein	Burns	Fligeltaub	Fligel
		Freedman	Freeman
Chait	Schneider		
Chapsky	Chapman	Garfinkle	Garfin
Charonsky	Charon	Gedalowitz	Cotlow
Cheimowitz	Harris	Gershenowitz	Gary
Cisarsky	Crain	Ginsberg	Gaines
Cohen	Allan	Ginsberg	Gainsley
Cohen	Baker	Ginsberg	Gilbert
Cohen	Coen	Goldberg	Berg
Cohen	Colman	Goldberg	Goldie
Cohen	Conant	Goldberg	Lyons
Cohen	Condon	Goldberg	Morton
Cohen	Conn	Goldberg	Wallace
Cohen	Corwin	Goldfish	Goldwyn
Cohen	Hoke	Goldman	Gale
Cohen	Justin	Goldstein	Gilbert

SOURCE: Records of the clerk of district court, Hennepin County.

APPENDIX

FROM	TO	FROM	TO
Goldstein	Gold	Mandelofsky	Mandel
Goldstein	Gould	Markowitz	Marko
Goldstein	Irwin	Mendowitz	Mendow
Goldstein	White	Michalovitz	Michals
Greenberg	Green	Moscowitz	Gold
Greenstein	Silverman	Moscowitz	Moss
Grossman	Gross	Moskovitz	Moscoe
Guttman	Goodman		
		Nachovnich	Nash
Haimowitch	Hymes	Nemerofsky	Numero
Halkowitz	Tokman		
Haselnus	Hayes	Percansky	Perkins
Hershkowitz	Hersch	Percansky	Villa
		Pinsky	Perry
Jacobs	Burt	Polinsky	Mitchell
Joselowitz	Joss		
Joseph	Shallett	Rabinovitch	Robbins
Judelowitz	Udell	Rauchwenger	Rauch
		Ravitzky	Ravine
		Robotnick	Roberts
Kabulnikoff	Cable	Rosenbaum	Rose
Kantrowitz	Kay	Rosenberg	Berg
Kaufman	Coufman	Rosenberg	Roberts
Kieferstein	Kiefer	Rosenberg	Roebern
Kone	Kane	Rosenberg	Rolfe
Krichefsky	Krishef	Rosenberg	Ross
		Rosenbloom	Rosy
Labovitz	Lyons	Rosenfield	Royce
Lachotzky	Lyons	Rosenstein	Rose
Lazarowitz	Babitz	Rosenstein	Roston
Lazarowitz	Lazarus	Rosenthal	Royal
Lebowitz	Lebow	Rosenzweig	Rose
Leibovitz	Lee		
Levin	Wilson	Sabeswitz	Sabes
Levy	Benedict	Sawitsky	Rose
Levy	Lee	Schmulowitch	Smiler
Lifschitz	Lifson	Schmulowitz	Smiley
Litinski	Litin	Schneider	Snyder
Lorberbaum	Lorber	Schneidman	Snyder
Lubetsky	Lubet	Schreiber	Berg
Lustgardten	Garten	Schulman	Schuman

JEWS IN TRANSITION

FROM	TO	FROM	TO
Schwartz	Swarthe	Sovitzky	Savitt
Shapera	Shaper	Spiegelberg	Sirmont
Shedlovsky	Shedlov	Sweetelsky	Sweet
Shmulewitz	Smull		
Shragowitz	Shragg	Tabachnick	Tanick
Shushansky	Shushan		
Silverman	Fox	Weksler	Juster
Silverman	Sills	Weisman	Wyman
Silverstein	Silver	Wiseman	Whitman
Slobotkin	Sabath	Wolkovitz	Wolk
Smilowitz	Smiler		
Sodomsky	Sanders	Yonolovich	Jacobson
Soliterman	Miller		
Solomon	Solon	Zelikoff	Zelle

Glossary

The letters (H), (Y), and (A) indicate words of Hebrew, Yiddish, and Aramaic origin respectively. The following symbols have been used to indicate the pronunciation of vowel sounds.

ă as in *art*	ei as in *ate*	o as in *us*
ah as in sof*a*	ĕ as in *end*	oh as in sof*a*
ē as in *ate*	ĭ as in *ill*	ŏ as in *all*
e as in b*e*lieve	ī as in *eat*	ū as in m*oo*n
er as in *urn*	ō as in *old*	u as in f*u*ll

Aliyah (ă lī yăh') — Literally, *going up.* Used to describe being "called up" to the reading of the Torah in the synagogue. Refers also to immigration to Israel. (H)

Arba kanfos (ăr bă' kăn fŏs') — Literally, *four corners.* A type of prayer shawl, with fringes on each of its four corners, worn under the upper garments during the entire day. An ever-present reminder of Judaism's sacred commandments. (H)

Avelim (ă vē līm') — Mourners, consisting of the nearest blood relations such as parents, brothers, sisters, or children. (H)

Bar Mitzvah (băr mĭts vah') — Literally, *son of the commandment.* A Jewish boy who has reached the age of 13, his religious majority. (H)

Bas Mitzvah (băs mĭts vah') — A recently instituted ceremony for girls approximating the Bar Mitzvah for boys. (H)

Berochoh (be rŏ chŏ'); plural, Berochos (be rŏ chŏs') — Literally, *blessing.* A special benediction or prayer uttered on numerous occasions. A means of expressing gratitude to God. (H)

Bes Hamidrash (beis hă mĭd răsh') — Literally, *house of study.* Study was one of the threefold functions of the synagogue, the other two being prayer and assembly. (H)

Blatt (blătt) — A folio or page of the Talmud. *Studying a Blatt* means studying the Talmud. (Y)

Brith (brĭth or brĭs) — Literally, *covenant.* The Jewish male child, on the eighth day after birth, was ushered into the Covenant of Abraham through the rite of circumcision. (H)

Cantor — An English word meaning *one who chants.* The cantor is usually a man of musical talent who possesses a knowledge of the Hebrew liturgy. The Hebrew word for cantor is chazan (chă zăn'). The cantor's function is to chant the service in the synagogue.

Challoh (chă loh'); plural, Challos (chă lŏs') — The Sabbath or festival white bread or twists. Originally connoted the observance of the commandment to contribute a portion of the bread to the priests. (H)

Chalutzim (chă lū tzīm') — Literally, *pioneers.* This term refers particularly to the pioneering Jews who have settled in the land of Israel. (H)

Chanukah (chă nū kah') — Literally, *dedication.* The Feast of Lights, celebrating the rededication of the Temple by the Maccabees. (H)

Chasid (chă sĭd') — Literally, *pious man.* A follower of the Chasidic movement founded by Israel Baal Shem Tob (Israel, Master of the Good Name). (H)

321

Chazan — *See* Cantor.

Cheder (chĕ' dĕr) — Literally, *room*. The old religious elementary school, usually a one-room school, privately owned and conducted. (H)

Chevra Kaddisha (chĕv rä' kă dī shä') — Literally, *holy association*. A society maintained by many congregations and some fraternal organizations whose members perform the sacred rites associated with burying the dead. (A)

Chumosh (chū mŏsh') — Literally, *five*. Refers to the Pentateuch or Five Books of Moses. (H)

Chupa (chū pah') — The bridal canopy, consisting of four poles attached to a square of cloth, giving the appearance of a tent. The term is also used for the marriage ceremony. (H)

Daven (dă' vĕn) — To pray. (Y)

Eicha (ei chä') — Literally, *how*. The Book of Lamentations begins with the Hebrew word *eicha* and is therefore referred to by this word. (H)

Esrog (ĕs rōg') — Literally, *citron*. One of the two major plants used in the services of the Feast of Tabernacles. The lulav (palm branch) is the other. (H)

Galus (gă lūs') — Literally, *exile*. Refers to the Jew's sense of living as a member of a minority people in lands of dispersion. All places of residence other than Palestine (Israel) have been regarded, since the expulsion, as galus. (H)

Gelt (gĕlt') — Literally, *money*. Often refers to gift money, as in *Chanukah gelt*, a gift on the Feast of Lights. (Y)

Gemarah (ge mă räh') — Literally, *learning*. That part of the Talmud which was created after the completion of the Mishnah. (H)

Get (gĕt) — A Jewish bill of divorcement. (H)

Goy (gōy) — Usually refers to a Gentile. Literally, the word means *nation*. Used in the Bible as in *Goy Kadosh*, a holy nation. (H)

Greggers (grĕg' gers) — Noisemakers used on the Feast of Purim (Lots) to drown out mention of the name of Haman when the Book of Esther is read in the synagogue. (Y)

Haftorah (hăf tō räh') — The portion from the Prophets read after the weekly reading from the Pentateuch. (H)

Haggadah (hă găd däh') — Literally, *narrative* or *story*. The text of the Passover home service, recited on the first two nights of Passover. It tells the story of the Exodus from Egypt and extols the God of freedom. (H)

Hallel (hă lēl') — Psalms of praise of God taken from the Book of Psalms. (H)

Hespod (hĕs ped) — Literally, *eulogy*. Usually delivered as part of the funeral service. (H)

Kaddish (kă dĭsh') — Literally, *sanctification*. The doxology recited especially in memory of the departed. (H)

Kashrus (kăsh rūs') — The system of dietary laws practiced by observant Jews. (H)

Kesubah (ke sū bah') — The Jewish marriage document or contract. (A)

Kiddush (kĭd dūsh') — Literally, *sanctification*. The benediction chanted over the cup of wine on Sabbaths and festivals, declaring the sanctification of these holy days. (H)

Klose or Klaus (klōse or klows) — The vestry room of a synagogue, used for prayer and study. (Y)

Knädlach (kneid' lăch) — Dumplings made of meal, usually eaten with soup on the Passover. (Y)

Kol Nidre (kōl nĭd rei') — Literally, *all vows*. A prayer chanted in the synagogue on the eve of Yom Kippur (Day of Atonement). (A)

Kosher (kō sher') — Food that is ritually acceptable in accordance with Jewish religious practice. (H)

Kosher le Pesach (kō sher' le pe săch') — Foods that are ritually acceptable

GLOSSARY

for use on Pesach (Passover) in accordance with Jewish religious practice. (H)

Kugel (ku gĕl) — A Sabbath pudding usually prepared with noodles. (Y)

Latkes (lăt′ kes) — Pancakes usually made of potatoes or matsoh meal. (Y)

Litvakes (lĭt vă′ kes) — Lithuanian Jews. (Y)

Lulav (lū lăv′) — The palm branch, used as a symbol at the services on the Feast of Tabernacles. (H)

Maariv (mă ă rĭv′) — Evening prayers. (H)

Matsoh (mă tsoh′); plural, Matsos (mă tsōs′) — Literally, *unleavened bread.* The matsoh is eaten on the Passover instead of ordinary, leavened bread. It is a reminder of the unleavened bread eaten by the Hebrews when they hastily began the Exodus from Egypt. (H)

Megillah (me gĭl lah′) — Literally, *scroll.* The Book of Esther is one of the five books of the Bible known as megillos or scrolls. (H)

Melamed (me lă mĕd′) — Literally, *teacher.* Refers to a teacher of elementary Hebrew subjects. (H)

Menorah (me nō rah′) — Literally, *candelabrum.* The seven-branched candelabrum used in the ancient Temple in Jerusalem. There is also the Chanukah menorah, consisting of eight branches, used on Chanukah, the Feast of Lights. (H)

Mezzuzah (me zū zah′) — Literally, *doorpost.* A small case, usually wood or metal, containing a parchment scroll, attached to the right doorpost of the entrance to the home and often to doorposts of living rooms within the home. On it are inscribed biblical verses. (H)

Minyan (mĭn yăn′); plural, Minyanim (mĭn yă nīm′) — Literally, *number.* A minyan or quorum of ten males above the age of thirteen is required for public worship. The plural, minyanim,

is used in the sense of small congregations of worshippers. (H)

Mishnah (mĭsh nah′) — That part of the Talmud consisting of statements of the law by scholars known as tanaim (tăn ă īm′). Collected by Rabbi Judah Ha-nasi and completed by the beginning of the third century C.E. (H)

Mishnayos (mĭsh nă yōs′) — The plural of Mishnah. (H)

Mitzvah (mĭts vah′); plural, Mitzvos (mĭts vōs′) — Commandment or prescribed religious observance or duty. (H)

Mohel (mō hĕl′); plural, Mohelim (mō ha līm′) — One who performs the rite of circumcision. A mohel must be qualified by both piety and experience. (H)

Motzi (mō tsī′) — A contraction of ha-motzi. Literally, *who brings forth.* The prayer before eating bread. The grace before meals. (H)

Payos (pē yōs′) — Literally, *corners.* Usually refers to ear locks. It was the practice of many East European Jews not to cut the hair of "the corners of the head." (H)

Pesach (pĕ′ săch) — The Feast of Passover, on which, according to biblical account, the Pesach or paschal lamb was to be eaten. The festival commemorates the Exodus from Egypt. (H)

Pidyon Ha-Ben (pĭd yōn′ hă bĕn′) — The redemption of the first-born son on the thirty-first day after birth. (H)

Purim (pū rĭm′) — Literally, *lots.* The festival whose history is recorded in the Book of Esther. Called Purim because Haman had cast lots to discover the day most favorable to his plan of destroying the Jews. (H)

Pushke (push′ ke) — A charity box. There were usually many such boxes (pushkos) in the Jewish home, each representing a different charitable cause. (Y)

323

JEWS IN TRANSITION

Rav (răv) — Literally, *master* or *teacher*. Refers to the spiritual leader or rabbi. (H)

Rebbi (rĕ bĭ') — Literally, *my teacher*. Usually refers to a Hebrew teacher of primary subjects. (H)

Rosh Hashonah (rōsh hă shō nah') — The Jewish New Year. Observed for two days by Orthodox and Conservative Jews. These are regarded as days of judgment by God of Israel and mankind. (H)

Seder (sē dĕr) — Literally, *order*. The service in the home on the first two nights of Passover, in which the story of the Exodus from Egypt is recounted and the importance of human freedom is stressed. (H)

Selaim (se lă īm') — A biblical word meaning *silver coins*. (H)

Selichos (se lĭ chōs') — Prayers of penitence. A special group of these penitential prayers are recited on days preceding the high holy days. (H)

S'forim (se fō rim') — Literally, *books*. Usually refers to books of religious content. (H)

Shabbas (shă băs') — The Sabbath. Weekly day of rest starting Friday at sunset and ending Saturday at sunset. (H)

Shabbas Shuvah (shă băs' shū vah') — The Sabbath between Rosh Hashonah (New Year) and Yom Kippur (Day of Atonement) is known as the Sabbath of Return. (H)

Shadchen (shăd' chĕn) — The marriage broker who, particularly in East European countries, arranged marriages with the consent of parents by introducing marriageable young people to their families and to each other. (H)

Shamos, Shamosh (shă' mōs, sha mōsh') — The sexton, who acts as the caretaker of the synagogue and also performs certain religious services. (H)

Shavuot (sha vū ōt') — Literally, *weeks*. The Feast of Pentecost or Feast of Weeks. Occurs seven weeks after the second day of Passover and commemorates the giving of the Ten Commandments at Mount Sinai. (H)

Sheitel (shei' tĕl) — The wig formerly worn by married women. Rabbinic law required that married women should not expose their hair. (Y)

Sheva Berochos (shĕ' vă be rō chōs') — Literally, *seven benedictions*. The prayer solemnizing a marriage consists of seven benedictions. (H)

Shiva (shĭ vă') — Literally, *seven*. The seven days of mourning. Requires abstention from usual work. Mourners remain at home during shiva. (H)

Shochet (shō chĕt') — One who slaughters animals or fowl according to Jewish ritual. Must be an observant Jew and must be certified by a rabbi as proficient in the knowledge of laws pertaining to slaughter. (H)

Shomer Shabbas (shō mēr' shă băs'); plural, Shomrei Shabbas (shōm rei') — A strict observer of the Sabbath. (H)

Shulchan Aruch (shul chăn' ă rūch') — Literally, *prepared table*. The code of Jewish laws, prepared by Joseph Caro, which deals with all legal and ritual questions that may be raised by the average Jew. (H)

Shule (shūl) — A synagogue. (Y)

Succah (sū cah') — Literally, *booth* or *hut*. The Succah was to be erected for the festival of Sukkot. (H)

Sukkot (sū kōt') — The Feast of Tabernacles or Feast of Booths. Also known as the Feast of Ingathering. (H)

Tallis (tă lĭs') — Prayer shawl worn over the outer garment primarily for morning prayer. (H)

Tallis koton (tă lĭs' ko ton') — A small prayer shawl worn under the outer garment by a Jewish male. (H) *See also* Arba kanfos.

Tachrichim (tăch rĭ chīm') — White linen burial shrouds. (H)

Tefillin (te fĭ līn) — Phylacteries. Used during daily morning prayers except

324

GLOSSARY

on the Sabbath and holy days. Two small leather boxes with narrow leather straps, worn on the arm and over the forehead. Each box contains parchment on which are written biblical verses. (H)

Teitch-Chumosh (teitch chū' mosh) — A Yiddish translation of the Bible, illustrated by fable, legend, and folklore, with homiletical emphasis. (Y)

T'hillim (te hīl līm') — The Hebrew name of the Book of Psalms. (H)

Tishah B'Av (tī shah' b'äv) — The ninth day of the Hebrew month of Av. The anniversary of the destruction of the Temple in Jerusalem. A day of mourning. (H)

Torah (tō rah') — In a limited sense the Five Books of Moses, the law, or the Bible. More broadly, Torah refers to all of Jewish learning and culture, both biblical and rabbinic. (H)

Trefoh (trē foh') — Nonkosher food, forbidden because it has not been prepared in accordance with Jewish ritual. (H)

Tzedokoh (tse dŏ koh) — Literally, *justice, righteousness.* Frequently refers to charity or philanthropy, following the biblical principle that charity was to be given not out of pity, but as a matter of justice. (H)

Tzitzis (tsī tsīs) — The fringes attached to the four corners of the prayer shawl, the tallis. Fringes are the visible reminders of God's commandments. (H)

Viddui (vĭ dūī') — The confession of sins recited by a dying person. (H)

Yahrtzeit (yăr' tsite); plural, Yahrtzeiten (yăr' tsitĕn) — Observance of the anniversary of death of members of one's family. In the plural, anniversaries of death. (Y)

Yarmelke (yăr' mĕl kĕ) — Skullcaps worn as head covering either at prayer or at home. (Y)

Yeshivoh (ye shī voh') — Academy of higher Jewish learning where the Talmud was the major subject of study. (H)

Yeshivoh Bochurim (ye shī voh' bŏ chū rīm') — Students of the yeshivoh. (H)

Yichus (yī chūs') — Pedigree or lineage. One has yichus if one is a member of a family of excellent lineage and repute. (H)

Yiddishkeit (yĭd' dĭsh kite) — Jewishness. (Y)

Yizkor (yĭz kōr') — Literally, *May He remember.* The first word of the memorial prayer for the departed. (H)

Yom Kippur (yōm kĭ pūr') — The Day of Atonement, the holiest day in the Jewish calendar, observed by prayer and fasting. (H)

Yomim Noroim (yō mīm' nō rŏ īm') — The *awe-inspiring days.* Refers to Rosh Hashonah and Yom Kippur, the days on which divine judgment is passed on mankind. (H)

Zemiros (ze mī rōs') — Table hymns sung at the Sabbath meal. (H)

Index

INDEX

Conservative Judaism, 76
Council of Jewish Women, 16–17, 25, 31, 196, 197
Council of Social Agencies, 45, 48
Council on Human Relations, 8, 55–56
Courtship, 129–30, 131–32, 134–35, 268
Cremation, 147
Crime, 202–4

Day of Atonement, 104–5, 258
Death, annual rate, 138
Death rites, 139–45
Deinard, Dr. Samuel N., 33–35, 152
Die Shabbosdige Post, 177–78
Dietary laws, observance in early days, 15, 23, 226, 234, 236, 237–38, 252, 255, 272, 275; Orthodox, 83–84; today, 84–90, 137, 240–41; Passover, 106, 107–8
Dilling, Elizabeth, 50
Discipline, parental, of immigrant generation, 222, 226, 228, 231, 255–56, 257, 273–74, 286–87, 290–91; of present generation, 244, 259, 260. *See also* Family, Parent-child relationships
Discrimination, *see* Anti-Semitism
Divorce, 200–1
Dowry, 132

East European immigrants, 17–27; reasons for immigration, 17–18, 217; life in Minneapolis, 18–27; attitude toward German immigrants, 31–32; aided by Germans, 36; religious practices, 75–76; marriage customs, 129–30; fraternal orders, 173–75; use of Yiddish, 175; personal histories, 213–27, 252–56, 265–73
Education, *see* Adult education, Hebrew education, Learning, Secular education
Elchanan, Rabbi Isaac, 216
Elopement, 134
Emanuel Cohen Center, 40–41, 182
English language, use by early settlers, 15, 19, 21; use in services, 118, 133, 136, 144, 165, 166; names, 123–25; spoken by rabbis, 153. *See also* Hebrew language, Yiddish language
Ethnic groups, 5, 299–300

Excommunication, 66
Fair Employment Practices Commission, 57
Fair Employment Practices Ordinance, 56
Family, 189–208; size, 7, 194–95; pattern of early settlers, 15–16, 20–21, 130–31; changing pattern, 78, 193–94, 195, 198–99, 200. *See also* Marriage, Parent-child relationships, Women
Father, changing role, 78, 193, 195. *See also* Discipline
Feast of Booths, 113–15
Feast of Lights, 115–17
Feast of Lots, 117–19
Feast of Tabernacles, 113–15
Felsenthal, Julia, 39–40
Food, Jewish, 15–16, 74, 75, 91, 107, 110, 115, 230–31. *See also* Dietary laws
Fox, Anna L., 39
Fraternal organizations, 24, 173–75, 255
Free Employment Bureau, 36–37
Friday evening observance, 91–95
Fundamentalist groups, and anti-Semitism, 54–55
Funerals, 139–41, 142–44, 282

Gemarah, 71
Gemilas Chesed burial society, 146, 159–60
German immigrants, 12, 13–17; attitude toward East Europeans, 21, 31; religious beliefs, 74–75; in personal histories, 279–83
German language, 15
Ghetto, *see* Segregation
Ginzberg, Rabbi Chaim, 162
God, traditional idea of, 72–73; changing idea of, 80–81, 293; belief in, 104. *See also* Prayer
Gordon, Dr. George J., 24, 32–33, 177, 179–81
Goslin, Willard, 57
Governor's Interracial Commission, 57
Greener Shul, 161
Gymal Doled Club, 24–25, 40–41, 62–64, 236–37

Hadassah, 34–35, 191–92, 196

327

INDEX

University of Minnesota, 3, 25, 48, 49, 186–88

Vidukla, Lithuania, 213, 216
Vilna, Lithuania, 215, 217

Waite, Edward F., 203
West Side, 7, 30–31
Women, in early community, 16; status, 193–98, 214, 225; participation in community organizations, 48, 196–97; employment for, 131, 198–99
World War II, Jewish contribution, 8, 10

Yeshivos, 217
Yiddish language, 175–78; use in early community, 21, 133, 153, 175–78, 228–29, 230, 253, 256, 258, 270, 272, 273, 294; newspapers, 177–78
Yizkor services, 112–13, 144–45
Yom Kippur, 102–3, 103–6, 282
Youngdahl, Luther, 57
Youth Aliyah, 35

Zietlow, Carl, 57
Zionism, in early days, 26–27, 34–35, 38; today, 197, 250, 262, 290, 306–8